Praise for *How to Raise a Boy*

"Michael Reichert's highly readable and important book reveals how we have failed boys by gendering our human capacities to think and feel, with the latter being considered girly and gay and thus put on the bottom of our hierarchy of values. He underscores the similarities between boys and girls, or among all humans, in their social and emotional needs and capacities. Recognizing this simple and empirically proven fact is key to his proposed solutions to foster boys' natural capacities to connect to themselves and others. A must read for all who care about boys and men."

> —Niobe Way, Professor of Developmental Psychology at
> NYU and author of *Deep Secrets: Boys' Friendships and
> the Crisis of Connection*

"Michael Reichert weaves a lovely tapestry of stories, experiences, insights and reflections acquired over a long, distinguished career guiding boys and young men. A must read—not only for parents of boys but also for educators, administrators, and counselors entrusted with the responsibility of championing boys' education and development."

> —David M. Armstrong, Executive Director of
> The International Boys' Schools Coalition

"From years of work with boys and young men, Michael Reichert is well positioned to explain the dire consequences of how we raise boys to be men. With deep compassion guiding both his work and his writing, he points to positive directions to bring change. A must read for parents, teachers and, really, for us all."

> —Michael Kaufman, author of *The Time Has Come:
> Why Men Must Join the Gender Equality Revolution*

"The battle for our sons' souls rages on. Parents, policymakers, and teachers are worried, as they should be. Pundits debate whether boys should 'man up' or whether it's manhood itself that is the problem. Into the debate Michael Reichert offers this bright light: boys need more connection, not less. They need care, not carelessness. They need parents, teachers, and all of us being courageous enough to let boys simply be the full-hearted human beings they want to be. And to love them and support them all along the way. *How to Raise a Boy* is a much-needed contribution to the discussion."

> —Gary Barker, founder and CEO of Promundo

"In this important new book, Michael Reichert draws on years of experience in the field and his vast knowledge of research on gender and adolescent development to present helpful ideas to parents and educators who seek to raise healthy boys and young men. Written in a sensible, clear, and compelling manner, this book is chock-full of wisdom and practical suggestions. At a time when we have so much evidence that many boys are in trouble, we finally have a book that offers the insights and practical guidance we need to raise boys!"

—Pedro A. Noguera, PhD, Distinguished Professor of
   Education and faculty director, Center
   for the Transformation of Schools

"This book is a must read for anyone who has, or expects to have, a boy in their life. Dr. Reichert punctuates theory and research with real life vignettes from his own extensive clinical practice, powerfully bringing the pages to life. He explodes many of the myths about boys that stand in the way of healthy relationships with their parents and peers. He carefully guides parents through strategies that enhance their positive influence on their sons, thereby ensuring that they can thrive in an increasingly confusing and complicated world."

—Dennis J. Barbour, Esq., president and CEO of
   The Partnership for Male Youth

"Michael Reichert has spent three decades working to understand how boys think, feel, and act. In *How to Raise a Boy*, he distills that learning into ten chapters that focus on the challenges boys face today, and on how the adults in their lives can help boys navigate the risks and develop into good men. His advice: purposefully intrude on your son's privacy to become part of his life! Boys are equal to girls in their capacity to commit their hearts—but only to those they trust. Highly recommended for all parents and educators."

—Dr. John Nagl, Lieutenant Colonel, US Army (retired),
   and ninth headmaster of the Haverford School

"Through a range of topics including love, violence, integrity, self-respect, hope, social development, peer bullying, and peer support, Dr. Reichert has written a treatise for anyone seeking to know young men of today and to set in motion the necessary steps to improve the trajectory of young men's lives.

His analysis of the issues elevates our understanding of the power that relationships have to combat and better prepare the youth for an ever-changing society; strengthening their chances for safety, satisfaction, and success. . . . His good counsel speaks directly to the men and women of our nation providing a road map to move us away from old and false ideas and toxic stereotypes that do nothing but constrict, and replace them with fresh beliefs and empowering practices that redefine and enlighten masculinity in healthy ways."

—David C. Banks, president and CEO of
The Eagle Academy Foundation, Inc.

"Michael blends the wisdom of being a loving parent and a caring clinician to help us listen to, understand, and honor our sons and the boys in our lives, in order to assist them to be their best and truest selves."

—David L. Bell, MD, MPH, medical director of
The Young Men's Clinic at NewYork-Presbyterian,
The University Hospital of Columbia and Cornell

"Reichert has woven together a must read that thoughtfully describes how to support boys to thrive. He draws on findings from cutting edge research (his own and others), practice as a clinician and educational consultant, and first-hand experience as a parent, to illustrate their needs for us to appreciate them as individuals, and to work to have meaningful relationships with them."

—K. Ann Renninger, Dorwin P. Cartwright Professor of
Social Theory and Social Action, Department of
Educational Studies, Swarthmore College

"*How to Raise a Boy* is a book of positivity and hope for navigating the complex and often fraught journey of raising boys to be good men in today's world. Through fascinating stories from boys and their caregivers, it provides valuable and practical insight into the utmost significance of relationality and the power of connection in dismantling the harmful gender norms of the 'boy code' that compromises the lives of all of us."

—Amanda Keddie, Professor of Education,
Deakin University (Australia)

"In the ten years since my book about boys' troubles came out, I have spoken to countless parents and educators about their worries. Over this same period things have not gotten any easier for boys—in fact, it is more important than ever for families to nurture men of character, emotional intelligence, and resilience. In his groundbreaking book, Michael Reichert combines a unique blend of research, clinical insight, and personal experience to offer an encouraging approach to raising our sons. If you have a son, or a grandson, or a nephew or a brother, buy this book."
—Peg Tyre, *New York Times*–bestselling author of
The Trouble with Boys

"No one writes more powerfully about how much boys need loving relationships to become healthy men. With the training of a researcher and the soul of a clinician, he has looked deeply into their hearts and lives; he sees behind their underachievement and gaming addictions and recognizes their yearning for connection and friendship. If you are the parent or teacher of a boy, if you love a boy, you should read Michael Reichert's *How to Raise a Boy*."
—Michael G. Thompson, PhD

"*How to Raise a Boy* gives parents a thoughtful, honest, and ultimately hopeful map for raising a son today. Without shying away from the tremendous challenges boys face, Michael Reichert does what he has done for so long for so many: give brilliant insight and advice that help so many boys become confident men of purpose and character."
—Rosalind Wiseman, author of *Queen Bees and Wannabees* and *Masterminds and Wingmen* and founder of Cultures of Dignity

HOW TO
RAISE A BOY

THE POWER OF CONNECTION
TO BUILD GOOD MEN

MICHAEL C. REICHERT, PhD

A TarcherPerigee Book

tarcherperigee

An imprint of Penguin Random House LLC
penguinrandomhouse.com

TarcherPerigee with tp colophon is a registered trademark of
Penguin Random House LLC.

Most TarcherPerigee books are available at special quantity discounts for bulk purchase for sales promotions, premiums, fund-raising, and educational needs. Special books or book excerpts also can be created to fit specific needs. For details, write: Special Markets@penguinrandomhouse.com.

Library of Congress Cataloging-in-Publication Data

Names: Reichert, Michael, author.
Title: How to raise a boy : the power of connection
to build good men / Michael C. Reichert.
Description: New York : TarcherPerigee, 2019. |
Includes bibliographical references and index.
Identifiers: LCCN 2018049608| ISBN 9780143133209 (hardback) |
ISBN 9780525504986 (epub)
Subjects: LCSH: Boys—Psychology. | Achievement motivation in boys. | Child rearing. |
BISAC: FAMILY & RELATIONSHIPS / Parenting / General. | FAMILY & RELATIONSHIPS /
Life Stages / Teenagers. | SOCIAL SCIENCE / Men's Studies.
Classification: LCC BF723.M56 R45 2019 | DDC 649/.132—dc23
LC record available at https://lccn.loc.gov/2018049608

Printed in the United States of America
1   3   5   7   9   10   8   6   4   2

Book design by Elke Sigal

APPRECIATION

In the end, I am grateful for my own family—my partner,
Sharon, whose faith, generosity, and fierce commitment to justice
have steadied me; my sons, Mike and Kier, who have helped me
keep it real; and my grandson, who provides daily witness
to how boundlessly boys enjoy being alive.

CONTENTS

✍

CHAPTER I

CONFINED BY BOYHOOD

A few years after my first son was born, I began work at a historic boys' school outside Philadelphia, the Haverford School. The school had long been dedicated to the care and education of boys, but nearly one hundred years after its founding had begun to question its core mission. Market studies indicated that many families were leery of educating boys apart from girls; conversion to coeducation swept the country as concerns grew that schools for boys violated the spirit of gender equality.

Prior to any thought of a formal role at the school, I had been asked to give a talk to parents about boys' vulnerability to chemical dependency and other risk behaviors, a specialty of my clinical practice. Afterward, I had a conversation with school administrators about a high-profile student who struggled with drug use, leading ultimately to an intervention, inpatient treatment, and a very public hug with the head of the school at graduation expressing gratitude for the lifesaving support he had received.

By that point, I had assisted many boys and their families through similar challenges, informed by an experience of my own—a terribly painful one some years before. In the late spring of my twenty-fourth year, my younger brother was killed in a car accident. Though he'd had troubles throughout adolescence—drinking, drugs, and disconnection from both school and family—things had begun to look up. There were many signs of healthier choices as he turned eighteen. That evening, he'd been hanging out with a friend. They had been drinking, perhaps also drugging, and he'd gotten into the passenger seat of his friend's car heedless of the risks. The friend lost control while speeding down a hill and crashed into a large, old tree in a neighbor's front yard. I will always remember the doorbell ringing at two in the morning, the policeman asking if this was where my brother lived, and the searing image he described of my brother and his friend inside the fiery wreck now wrapped around an unyielding tree.

Earlier that same year, I had begun my first postcollegiate job as a counselor at family court, assigned to the juvenile presentence unit. Through the revolving door of the court came a deluge of adolescent males caught up in various delinquencies: stealing, fighting, not attending school, running away from home, robbery, car theft, and even homicide. It fell to me to consider their trajectories, weigh their struggles and strengths, and make appropriate recommendations to the judge regarding consequences. I would read through the often heartbreaking police and school reports, meet with the youths and their caregivers, and try to imagine how they might avoid future trouble.

In those days just after the accident, while my brother clung to life in the hospital intensive care unit, and my family kept a bedside vigil, I grappled with what was happening. There was a common thread—an unspoken tragedy—at work in both my brother's and my clients' stories: their maleness. In each case, a confounded sense of self, some degree of numbness and cluelessness, disconnection and mental isolation, lay behind choices that ranged from self-defeating to self-destructive. In the mid-1970s, there was little understanding of what the Canadian activist and scholar Michael Kaufman would memorably describe as a "strange combination of power and powerlessness, privilege and pain" in male development.[1] And there was even less appreciation for boys' fundamentally relational human natures—the reality that human development happens in relationships with those offering care.

But, buoyed by the successes of the women's movement, a men's movement had begun to sprout. Though still inchoate and fitful, the movement was premised on the idea that boys and men suffer costly losses. As caregivers—parents, teachers, communities—pass traditional masculine values along to male children, what results, according to Harvard Medical School psychologist William Pollack, is "the traumatic abrogation of boys' holding environments."[2] Too many boys lose their intimate connections and emotional voices early in their lives. Once detached from their relational anchors, boys are vulnerable to the temptations of the times and lose touch with their sense of who they are.

That is what I was seeing in my days at family court, what I saw in my own brother, and, later, what I saw in the young man I helped into rehab. Each was affected by a Darwinian masculine code that is corrosive for their human development, their virtue, and their well-being.

I felt called upon to do something. After that talk to parents, and with the loss of my brother in the back of my mind, when the school asked me to come on as its consulting psychologist, I accepted, believing it would provide an opportunity to focus on another new role, as father to a son. Through the late eighties, nineties, and into the new century, while my son grew to manhood, and I grew in understanding as his parent, the school also evolved. Following a searching strategic planning process, it recommitted to boys with new rigor and established a program called

On Behalf of Boys. We launched it in 1995 with a national advisory board, new educational programs for parents, and wide-ranging research projects.

Frankly, I was worried about my son and what life might have in store for him. More alarms had begun to sound for boys—that they were falling behind in school and failing to get traction in their lives; that they were "at war" and "in crisis."[3] My commitment was furthered by the birth of a second son. By then, it had become clear that their mother and I could never circle our wagons tightly enough to stave off the seductive influences that sweep away many boys. The best we could do, I concluded, was to take a stand for the worth, innocence, and possibility of boys in a way that would be visible to our sons.

Routine casualties are an inconvenient truth about boyhood. Boys from every walk of life do not pass successfully on to manhood, especially when masculinity is compounded by stresses such as racism and poverty. In a 2009 journal article titled "The State of American Boyhood," psychologist Judith Kleinfeld of the University of Alaska was particularly concerned about "disconnected" youth, a group twice as likely to be male as female and more likely to be of color than white. In concrete and measurable ways, these disconnected males show up at the wrong end of gender gaps in education, employment, and civic participation. What's more, as they reach maturity, many carry their disconnectedness into their lives as adult men. Particularly in the new world of knowledge-based, globalized economies and expanding gender equality, boys must be thoughtfully prepared. The historic model of boyhood, unchanging for generations, is woefully behind the times. Demographer Tom Mortenson of the National Center for Public Policy and Higher Education, a nonprofit research organization, has written, "Men are not adapting easily or readily to this new world. A growing share of men are not adapting at all, and, as a result, their lives are falling apart."[4]

What can be done to ameliorate the losses of boyhood? How can we protect the boys in our care from threats built into boyhood? How can we ensure that our sons are well prepared for and well launched to manhood? Over the course of my career as a psychologist, I have talked, studied, and worked with thousands of boys and young men since my brother's accident. In my research, young males around the world have shared accounts of their hopes and hurts, successes and setbacks. These stories reveal how the lives offered to boys actually *feel* to them—how limited opportunities often chafe against their human natures; how they may be left feeling lonely and neglected or find themselves misunderstood and misdiagnosed.

As a result of this compelling narrative evidence, I have come to agree with British sociologist Caroline New, who proposes that there is, indeed, a "systematic mistreatment" underlying boyhood, and that those of us responsible for its design and maintenance—not boys themselves—must fix its flaws.[5] We will find ready partners in boys themselves, who have a keen interest in being seen as they are, hearts beating loudly behind the masks they must wear. But to repair boyhood, we must first acknowledge its problems and reach a common understanding of their causes.

That is harder than it might seem. I expected On Behalf of Boys would be a welcomed program that would inspire more careful consideration of what boys need. But right from the start, things got complicated. Those members of the school community comfortable with tradition scorned the very mention of gender regarding boys, while those who were feminists feared a plot to take boys into the woods to trumpet their masculinity. A columnist for the local paper, catching wind of the controversy, mocked the initiative and invoked an underlying fear: "Boys shouldn't have to be brave. They shouldn't have to strive to produce. Boys should be more like . . . well, girls, I guess."

The truth is that prejudice and stereotypes show up very early in a boy's life, shaping and skewing how even the best intentioned of us think about him. In her intensive study of four- and five-year-old boys, Stanford University psychologist Judy Chu observed how parents and teachers limit "how it is possible for boys to be." She witnessed a hardening of identity in some of the boys, a closing off of options, and an "overcompromise" with cultural norms and pressures that build in their relationships. Over the two years of her immersion in their classrooms, open and authentic boys became more guarded and less spontaneous. She wrote, "What is often perceived and described as natural to boys is in fact not a manifestation of their nature but an adaptation to cultures that require boys to be emotionally stoic, aggressive, and competitive if they are to be perceived and accepted as 'real boys.'"[6]

In my own experience, I find that masculine stereotypes are ubiquitous and unconscious, and influence how we regard boys nearly from conception. A friend, a high school biology teacher, was pregnant some years ago with twins and said to me, "I know which one is a boy." Curious, I asked how she knew. She explained, "He's the one who kicks me." Niobe Way, a developmental researcher at New York University, concluded from her research that popular ideas about boys have little basis in evidence and even less in their actual needs. Contrary to the conventional belief that boys prefer autonomy and are not interested in close bonds, those in her studies told her they would die or go crazy without their friends. She warns that cultural clichés about boys lie behind flawed family and educational practices and the tired, familiar failures of underperformance, isolation, addiction, and bad behavior.[7]

Early in my first go at being a parent, cultural prejudices I was hardly aware of came to the fore, sometimes awkwardly. Our family lived in one of the row house neighborhoods for which Philadelphia is famous. Right down the street was a small playground where gangs of pre-teen boys gathered daily for games of stickball and basketball. My son was an eager athlete and loved playing, but he was unprepared for what came to pass as the boys he played with grew older and approached adolescence. Despite years together, laughing and riding big toys up and down the block, several grew angry and mean and seemed to forget their friends. Ultimately, the group, spurred by them, turned against my son, excluding him and sending him from the playground. He trudged home, tail between his legs, time after time.

Rather than just let him sit watching television or playing video games alone, at first I played with him and tried to bolster his confidence so that he could try again at the playground. But one Saturday morning, as I recovered from an intense week, when he headed home from the playground once again I met him at the front steps and told him he could not come into the house. "You have to figure this out," I said. "I'll stay here with you as long as you need, but I cannot let you just give up." He tried to push past me, humiliation and frustration quickly turning frantic and explosive. He exclaimed that he did not want to go back down the street and melted down, screaming and crying over and over, trying to slide by while I blocked his way. I kept saying, "You can do it. You don't have to give up." A neighbor came out, concerned about what must have sounded like child abuse.

Was I helping? Or was I merely passing along the cliché that a boy should never shy from a fight? Was I teaching my son the terrible lesson that he must solve problems no matter how afraid or undone he feels? In responding to what I perceived to be a critical threat to my son's future on our street, I was also responding to something deep within me. How much was I motivated by my own fear that my son might be driven from the playground, from boyhood's pleasures, and exiled to a smaller life?

I was lucky. I had found a way to answer such soul-searching questions. Shortly after college, I joined a peer counseling network, a serendipitous turn that changed my life and eventually led to my chosen career. I learned to listen to others and, in turn, to be listened to by them in a deep, patient, and straightforward way. I worked within this network of ordinary people to resolve tensions and prejudices that had interfered with our healthy functioning. That was it—a people's movement for restoring the ability to be present and creative in relationships rather than bound by old relational patterns. As I took regular turns to talk, cobwebs cleared, long-held tensions eased, and my capacity to be honest with myself grew tremendously. From this practice of listening to others, I also became more attentive in general. Over the years, these opportunities to sort through my reactions, feelings, and thoughts helped me cope with hard challenges like my brother's death and to gain perspective on biases built into my own boyhood that limited how I saw the world. I could even recognize when my reactions to my sons had more to do with my life than theirs.

In this instance, after further self-examination, I realized that I was attempting to achieve a tricky balance between telling my son I was sorry his friends were mean to him and holding out a belief in his power to make his life work, whatever the obstacles. I wanted to pass along an important lesson I wished I had understood earlier than I did: that he could choose his own perspective, no matter how hopeless or stuck he felt. Later, in a calmer moment as we sat together, I tried to convey this message so that he could hear me without the upset, fear, and frustration he had been feeling, but I am sure some worry still came through. With so much upset of his own, mine may only have amplified the emotional volume.

Parents of boys often feel urgent. Their son is behaving a certain way—lackadaisical in school, self-centered at home, defeated by his peer group, unkind toward his sister or brother, insufficiently aggressive on the sports field, anxious or angry or shy—and parents cannot take it anymore. They intervene with a hand heavy with worry or irritation. They try to give advice and become even more frustrated or alarmed when their sons cannot hear them.

Fortunately, my son and I survived that moment on our front

steps, though there would be many others to come. He has become a wonderful, patient teacher of boys and a warm father to a son of his own. I am not sure he got my intended message. But, like every boy, he has had many, many gut-check moments and has certainly had to find his own courage. Our relationship has survived many challenges, and I believe he understands that even when I go about it clumsily I am still willing to help him with life's difficult puzzles.

The Boys We Have

In a group for parents of teenage boys, I posed this question: Can you tell me a time that someone—a teacher, a coach, or a mentor— made a positive difference for your son? Each mother and father came up with a heartening example. As they told these stories, the tone in the room warmed. All of us had said a common prayer, longing for our boys to have good lives, to be safe, to plant deep roots, and to reach upward for their dreams. To find help was the greatest of blessings!

I was struck by how strong parents' emotions were as they told their stories of someone giving their sons a hand. One father spoke about a time his son lied to a teacher after being caught doing something wrong. He made no excuses for his son's behavior; he had been worried about this bad habit and how it might hold his son back. As the boy's luck went, he was assigned to the same teacher the following year for math. But instead of harboring a bad impression of the boy, the teacher let him know that he had simply made a mistake and would be given a fresh slate. He made himself available for extra help and spoke to the boy about how sure he was that he could do really well in the class. At the end of the year, the boy had achieved higher grades than ever, had developed new self-confidence as a mathematician, and regarded the teacher as one of his favorites.

Another parent told about a time her son became ill and needed extended hospitalization. During the time in the hospital, not only did his teacher communicate with him regularly about his schoolwork, helping him to keep up with the class, but he also came to visit the boy, bringing with him notes from the other classmates. The mother explained how she felt toward that teacher:

"It just made me feel that his dad and I weren't the only ones worrying about him; that there were others out there who cared as well. This person went out of his way to visit him on his own time and see how he was doing. He didn't have to do that. I knew he was a fantastic kid, but it was the knowledge that other people also knew he was special that struck me. I'll be forever grateful to him."

Yet another mother told a story about a coach who had taken special trouble to help her son master the skills of the sport, to a point that he achieved notice from coaches at the regional level. When I asked what she had felt as she observed their relationship, she said, "Relief."

"Relief?" I asked. She explained:

"What it's done is given him a belief in himself. My greatest fear is that he wouldn't identify what it is about himself that is special. Now I believe he has something in his life: a reminder that he can forever recall."

Perhaps these are common sentiments whenever parents talk about their children. But it seemed to me that there was a particular charge because we were talking about boys. What was unsaid was the great uncertainty parents feel about boys, particularly today. There are so many ways things can go wrong with a son. According to David Stein, author of *Unraveling the ADD/ADHD Fiasco*, boys' behavior often elicits severe consequences. For example, he reports that five boys are diagnosed with some sort of psychological "disorder" for every one girl.[8] A 2012 paper on the sex preferences of adoptive parents found that girls were favored nearly 30 percent more than boys. The researchers' explanation: girls are viewed as "less risky."[9]

Particularly in these new times, when expecting fathers learn that they will have a son, it can be unsettling. The actor Justin Baldoni, best known for his role as Rafael Solano in the CW show *Jane the Virgin,* shares in talks and writing about the time his wife was pregnant with their son. "There was another emotion building inside me as my wife's belly expanded: terror," he wrote recently. What was so frightening? Playing the part of a matinee idol male, Baldoni confessed that he developed an unhealthy relationship to his body and was worried that his son would emulate him. "I didn't want him to be anything like me. I want him to know better, feel better, and do better than I do."[10]

Everyone has a story of a boy who has run into trouble. Like this one involving a seventh-grade boy.

At the time his mother called me, David was wildly out of control: though very bright, he was failing in school due to little effort and frequent misbehavior; he was defiant to his parents, and mean, sometimes abusive, toward his younger sister. His mother had tried a parenting support network, but their suggestions of tough love only escalated her conflicts with her son. When I met privately with David, I discovered that he truly believed that his mother did not like him, much less love him. In the heat of their bitter arguments, she would lose self-control and say things like "I hate being your mother." It had apparently been like this for some time, and as David entered adolescence, he grew more vehement in rejecting her efforts to parent him.

I met alone with Lily to ask how she felt toward her son, and she admitted that he had been difficult for her from the beginning, while her daughter, coming several years later, had been a dream. As she discussed her first birth and David's infancy, it became clear that Lily had experienced a postpartum depression and that her son's needs had felt like nails on the blackboard to her. Scared and overwhelmed, when David would cry out for her, Lily often felt irritated and withholding. The relationship she established with her son on these terms simply increased in volume and anger as he grew to become a teenager.

David was actually quite likeable alone with me, and over time we forged a bond. He could tell that I enjoyed talking with him and thought he was talented and decent. We would laugh together, and I was careful not to blame him for his fights with his parents, his poor marks, or his conduct problems, instead offering that he had done the best he could, all things considered. Eventually I was able to leverage our connection to point out the self-defeating nature of his behaviors, and he was able to acknowledge that he wished things were better. I also intervened with David's parents, recommending a moratorium on coercion and punishment and coaching his mother, in particular, to rebuild the relationship by summoning her delight in her son. Given that her son was a strong, physical boy who loved to roughhouse, I encouraged her to start pillow fights and lighthearted roughhousing with him.

Things went up and down. David remained skeptical of his mother's commitment to him, and Lily struggled not to condemn him for his disrespect and lack of appreciation for her efforts. But as he grew and became more interested in relationships with girls, I upped the ante. I explained that the kind of relationship he had with his mother—his attitude toward her, his experience of closeness and trust with her—would set a framework for other relationships. I recommended a healthier intimacy in order to put their painful past fully behind him. I also proposed zero tolerance for any mistreatment of his sister. Over time, with his mother cheering him on, David was able to overcome the bad relational habits that he had acquired during their early years.

At Thanksgiving time in ninth grade, after not having seen him for some months, I received the following email from his mother:

> I just wanted to touch base with you about David. It's been a good thing that I haven't been in touch sooner. Anyway, he is doing fantastic. I hope I'm not jinxing myself by sending you this email. But I often think of you and how much progress we made while working with you. And now, finally, the fruits of my labor are paying off. He is much more involved with his dad and me. He's a little bit nicer to his sister. (I don't think he'll ever be really nice to her until he is an adult.) Also, he takes more responsibility for his actions and admits when he's wrong. Most importantly, he is allowing me to be his mother. I can't thank you enough for all your help. It has been absolutely priceless!

This family was in trouble, and David was on the verge of going south in ways that could affect the rest of his life. In the course of my assessment, I concluded that the family's crisis was the result of a bad theory: the parents believed that their son was willfully misbehaving and was simply testing their limits in an angry contest for power. Their theory led them to believe that force and moral blame were the best responses.

My intervention went in an opposite direction, suggesting that there is a hardwired need for boys to form trusting attachments to their parents. I regarded David as traumatized by his mother's rejection, ambivalence, and withholding, and talked with them both about how Lily's early parenting struggles had gotten their relationship off to a bad start. Validating David's sense of being wronged while also validating his mother's lovingness and right to be respected allowed both to feel that I understood. I was then able to take a hard stand with David for better behavior, calling upon him to be the type of man—older brother, son, student, athlete—he really wanted to be.

For families seeking help with their sons, it is important to frame their crises as an opportunity to rethink ideas that are not working. A more accurate set of assumptions is called for. Once it is understood how things have gone awry, a new approach can be devised—one likely to include a deeper reckoning with the boy's need for connection. In many families, a pronounced disconnect can arise between what parents had hoped for in a son and who a boy actually is. Dependent on their parents' acceptance and love, boys have little choice when these come with a price. Most initially work hard to fulfill their parents' hopes and expectations; some conclude that their best efforts will likely fail and look elsewhere to meet their needs. But conformity and striving to please have a downside: a boy's cynical conclusion that his home in the world is contingent upon satisfying other's needs. The conditional nature of parents' love leaves many boys feeling insecure.

It is as if parents believe that they can order up a particular type of boy to fit their dreams or, barring that, force the one they have into a preferred mold. How many boys have heard from their parents some version of the message that they need to "man up"? "Try harder" at school or sports. "Achieve." "Suck up" their feelings and show more "grit" and determination? Old-school masculine ideas that trying harder is the answer to everything ignore scientific insights about how grit develops and how motivation is deeply interwoven with a boy's emotional state. The problem with trying to fit a boy into a predetermined identity is the message he receives about the person he actually is: that he is not good enough.

The Man Box

The British writer and author of *1984*, George Orwell, was a policeman in colonial Burma as a young man. In his 1936 essay "Shooting an Elephant," basely loosely on this experience, a policeman struggles with the assignment to kill an elephant running amuck through the streets. Not only must he shoot the animal but also he must appear coldly efficient and free of any conflict as he does so. A quote from this story opens the movie *The Mask You Live In*, an official selection of the 2015 Sundance Film Festival that "follows boys and young men as they struggle to stay true to themselves while negotiating America's narrow definition of masculinity." As Orwell wrote, "He wears a mask and grows to fit it."[11]

Actually, the metaphor of a mask downplays the extent of boys' losses. A study released in 2017 by Promundo-US, a global leader in educational and community-based programs for men and boys, employed a stronger image: the act-like-a-man box. What's in or out of the box is determined by behaviors that are okay and not okay for males: self-sufficiency, acting tough, physical attractiveness, homophobia, hypersexuality, aggression, and control are all in. The researchers surveyed a representative sample of men aged eighteen to thirty in the United States, the United Kingdom, and Mexico, and found striking differences in levels of violence, bullying, sexual harassment, depression, and suicidal thoughts between young men "in" and "out" of the box. The research team concluded, "The troubling effects of the Man Box are severe, real, and troubling. The majority of men who adhere to the rules of the Man Box are more likely to put their health and well-being at risk, to cut themselves off from intimate friendships, to resist seeking help when they need it, to experience depression, and to think frequently about ending their own life."[12]

Early gender researchers such as Sandra Bem, who pioneered the study of polarized gender roles and stereotypes, established that boys are held more rigidly to gender norms than girls are. It is one thing for a girl to be a "tomboy," but another altogether for a boy to be a "sissy." Both in homes and on playgrounds, boys are corrected more strenuously if they veer off the prescribed course. In her book *The Courage to Raise Good Men*, family therapist Olga Silverstein cited a research study in which a mother holding an infant—dressed in white, and not readily identifiable as either a boy or a girl—sat in a doctor's waiting room. When the nurse called for the mother, the woman politely asked others in the waiting room if they would mind holding "my daughter" or "my son" while she briefly consulted with the doctor. A hidden camera recorded what happened. When identified as female, the infant was held close, talked to, and played with; when identified as male, often the child wound up on the carpet playing with a set of keys.[13]

Mothers play an important part in the masculinizing drama. For her 2013 book *The Mama's Boy Myth: Why Keeping Our Sons Close Makes Them Stronger*, journalist Kate Stone Lombardi interviewed mothers of sons to explore how cultural pressures influenced their relationships. She learned that there are strong prejudices bearing down on mothers to push their sons away, even against their better judgment. She wrote, "For at least a century, the common wisdom about mothers and sons has been something like this: a mother who stays emotionally close to her son after he reaches, say, the tender age of five, is acting inappropriately. She's that smothering mother destined to prevent her boy from growing up to be a strong, independent man."[14]

The Promundo study asked about different sources of pressure to conform to traditional masculine norms. Among young men in the United States, 60 percent agreed with the following statement: "My parents taught me that a 'real man' should act strong even if he feels nervous or scared." In terms of the lessons of their boyhoods, there was remarkable consistency between what families and the broader society asked of them. Three in four respondents agreed, "Guys should act strong even if they feel scared or nervous inside," and 68 percent agreed, "A guy who doesn't fight back when others push him around is weak."[15]

A boy's training in masculinity, begun in his family, accelerates in school. Observing her group of four-to-six-year-olds through preschool and kindergarten, Judy Chu witnessed how boys transitioned from being direct, articulate, attentive, and present in their relationships to pretending and keeping things to themselves. They became, according to Chu, "cynical" and "sober," less "exuberant" and more "discontented." Boys' development, she concluded, proceeds from "presence to pretense via posturing" as boys realize it is not who they are but how they play the part that matters.[16]

Boys' losses extend well beyond pretending. Exaggerated ideas about masculinity, pervasive in the culture and conveyed by media images, games, and television, goad boys to extreme behavior. In Chu's study, the boys formed a "Mean Team" and set out "to bother people"—particularly the girls in the class. Whatever feelings of empathy individual boys might have harbored were overridden in their groupthink.

Though the late nineties brought growing concern that all was not right in boys' lives, problems of boyhood persist to this day. According to the US Centers for Disease Control and Prevention (CDC), parents of boys aged four to seventeen seek help from health care or school staff at rates nearly twice those of girls. In addition to impulsive risk taking, inattention, and conduct problems, boys lag behind girls in the social and behavioral skills that facilitate success in school; they are more often fidgety, disengaged, defiant, and unregulated. Being disruptive and unable or unwilling to heed adult limits, boys evoke corrective action from teachers. They are the primary recipients of disciplinary sanctions and medication prescriptions, even though, as the esteemed University of Minnesota child development researcher L. Alan Sroufe argues, "to date, no study has found any long-term benefit of attention-deficit medication on academic performance, peer relationships, or behavior problems."[17]

Boys are also far more likely than girls to act in ways that increase the risk of disease, injury, and death, to themselves and others: they carry weapons more often, engage in physical fights more often, wear seat belts less often, drive drunk more frequently, have more unprotected sex, and use alcohol or drugs more often before sex. The correlation between these masculine norms and uncivil behavior is troubling. In another crosscultural study, Stony Brook University anthropologist David Gilmore found that various practices of misogyny, which he terms a "male malady," are best understood as a manifestation of the struggle to suppress whatever men perceive about themselves as feminine. He wrote, "Men who hate women hate themselves even more."[18]

Life within the box or behind the mask is not merely confining but also erodes boys' goodness and virtue. Shielded by a mask, presenting an inauthentic front, boys become isolated and unmoored, losing the "true north" of connections to others for their moral compasses. Pretense trumps authenticity, a "cool pose" beats sincerity, and academic disengagement replaces commitment. Whatever parents teach their sons about fairness, integrity, and sincerity is undermined in a "bro" culture of peer policing and *Animal House* celebration. Compelled to conform, boys are vulnerable to forces designed specifically to co-opt their minds and hearts. Cut off from their families, for example, boys are more susceptible to the marketing pitches of a pornography industry that distorts human sexuality and love. The list goes on.

The Good News

Fortunately, there is a solution to the problems of boyhood. If we muster the courage, we can open ourselves to boys' actual experiences and work to build a boyhood that permits our sons to be who they are. The spate of books about boys in the late 1990s offered important insights. But the books tended toward one or the other of two polarized views: (1) that boys are biologically driven toward rambunctious play, gratuitous aggression, and incessant risk taking or (2) that they are naïve innocents, victims of social oppression, suffering in silent pain. In both cases, boys are victims, either of their genetics or their social ecologies. What was missing is the lovely and inspiring part played by a boy's own imagination for his life.

But I am optimistic that a historic breakthrough is currently in the making. Though boys continue to be subjected to myths and prejudices rooted in the past, and new, healthier ways for being male have not yet replaced old paradigms, contradictions between economic realities, family dynamics, and traditional norms make boyhood's reinvention inevitable. As new social demands reveal the stark limitations of the old boyhood, fresh ideas will gain currency.

Here are several examples on a small scale hinting at what's possible:

When a historic boarding school went coeducational after 150 years as a school for boys, it developed an attrition problem it had never faced before. Just a few years after girls entered, ninth- and tenth-grade boys began dropping out. I was called in to meet with male students, their families, and their teachers to find an explanation for the boys' new unhappiness. It wasn't hard: under everyone's noses—so taken for granted that it was practically invisible—was a hazing system that encouraged older boys to mistreat younger ones, but with no parallel among girls. Boys entered a school steeped in harsh man-making rituals, underwent considerable abuse, and received a promise that they could take advantage of the new boys who came after them. It was a proud tradition, defended as character building and tacitly endorsed by parents, teachers, coaches, and school administrators. Only, with girls having such a different experience, it was harder and harder for younger boys to tolerate. The way the school had always done things, its model for the development of boys, was disrupted.

I offered my evidence for a link between hazing and the attrition problem, and school leaders took strong action. They restructured their program for younger boys, emphasizing safety and mentoring, and made steady progress eliminating its peer hazing tradition, the "rat" system. Though stubbornly resistant to change, hazing gradually receded from boys' relationships, and the school's attrition rate fell. Today it is on a strong footing as a modern institution.

A second example arose in the question-and-answer period following a talk I gave to parents. It was clear that what had brought them out on a wintry weeknight was hope for help with boys they worried about. Both mothers and fathers shared quite personal stories of anxiety, loss, frustration. One mother raised her hand. She explained that she was a single mom, separated from the boy's father, and that her son had become harder and harder to deal with. He was withdrawn, surly, and rejected her authority to place limits on him.

She asked, "Is this normal, and should I just let his father take care of him now that he is a teenager?"

There were nods of understanding and even agreement across the audience. I have heard this question in some form or other from the start of my work and have come to expect it. I have even been on panels with experts who have confidently asserted that, of course, it takes another man to initiate a boy into the fraternity of manhood. One expert, in fact, has advised that it is the mother's role to "build a bridge to the father" for her son.

There are problems with this view, on several levels. First, there is no evidence that only another man can support a boy to become a man himself. In fact, such mentoring most often ensures the perpetuation of traditional ideas. That's not to say that boys cannot learn important things from rubbing shoulders with an older man: how he gets up, shaves, relates to his partner, conducts his affairs. Boys love to see what other males have figured out. In the absence of real contact, in fact, boys are more vulnerable to exaggerated views. But an emphasis on learning masculinity can obscure the more vital development of the boy's humanity and his acquiring skills necessary for success in modern society.

This is what I said to that mother: "As much as I value strong relationships between boys and their fathers, the idea that mothers should back away from their own relationships out of fear that they might spoil their sons' masculinity—turn them into mama's boys—violates everything developmental scientists understand about the child's need for a secure, dependable attachment. Boys, just like girls, have basic human needs that are ignored only at peril. The child who does not have the unconditional acceptance and love of a parent—or someone, somewhere—will be less bold, less confident, more vulnerable to a host of negative influences."

"Please keep your son close to you," I urged her. "Knowing that he has you standing right behind him as he goes out into the world will make all the difference to him."

There were nods from the fathers and looks of surprise, gratitude, and renewed confidence on the faces of the mothers. What struck me was how captive this mom was to bad ideas that violated nearly all of her parenting instincts—and how ready she was for permission to trust those instincts.

The third example came in a violence prevention program developed for early-adolescent boys in neighborhoods in and around Philadelphia. Because the link between becoming violent and witnessing or experiencing violence is strong, my research team began by assessing boys' exposure to violence: fights, witnessing shootings or hearing gunshots, directly experiencing crime and personal threats. The goal was to build a program grounded in real data about the frequency and severity of experiences that evoked the fight-or-flight response characteristic of acute stress reactions.

We found chilling levels of violence. Despite the evidence of abnormal environmental stressors, we encountered skepticism from our funders and advisory board about whether these boys could benefit from an intervention that would aim both to protect them and help them recover from toxic stress. Some argued that the stresses were too severe, the boys too far gone, their resources too thin, community norms promoting violence too strong. Old racial, class, and gender prejudices were offered; ideas that would have kept things just as they were.

But pressures to prevent at-risk boys from becoming twice victimized were persuasive. We organized after-school groups and found quickly that many boys were all too happy to meet with other boys and an adult leader to talk through how they felt about various aspects of their lives. Many boys showed up for years, in fact, to talk, play games, and generally work through tensions they were confronting at home, in school, and around the neighborhood. The open discussions allowed them to be honest about what they felt and, evaluation research confirmed, made them less vulnerable to blindly reenacting violent scenarios.

When asked, many boys shared the sentiment voiced by Terrence, that though he sometimes had to defend himself with force, he "don't love no fight." A younger boy, Juan, elaborated on his view:

"Usually, I'm a person that doesn't like to fight. Like, I'm like a ladies' man. I don't fight. Usually, well, I'm a lover not a fighter, right? I write poems. I do different stuff."

Raising Good Men

In each of these examples, a truer read of boys overcame historic prejudice. With a commitment to boys' human development as the starting point, very different outcomes in families, schools, and communities come into focus. Ethicist Martha Nussbaum of the University of Chicago Law School has suggested the goal of "what people are actually able to do and to be" as a morally appropriate measure of whether a child receives proper care.[19] In her view, what defines an ethical society is its creation of conditions—resources and relationships—that allow children to translate innate capabilities into actual abilities. What sort of boyhood might allow boys to realize their full human capacities?

Converging lines of research point in a single direction. According to psychologist Niobe Way, "What makes us human is our relational and emotional skills, and we must figure out ways to strengthen these critical life skills."[20] Yet she observed a marked shift in the quality of boys' connections from early to later adolescence. While younger boys were able to care, connect, and share intimacy and vulnerability with one another throughout much of their childhoods, cultural pressures became unavoidable for adolescent males. Pulling away from their close friends in response, boys lost touch with primary sources of connection and sharing. They even lost their willingness to express themselves emotionally for fear that they would be perceived as "gay." Though they found life without their friends bleak and sometimes unbearable, few boys were able to swim against the strong currents. Most wound up in the familiar destination of emotional constriction, social isolation, and personal inauthenticity.

Way's research coincides with research from other, diverse fields. New studies into brain development underscore how far off base traditional assumptions have been. Psychiatrist Amy Banks of the Jean Baker Miller Institute at Wellesley University argues that how independence and individuality are conceived, at the heart of boyhood's value system, goes against the very design of their human anatomy. She goes further, in fact, and adds that the relatively new field of relational neuroscience teaches that relationships are not merely nice, serendipitous extras, but are essential to human well-being. Every person, male as well as female, is "built to operate within a network of caring human relationships."[21] When people are cut off from their connections, a negative neural cascade results. Health and happiness are a function of the vitality of these relational connections.

The proof is in our brains and bodies. Banks identifies four separate neurobiological systems designed to ensure that each person is in sync with others: the smart vagus system, that helps us respond with appropriate emotion in social contexts; the dorsal anterior cingulate cortex, that moderates our responses to social exclusion and pain; the mirroring system, that helps us read others and respond emotionally to them; and the dopamine reward system, that governs experiences of pleasure in relationships. Such neuroanatomical insights have important implications for parenting.

In their book *Parenting from the Inside Out: How a Deeper Self-Understanding Can Help You Raise Children Who Thrive*, Dr. Daniel J. Siegel and coauthor Mary Hartzell challenge the traditional view that boys develop as "boys" because of their male biological inheritance. "Experience *is* biology," they argue. "How we treat our children changes who they are and how they will develop."[22] It is the "interpersonal neurobiology" underlying the formation of children's mental models that guides how they relate to others: "Neurons that fire together, wire together," according to the Canadian psychologist Donald Hebb.

Siegel and Hartzell cite findings from a landmark child development study in which researchers administered parents the Adult Attachment Inventory (a scale that measures the quality of the parent-child bond) and discovered that the test predicted the quality of their children's attachments in subsequent relationships with 85 percent accuracy. For "Boys will be boys" claims, this means that just the opposite is true: "Interactions with the environment, especially relationships with other people, directly shape the development of the brain's structure and function," Siegel concludes.[23]

Boys at early adolescence are vulnerable. Hardwired in each

boy's heart is a profound faith in those taking care of him. Each can be let down, overcome like the canary in a coal mine by developmental conditions that do not provide enough oxygen: relational connections, help, safety, love. It is not necessary to submit boys to punishing rituals to harden them; nor should we abandon boys to prepare them for autonomy. What so many parents underestimate is the nourishing goodness of our relationships. Open and susceptible to a wide range of influences beyond their families, what grounds boys is how well they can bring those who care to mind, hold us in their hearts, and remember that they are not alone. None of us can make his or her sons invulnerable—but we should never discount the power of our connections to strengthen them and keep them safe.

Psychologist Alison Gopnik of the University of California at Berkeley objects to approaches to raising children that overmanage them toward predetermined outcomes. Reviewing research on child development, she contends that parents and others have been drawn to the wrong metaphor. She observes that it was only in the beginning of the mid-1950s, as family life shifted in response to new patterns of work and consumption, that the concept of "parenting" came into vogue. Parenting, in this new view, was like the work of carpenters who take a piece of wood and fashion it into something predetermined, like a table or chair.

By contrast, to Gopnik, being a parent is like being a gardener: "When we garden, on the other hand, we create a protected and nurturing space for plants to flourish."[24] Supported by neuroscience and laboratory studies, she explains that children are not really projects and that parenting is less about outcomes than it is about *relationships*. "To be a parent—to care for a child—is to be part of a profound and unique human relationship, to engage in a particular kind of love," she writes. Not that the work of parental love is without rigor or demands; it is highly purposeful.[25] Gopnik adds:

"Love doesn't have goals or benchmarks or blueprints, but it does have a purpose. The purpose is not to change the people we love, but to give them what they need to thrive. Love's purpose is not to shape our beloved's destiny, but to help them shape their own."[26]

Boys are not mere robots, reflexively donning the badges of boyhood. They make choices, trying on one thing or another, from options that are limited, sometimes severely limited, and often foreign to their own values. They calculate and search for openings; the chance to be themselves. When contexts are harsh and masculine norms rigid and unyielding, with gangs of boys policing the group norm and ready to jump on one another, boys feel alone, overmatched, and hopeless. But in quality relationships, equality, authenticity, and love blossom as boys grow into their visions for themselves as men.

Recognizing how relational boys are can revolutionize boyhood. There are many times when pressures to conform will be overwhelming even to the most courageous or creative boys. But when a boy finds sufficient support that he can keep his own mind and hold on to his heart, he is more likely to take a healthier, more adaptive stance when those circumstances change. The best way to prepare boys for the world ahead is not to train them to follow outdated standards but to permit their humanity to flourish. As Gopnik maintains, "Even if we humans could precisely shape our children's behavior to suit our own goals and ideals, it would be counterproductive to do it. We can't know beforehand what unprecedented challenges the children of the future will face. Shaping them in our own image, or in the image of our current ideals, might actually keep them from adapting to changes in the future."[27]

I headed up a series of global studies investigating which educational strategies work for boys. My colleagues and I were led to an urgent realization by thousands of teachers and boys. When boys are relationally engaged, paid attention to, known and understood as they know and understand themselves, they will *try*. When they are effectively reached, boys who are failing and underperforming become engaged, improve, and excel. Boys who are distracting and oppositional in class become attentive, respectful contributors. The direction offered by relationships' role in realizing boys' capacity to commit was not limited to school. Attentive, caring relationships *transform* boys—especially boys struggling or in peril.

The real magic of boys' relationships with their parents, teachers, coaches, and mentors lies in how they are internalized, actually forming their minds and hearts. What we refer to as character strengths are less a product of genetics or constitution than of nurturing. Children are more likely to develop ambition and compassion under developmental conditions that cultivate these qualities. Virtues are not learned from preaching or lectures. Rather, virtues and character strengths are outcomes of children's experience as they face challenges, make decisions, and incorporate life lessons into their emerging senses of self. In the same way that boys have been falling behind in education as a result of an inadequate understanding of their relational needs, too many boys fail to develop the virtues and strengths they need largely due to confusion about the power of relationships to build character.

In 1993, William Bennett, the former US secretary of education under President Ronald Reagan, published *The Book of Virtues: A Treasury of Great Moral Stories*—a response to concerns heard around the country about the moral state of American youth. Other national efforts to promote the teaching of character also arose during that same period, most prominently the Character Counts! Coalition, a project of the Joseph and Edna Josephson Institute of Ethics, which touted "Six Pillars of Character": trustworthiness, respect, responsibility, fairness, caring, and citizenship. As the coalition explains on its website, "In personal relationships, in school, at the workplace—in life—who you are makes a difference! Character is not hereditary, nor does it develop automatically. It must be consciously developed by example and demand."[28]

But as the character movement grew, supported by federal

funding, scholars began to put a finer point on how character actually develops. Psychologist Marvin Berkowitz of the University of Missouri–St. Louis summarized the "science of character education." In Berkowitz's view, "it is clear that the primary influence on a child's character development is *how people treat the child*." In fact, the formation of a child's character begins very early, in parent-child relationships during the first year of life. He writes: "The development of an attachment bond, the powerful emotional relationship that develops between an infant and his or her primary caretaker (typically mother), may be the single most important step in the development of character."[29]

Nel Noddings, a legendary professor of education at Stanford University (and mother of ten children, grandmother of thirty-nine, great-grandmother of more than twenty), challenged the "long and checkered history" of character education and offered an "ethic of care" as an alternative approach.[30] She explained that children's values originate in their personal experiences of care: "We learn first how to be cared for, how to respond to loving efforts at care in a way that supports those efforts."[31] She worried about how well this care ethic was being nurtured in families and schools, and made a broad social claim for the critical nature of this work. "It is probably true," she wrote, "that one must learn how to be cared for and to care for oneself before learning to care for others."[32]

There is a real opportunity today to get boyhood right—perhaps for the first time. In the long history of childhood, social progress has come from periods of social foment. Concerns about an "end of men" may finally compel the honesty and courage needed to build new opportunities for boys. If so, boyhood scholars can provide a much better understanding of how boys learn, grow, and build virtue than ever before. Careful research that has actually *listened* to boys and identified threats to their flourishing can point the way to a more supportive, healthier, and more human boyhood.

In each of the chapters to come, I trace specific challenges and suggest strategies to guide all those supporting sons, students, and athletes. Though I share stories of boys from my work, the strategies will be more tactical than specific, more about *us* than about *them*. What I have to offer is more a stance than a recipe. If there is one thing I have learned from my own parenting, years of clinical care, community intervention, and observational research, it is that human development is a powerful, trustworthy force. When we get it right, when we meet our children's needs, they grow in remarkable ways. Boys rooted in strong attachments to supportive parents, teachers, mentors, and coaches are able to be themselves, and their humanity flourishes. Throughout *How to Raise a Boy*, I describe how to build and maintain strong connections with boys facing challenges in a boyhood that threatens to pull them away from their moorings.

And as we nurture all of their human capacities, including courage and integrity, I am confident that boys will surprise us with their reinvention of a boyhood well suited to this new world.

∽

CHAPTER 2

FREEING BOYS

There's a confusing paradox at the heart of male development. On the one hand, the determination of parents and schools to teach boys how to be men represents a sincere desire to help them. But even with the best of intentions, when parents become preoccupied with teaching boys lessons about being men, it can reduce their sons to projects and overlook their unique personalities for the sake of fitting them—often forcefully—into traditional boxes.

Boys have the ability to imagine for themselves lives that are entirely of their own design. Inspired by their dreams, they can and do *resist* all efforts to make them into something they are not. Rather than seeing this resistance as self-indulgence or willful avoidance, developmental scientists have come to understand it as an expression of a youngster's most basic human instinct for self-preservation. As he fights for who he is and wants to become, the child exercises the fundamental values of integrity and courage. In the eighties and nineties, studies of girls' resistance to the confines and sacrifices of sexist socialization showed how children naturally strive to express their true hearts.

But sometimes pressure to conform to social norms, even harmful ones, becomes overwhelming, and resistance is punishing. Whether a boy might submit to these pressures or resist them is puzzling. What are the conditions, internal and environmental, supporting a boy's healthy resistance?

Gender socialization is especially forceful with boys. In all of their relationships—with their peers, parents, and teachers—a system of rewards and punishments operates to suppress feminine qualities and press male children toward masculine ideals. Play styles, toys, chores, discipline, and patterns of adult-child interaction reinforce conformity to these norms. Because this socialization can violate basic instincts, male identity is said to be "fragile"—perhaps explaining why it is enforced so zealously. Claims of biological difference are backed up with pseudoscience. Whereas the mantra "Biology is destiny" is rarely applied to girls any longer, hormonal and brain-based explanations are so common with boys that the incongruity is seldom noticed.

Even experts struggle with masculine stereotypes. When psychologist Judy Chu initially met the six preschool boys in her two-year study, she was surprised. As she wrote in her book *When Boys Become "Boys": Development, Relationships, and Masculinity*, at first she "didn't know what to make of the boys' rowdy, rambunctious, and seemingly aggressive behavior."[1] A breakthrough occurred with a boy who, after greeting her warmly, made his hand into a gun and shot her; she looked away, unsure how to respond. But later that day, when he did it again, Dr. Chu smiled and pretended to shoot him back. The boy patiently explained that she was supposed to fall as if she were dead and gave her another chance. When she did as he instructed, he was pleased. Later, having established a connection, the boy asked to sit in her lap during story time.

As Chu became more aware of how her biases limited her understanding of what was happening, she sought to perceive "not only their physicality and 'aggression' (i.e., behaviors that reflected masculine stereotypes) but also their thoughtfulness and equanimity."[2] In their relationships, she observed boys who were "close, mutual, and responsive" with one another, shattering myths of males as individualistic, self-centered, and nonrelational.[3]

But over the two years she spent with them, the boys changed, becoming less authentic and more prone to posturing and pretending. Boys' first disconnection is from themselves, her research shows, setting off a stream of developmental losses and estrangements. Hiding from a boyhood that otherwise might condemn and punish them, boys adopt the only really safe option. It is a short-term strategy with long-term consequences.

Chu's mentor, the pioneering feminist Carol Gilligan, detailed the various ways children fight to preserve their integrity. Sometimes their resistance arises in psychologically healthy ways, especially when they find someone they can talk to about what they are experiencing. Sometimes their strategies are more internal, involving withdrawal and an inauthentic public pose. Though resistance is a boy's natural response to pressures to be something he is not, acute stress can push him to disconnect from himself when he is no longer able to stand his ground.

In Chu's research, there were many examples of boys' resistance, "primarily against silencing their selves, so to speak, and surrendering their sense of agency."[4] In my own research, I have found boys of all kinds who resist cultural pressures. But this basic insight applies to all of them: how well they preserve their humanness and authenticity, whether on the outside or privately, depends on the quality of the relationships they find in their families, schools, and neighborhoods.

Supporting Boys to Be Themselves

We can envision a new model for boyhood that begins, naturally, in relationships. For boys to resist masculine norms that are harmful, unhealthy, or unjust, they need at least one person who can support what matters to them. This "ally" can be a parent, a friend, a teacher, a counselor, an aunt or uncle—someone committed to them and to helping their personal dreams flourish. A relationship in which a boy can tell that he matters is fundamental to his ability to think for himself and to follow an independent course. A young man's self-confidence is not accidental or serendipitous but derives from experiences of being accurately understood, loved, and supported.

I learned about the power of recognizing boys' humanity in my first real job. Niles was an adolescent I met while working as a counselor at the state family court. On my presentencing unit, we had learned that a boy's likely prognosis could often be gauged by the thickness of his case folder—and Niles's was the thickest I had seen yet. His family members were all involved as clients and defendants with social services and the law. Poor, African American, consigned to underresourced schools in a town with a long history of segregation, Niles's family had experienced many adversities. In such a context, trusting relationships were in scarce supply. At the outset, I realized that trying to talk to Niles was not likely to be very productive. But after he revealed, in grudging, mumbled comments, that he liked to draw, I put a pad of paper and a box of colored pencils in front of him and invited him to draw while I worked us through the prescribed intake interview.

So many years later, the drawings Niles produced are still vivid in my memory. Bit by bit, over the course of subsequent sessions when I could simply sit with him and pay attention quietly, he sketched figures and scenes that depicted important parts of his life. I learned a great deal about him this way and was able to let him experience my interest in who he was in his own mind. As he shared his drawings, he would talk, and I could ask him about whatever the sketches represented.

Though our relationship took place in the context of court-mandated counseling while Niles awaited the judge's decision about his fate, he gradually participated more fully in thinking about what might happen next. He was a natural artist, his art representing an alternative to street-oriented activities. When his case was finally heard, the judge used his discretion to refer Niles to a residential school that had strong arts programs. Though I cannot say we became close, Niles taught me how listening and kindness make it possible for even toughened boys to reveal how they see themselves and to invest in their futures.

Connecting with boys seems quite basic but, in practice, is not always easy. Many boys build up habits of mistrust, detachment, and reticence. They learn to play it cool, showing little of what they actually feel and adopting a demeanor of indifference, boredom, or irritation. Confronted by these off-putting masks, parents and other caregivers can get confused and discouraged. Some may even give up or blame the boy, who seems unable to trust or respond.

After a talk for parents at a school recently, several fathers and mothers came up to me individually. The common concern was that they had lost their sons—to a group of peers, to anger or brooding silence, to video games and social media, and, occasionally, to romance. But whatever its cause, disconnection from their sons had left them feeling worried, bereft, and powerless. Knowing in their hearts that each child needs someone looking out for him, parents of boys who have become disconnected feel unsettled.

To each parent, I explained that real power, even when a boy is angry, stubborn, or closed off, actually resides with those in a position to reach for him. They have something to offer their sons—care and connection—that is ultimately irresistible. Paying attention, listening, and caring with confidence and persistence are critical resources for a boy's development. Even boys like Niles, who had been let down over and over again, cannot completely bury the need to be known and understood. When he receives the care and attention of an adult, a boy feels valued and valuable in and of himself. It is not just what he accomplishes, how he looks, or how well he performs that is important, but who he is. As a boy's self-concept is strengthened by the care and attention he receives, he is on much surer footing for the long-haul effort to resist the boy code.

When the power of their connections becomes clearer to parents, they may worry about times they are preoccupied or inattentive and let their sons down. But every human relationship cycles through periods of connection-disconnection-reconnection, I explain. In her research with teachers, Miriam Raider-Roth, a professor of education at the University of Cincinnati, discovered that push back from uncertain boys against teachers who are trying to engage with them sometimes causes the teachers to despair and to give up. In a 2012 paper, her research team explained, "In these situations, the resistance felt more personal to the teachers, and more threatening. . . . This kind of resistance also often led the teachers to 'let go' or 'step back' from their relationships with the boys."[5] But in my own studies of successful teaching approaches with boys, the relationships they recalled most fondly were often ones that had gone through periods of struggle and testing. It was the teacher's determination to reach them, persisting despite setbacks, that made the relationship so meaningful to boys.

Many boys hide their insecurities about learning behind a mask of indifference and passivity, or more openly in disruption and defiance. When they act disrespectfully or are uncooperative, teachers tend to become upset and angry. The very ways that boys act out their upsets produce upset among those who care for them, leading them to blame the boys and push them even further away. In Raider-Roth's study, a teacher who was having a difficult relationship with a young boy in his class described his anger toward the student as "profound"—a "deep-seated, unnerving raw emotion."[6] With little opportunity to process these strong reactions, it is unlikely that any teacher can perceive anything except the boy himself as the problem. Yet, as her team admitted, "[C]hildren acutely read teachers' presence and relational availability in the classroom and respond accordingly."[7] An angry, critical, or dismissive teacher is unlikely to reach the boy behind the mask.

Maintaining caring and connected relationships with boys can be particularly difficult. The boy who comes to school with an insecure or shaky attachment is more likely to avoid vulnerable dependence on his teachers. But as developmental psychologist Diana Divecha of the Yale Center for Emotional Intelligence remarks, attachment history is not destiny. Poor experiences with parents can be overcome by positive ones in later relationships. "Working models" that children build from hurtful experiences with their mothers and fathers can even be modified. Negative conclusions can be disconfirmed, hope resurrected. As we found in our research, teachers regularly manage to reach boys who have become mistrustful and antagonistic, overcoming their defensive barriers and transforming their life trajectories. As Divecha flatly summarized, "Children who have a secure attachment with at least one adult experience benefits."[8]

In fact, given how common relational ruptures are, both in general and particularly with boys, it is less important that caregivers maintain a steady, positive regard than that they monitor the quality of their connection with a boy; if it weakens or breaks, they must repair it. What differentiated successful from less successful relational teachers in my studies was how fully they understood their role as "relationship managers." Assuming responsibility for the relationship—going to great lengths to reach for a boy who has gotten stymied or stuck, in order to fix the breakdown—makes all the difference. According to Allan Schore, a neuroscientist at the University of California at Los Angeles (UCLA) Center for Culture, Brain, and Development, "Insecure attachment isn't created just by a caregiver's inattention or missteps. It also comes from a failure to repair ruptures."[9]

The relational challenges for those who care for boys must not be minimized, as I learned quite early in my career. Tony was one of the first boys I was assigned when I began a new job as a school counselor at urban schools in Philadelphia. An eighth grader, he was referred to me by a concerned principal who foresaw nothing but trouble ahead for him. The principal hoped that talking to a young male different from others in his life might afford him some perspective on a rigid masculine code that was sucking all light-heartedness and innocence from him. Son of an alcoholic father who was angry and violent, and whose idea of discipline was to haul off and punch his children, Tony at age thirteen already came off more as a little man than a boy. He allowed little softness or vulnerability to show.

Sitting in chairs in an office was not going to work with Tony, I realized upon first meeting him. For his second session, I put on a coat and invited him out for a walk through neighborhood streets. We meandered, led by Tony's whim, bound only by our limited time. I asked him about his week, gently bringing up issues that had come up at school, listening without judgment. I knew I would gain influence only if he would talk to me and over time open up to my point of view.

Some days Tony came angry and especially hard. Betrayed by practically every adult in his life, battered by his father and by street violence, the teenager had learned to respect only superior force. One day he had bruises on his face and explained that he and his father had fought the night before. I knew not to condemn his father, with whom Tony was already struggling to stay connected, but I had to let him know of my duty to report his father to Child

Protective Services if things crossed into child abuse. While I listened week to week, conflicted by how close the call was coming, I tried meanwhile simply to care and to show Tony that I was sorry for the violence and harshness of his life.

During one walk on a day in early spring when the air was just beginning to warm, I found myself thinking that Tony might be coming to depend on our time together. But just as I made this positive appraisal, Tony issued a new challenge: "Are you gay?" he asked accusingly. I responded simply, "Why do you ask?" Somewhat derisively, he answered, "You're not very tough, that's all." I was taken off guard by the statement until I realized that Tony was trying to make sense of a relationship with a male who was so different from others in his world. I realized that how I answered, how I revealed who I was, could be very important for him. I laughed with genuine embarrassment and said I understood that it was unusual for another guy to take an interest in him and not harbor some suspicious agenda. I also admitted that I was not skilled as a fighter and had never really been put to the test—a remarkable privilege. I did not know what it was like to have to be prepared to fight at any time. I turned his question around and asked, "I see you are a survivor and have had to fight hard for that. What's it been like?" In turn, he was taken by surprise but seemed to grasp my answer to his question. At least, he realized that I respected him and was not going to exploit him.

I would like to believe that by showing up consistently and not allowing myself to be put off by his moodiness, withholding, or disrespect, I managed to make some difference for Tony. I wanted him to see that there were adults who would reach for him, whose own feelings would not become the issue no matter how he acted. And that there were men who would not seek to dominate him or apply force in their relationships with him but would recognize that he was a boy and needed to depend on others for help.

The examples of Niles and Tony both represent a straightforward approach to boys whose withdrawal and cold shoulder became habitual: offer acceptance to the boy as he is. It comes down, at least at the start, to just listening. By paying attention to him and to whatever he cares about, asking questions and showing real interest, a caregiver signals interest in what a boy is thinking, feeling, doing—validating that who he *is* matters, not the part he plays. According to psychologist Michael Nichols, author of *The Lost Art of Listening: How Learning to Listen Can Improve Relationships*, "That validation is essential for sustaining the confirmation known as self-respect. Without being listened to, we are shut up in the solitude of our own hearts."[10]

Thus, I can recommend two basic tools for caregivers wanting to deepen boys' self-respect and enable their resistance, strengthening their resolve to fight for themselves.

Listening to Boys

When caregivers muster the willingness to simply listen and observe, without offering judgments or advice based on their own experience, it can make a world of difference to boys who are trying to develop confidence in their own judgment. When parents listen to their sons, they "bear witness," in Nichols's view, to the boy's experience and establish that he is not alone. Contrary to the stereotypic individuality promoted by traditional masculinity, the surest way to empower boys is to meet their dependency needs. Listening is the most important tool parents have for building boys' resilience.

Alone with their own feelings and reactions, children feel frightened and insecure. Research on secure attachments teaches that children who are able to depend on their caregivers are stronger, happier, and more confident. The self that a child becomes emerges from seeing himself in the eyes of significant others. From the earliest age through the rest of childhood, the most important experiences—the ones that contribute the most to his self-concept— happen in close relationships. Being alone is a primitive fear, counter to the most basic human instincts. Secure attachment is a precondition for independence. Simply listening is the most basic way to foster attachment.

Listening, of course, demands much more than accepting information. It involves an exchange that is more like receiving, understanding, and holding what is said. There is communication—words and meanings are exchanged—but on an emotional level, a deep resonance develops, allowing something primitive and visceral to happen: the one listened to is "known." The boy's self, aspects of who he is that are known and accepted by his listener, is strengthened. By contrast, the unknown self remains incomplete, searching for validation. For a boy who is not "well known," a split arises between his core self and the more public self unconsciously seeking validation, found too often only in a peer group that exacts its own price. As Nichols explains, "What never gets heard affects more than the difference between the socially sharable and the private; it drives a split between the true self and a false self."[11]

Listening certainly involves attention. It is hard to offer or sustain listening to someone else if your attention is dominated by pressing concerns. But more importantly listening is an emotional act. In listening exchanges between caregivers and children, the primary outcome is to soothe tense or upset feelings by the closeness, warmth, and understanding of a caring mother or father. According to neuroscientist Daniel Siegel, communicating emotions successfully is fundamental to an individual's sense of vitality and meaning. The sense of "feeling felt" that results for a boy when his parent tunes in to the emotional level of his experience actually can free him from bad feelings. As he offloads tensions to his listener, a boy notices his power to restore his own mind and his independence from the various pressures and threatening norms of his life. No matter what others think or want from him, he exists on his own. In this way, as Siegel and Hartzell write, "parents are the active sculptors of their children's growing brains."[12]

Effective listening, according to Nichols, involves "attention, appreciation, and affirmation." What listeners are trying to achieve is "empathic responsiveness," where the boy can tell that he is cared for, regardless of what he may feel or have done, and that his feelings are accepted and have not confused his listener or tied up that person in his or her own emotions. When parents are clear that empathic connection is the goal, what the boy does next or how he understands things is less important than affirming and strengthening his core self. Listeners learn to trust that boys will figure out things and are more likely to do so when they are not alone.[13]

A real problem is that it can be hard to listen to boys. Because deep listening involves both suppressing or setting aside their own emotional reactions while allowing whatever their sons are feeling to resonate in their hearts, parents are vulnerable to being hijacked by their own emotions. In certain situations, particularly when they are reminded of unpleasant encounters with the boy code, parents may have a limited capacity to "be with" boys. Their re-kindled upsets are on prominent display as their sons reach for their attention and compassion. How many conversations with boys go nowhere because a parent or a teacher feels compelled to give advice in hopes of saving the boy from an imagined danger? Instead of finding comfort and confidence, boys come away with more worries and doubts about their own abilities.

For parents, staying present while listening requires managing emotional reactions so they do not hijack the conversation. Siegel and Hartzell outline the "high" road and "low" road of our mind's response to emotional triggers.[14] The high road takes place at the top of the brain and involves reflection on the experience and coding of whatever feelings it arouses with language and thought. But the low road entails shutting down these rational processes in favor of primitive fight-flight-freeze reactions. The hallmark of low-road functioning is inflexibility.

Wanting a boy to believe that we truly want to know what he thinks and feels, parents have the problem that it is hard to fake attention. Strong feelings of worry, anger, or unconscious upset convey a sense of urgency that is hard to conceal. If parents' feelings frequently trump their ability to listen, boys will learn to stay away. The boy who becomes reticent and uncommunicative is typically one who does not expect to be heard. Building a boy's confident expectation that he will find someone who will listen to him requires that caregivers notice when their attention shifts to their own preoccupations. The strongest feelings are the ones that are hardest to keep perspective on. For many, these may seem less like feelings than legitimate concerns—nonnegotiable, bottom-line lessons good parents must impart to their sons.

Boys are especially prone to testing limits, forcing parents into authority roles that can interfere with listening. Contests over power can trigger parents' bad memories and lead to knee-jerk reactions. But to help a boy develop his own internal self-regulation, unreasonable or inappropriate behaviors should be met with a relaxed limit offered by a connected caregiver. Being relaxed when confronted with bad behavior is a key to effective discipline. What a boy who is acting badly is looking for is not permissiveness but someone who knows him well enough to recognize when he is "off" and needing to download the tension driving the misbehavior. The trick is to worry less about setting limits and focus more on learning what is causing the unreasonable behavior—connecting with the mind and heart behind the behavior.

When exercising authority becomes an end in itself, caregivers have effectively disconnected from the boy. Their attention is directed internally, and their emotional attunement with him is lost. Particularly when power struggles elicit feelings of frustration and anger, caregivers become preoccupied with vindicating their feelings. Strong emotions evoked in confrontations with boys often have their roots in "implicit memories": childhood experiences that the parent has forgotten but that nonetheless have the power to drive his reactions.[15] Unless caregivers want to return over and over again to these blind spots, when they notice their attention gravitating to internal concerns, it signals that something is unfinished and there is work to do.

Given how frequently ruptures occur in relationships with boys, perhaps even more important than listening are skills for recovering from emotional hijackings. When boys perceive that their caregivers will monitor themselves and bring themselves back from disconnections, they develop a happy expectancy: "I can count on my mother, father, coach, or teacher to stay in the relationship and not get so lost that they blame me, give up on reaching for me, and hold themselves apart from me." What Siegel and Hartzell call "toxic ruptures" are times when caregivers remain stuck on the low road, blaming their son for their upset feelings.[16] Random and idiosyncratic, relational breakdowns undermine a boy's trust.

Repair is always the responsibility of the caregiver. A boy is not in a position to reestablish connection when a breakdown has occurred in his relationships with parents, teachers, or mentors. It falls to the adult to exercise sufficient self-awareness that disconnections caused by harsh or angry reactions are monitored and repaired. Happily, perfection is not required. Boys will attach to the commitment offered, even when the caregiver has trouble staying connected or continuing to listen. When caregivers come back after losing it, with an honest acknowledgment that they got hijacked momentarily, boys learn an important moral lesson from their example. By simply saying, "I am sorry for getting so upset with you. Even though I didn't like what you did, my upset was more about my own experiences of being treated badly than what you did. I know you didn't mean to be hurtful." Boys are less able to absorb moral messages when they feel insecure or abandoned.

Special Time with Boys

Patty Wipfler, founder of the California-based parent education nonprofit, Hand in Hand Parenting, developed a set of tools to deepen parents' connections with their children:

- Staylistening (simply offering attention while a child lets off steam);
- Playlistening (following the child's lead in a game that invites laughter and joy);
- Setting limits (gently but firmly interrupting a child whose behavior indicates that he is upset);
- Special time (offering attention in dependable, child-centered ways).

These tools are relevant for children of all ages and enhance a parent's ability to provide the help boys need as they reach for goals that matter. As Wipfler, a mom and longtime parents' counselor, proclaims in her book *Listen: Five Simple Tools to Meet Your Everyday Parenting Challenges*, written with Tosha Schore, "The time is ripe to replace the focus on command and control in parenting with a focus on connection, sensible limits, and listening."[17]

With younger children, special time involves scheduling opportunities for the child to play, watch movies, read, or simply talk alongside his caregiver. The key is that the child decides how the time is structured and enjoys the opportunity to "spend" the resource of attention however he wants. The typical outcome is that, consciously and unconsciously, his sense of being known and cared for deepens and grows. This special time can also be applied to relationships with adolescent boys to powerful effect because older children, especially males, rarely find adults able to hang in with them.

Spending special time with an adolescent boy can mean lots of video games at the start, unfamiliar music, and gross or violent television movies and shows. Sometimes it means building forts, watching as the boy skateboards, playing one-on-one basketball (letting the boy win), or taking shots on a lacrosse goal in the backyard. The point is to reinforce the boy's appetite for the support of an adult who is not seeking to direct, dominate, or correct him. Simply offering attention and interest in whatever interests your son produces surprisingly powerful results.

Wipfler and Schore offer practical ideas for how to build special time into family routines. They suggest that the time be specifically named ("Any name will do, but there has to be a name") and a specific date and time set so that the boy can anticipate and depend on it.[18] For their own sakes, caregivers should begin with a shorter time commitment, perhaps fifteen minutes, to take measure of their attention and ability to follow their son's lead. The time can be built up to an hour or longer as confidence and better command of their attention is achieved. Screening out distractions is often a challenge—but it is a satisfying pleasure to focus on your youngster and simply enjoy the relationship. The point is to be pleased with wherever the boy's mind goes and however he expresses himself, enabling an unparalleled degree of understanding that leaves both child and parent feeling close.

Invariably, once a boy expects attention and comes to believe that it will be available, he will make extraordinarily good use of it. Being with a boy, accepting him by following his lead in play or conversation, evidencing a desire to know him by paying attention to whatever he wants to do or say, is a profound act of validation that builds a stronger, more confident sense of self. Offering regular special time is like putting money in the boy's bank: it safeguards him against whatever stresses lie ahead.

Well before I became a psychologist, and even before I had sons of my own, I attended workshops with Wipfler and others who practiced these tools. I had become especially interested in the power of connection to promote healthy male development. A friend I met at one of the workshops, a single mother with a twelve-year-old son, asked me if I wanted to spend some time with him. Jimmy was a vigorous boy who loved playing sports, though he was also quite sensitive. At times he was willful and wild. I also loved sports and thought I was up for the challenge. I made a commitment to spend time once a week with him as a way to deepen my own understanding of boys and in preparation for one day becoming a parent myself. In addition to helping my friend and her son, I believed I would learn a great deal about myself.

The first time I came to their house, his mother explained that I was a friend of hers interested in getting to know him. She, Jimmy, and I hung out together that afternoon, following his lead in whatever he chose to do. On a Little League baseball team at the time, Jimmy naturally wanted to play running bases and to throw the ball around. For one stretch, I pitched, his mother caught, and Jimmy took a long turn at bat. At the end of our time, I asked him if I could come again and hang out. He said, "Sure." The pattern we established extended over the next year: I'd stop by once a week at a time we had set aside. I never had to explain more to him about my interest in being with him—in a basic sense, young people expect that adults will want to be with them. But I did have to assure him, week after week, that I would be back. His father and mother had divorced some years ago, and he had some qualms about things he'd counted on disappearing.

In a short while, Jimmy came to depend on our time. We'd go off into the woods near his house, and he would show me all of his special places. Or we'd go for a ride to McDonald's when he got hungry. During special time, I challenged myself to pay attention to Jimmy, not to initiate an activity or otherwise modify what he wanted to do. My internal battle was with not taking over and not moving our focus to something more interesting to me. My mind regularly wandered to concerns or worries I had. I had to catch myself and bring my attention back to Jimmy and to the present moment repeatedly.

I got to know Jimmy better and better. Sometimes, as he came to trust me more, he became difficult—uncooperative, easily annoyed, making unreasonable demands—seeming to set up tests where I would have to say no and provide him with a limit. At these times, his feelings would flare, and he became angry, sulky, even teary, bringing a slew of painful emotions to the surface. He was sometimes rude or disrespectful. If I managed to keep my confidence and composure, not taking things personally or becoming upset at him in response, he always came through more relaxed and open to me. Our relationship grew. Overall, the chance to practice a relational approach with a teenage boy was invaluable. I learned a great deal from Jimmy.

There were many times when his behavior might have earned a reprimand. But because I was practicing a discipline—a listening approach to relationship building—I bit my tongue and learned how important it is to monitor and gain control over knee-jerk tendencies to judge boys and correct them. I knew I could assert my greater power but did not want merely to dominate Jimmy. I also believed that I did not need to teach him how to behave but rather support him while he struggled to regulate himself. Too often, parents and others react unthinkingly, simply passing along rules and relationship styles from one generation to the next. Often, we think that advice—"What I did at your age . . ."—is the best way for boys to improve their own judgment, without being realistic about how different the times and challenges are.

There are several rules to get the most out of special time: not giving advice, not dividing attention among other tasks, not talking to others or interrupting the time that's been promised, and not modifying the activity the boy has chosen, no matter how hard it might be to see its point. The main rule, though, is to keep your attention focused on the boy and to maintain a connection with him whatever he might do. That in itself will be a challenge for every caregiver, because most of us function with a shortage of attention. How many of us were paid attention to and listened to like this? Who had a parent or teacher so interested that he or she put aside everything simply to listen to us and play with us? Most adults proceed about their business only rarely, if ever, getting to share our deepest thoughts or feelings. We all suffer from attention deficits.

When we manage to stay with a boy during special time, what can we expect? Especially at the outset or in relationships with boys who have grown apart from us, we can expect to be tested, as many boys have become quite skeptical. It is as if they are thinking, "I'll bet Mom and Dad won't want to be with me if I show them all of what's inside me," or "I doubt they can hang in when I do what I really feel like doing." Over the year I spent time with Jimmy, he sometimes upped the challenge, and I would become confused. I didn't know what to do. Once, for example, out of nowhere, he began to sulk and withdraw on the ride home from McDonald's. In dramatic fashion, he went from being engaged and happy to turning away from me in the seat, looking out the window and pouting, refusing to answer when I asked him what was wrong. I had no idea what flipped the switch and felt worried and a bit manipulated. "What's up with this?" I muttered to myself.

But to Jimmy I remained patient and open as we arrived at his house, where he ran to his bedroom and closed the door. Following him, I sat outside the door and decided not to barge in but to talk through the door, reassuring him that whatever he felt was okay with me and that I was not going anywhere. Through the door, I could hear muffled sobs, but for a long time there was no reply. Eventually Jimmy came out again, and I simply smiled at him and followed him out to the backyard, where he picked up a bat and ball and resumed our play. I realized that Jimmy was still unable to tell me directly when he felt overcome by upset but also understood that by staying with him through the storms—not making a big deal out of it—I had passed a test. He had found that I would neither judge him nor leave.

The various ways that boys test caregivers in the course of a special-time relationship are not intended to push them away but unconsciously to settle a question in their minds: "Can this person handle me?" As the tests confirm that the attention and care are real and dependable, that there is a capable adult available for a relationship, the boy typically invests more and more hope: "Maybe I can really count on this."

Special time, even when it is going well, may lead to upset. Sometimes the boy will open up and talk about things that trouble him—even about the caregiver directly. Sometimes, especially when he feels ashamed, painful emotions may be masked or guarded until the boy achieves even greater confidence. When listening to a boy's hurt feelings, it is important to follow his lead and not allow curiosity to take over. The boy determines how much and how quickly he shares what's on his mind.

Sometimes boys have a hard time putting difficult feelings into words and set up situations that allow them to display the feelings in the context of play. Jimmy, for example, would sometimes "hurt" himself while playing baseball or basketball and fall to the ground, crying. My role was to take his hurt seriously, even if I did not perceive how it had happened, and to patiently pay attention while he complained. I saw that a buildup of frustration and fear had arisen around playing sports and that he was simply showing me how he struggled and stretched to meet the competition and challenge.

Offering special-time opportunities to boys will engage caregivers' most generous spirits, not to mention their discipline and focus. Some days will be easier than others. On the hard days, it will seem as though every moment brings another distraction, another intrusion, pulling your mind from your youngster to some other pressing matter. Stretched thin by too many demands, few caregivers have the slack to sustain their full attention on a child, especially when all he wants to do is play games. But it helps to remember that under cover of the game, the boy is doing vital work. He is establishing in his mind and heart that he matters so much to his caregivers that, even when they are pressed by important adult business, they make time for him. He is fortifying himself for the challenges of boyhood. Simply by trying and by coming back when they get thrown, a caregiver is offering a great gift.

∽

CHAPTER 3

BOYS AND THEIR HEARTS

In chapter 1, I introduced you to the 2017 "Man Box" study, in which younger men in the United States, United Kingdom, and Mexico were surveyed. When I first saw the report on the study, one set of findings leapt from the page: among eighteen-to-thirty-year-olds subscribing to a traditional masculine identity, three of four said they "experienced little pleasure in doing things" at least once in the last two weeks; two of three said they felt "down, depressed, or hopeless"; and two of five said they'd had "thoughts of suicide."[1] The prevalence of unhappiness among these young men bore witness to the especially poor fit of their identities as males with their human hearts. Forced to censor thoughts and feelings, life for these young men had become more performance than authentic experience. They were lonely and discouraged, missing out on the ease and uplift that comes with emotional connection.

Popular culture holds that women do feelings while men do action. But from a time when that was just how things were, everything has changed. Women have challenged biases about their capabilities by demonstrating how ably they both feel and act. Likewise, recent research indicates that stereotypes about male emotional incapacity may be equally mistaken. In fact, according to a number of new surveys, today young men are more invested in taking care of their mental health than their physical well-being. They understand that managing their minds is key to a good life. The NBA basketball player Kevin Love made a big splash off the court this year by going public about having a panic attack that disrupted his play in a key game. For the first time in twenty-nine years, he was forced to consider his emotional life and decided to serve as a role model for other males who ignore how they feel. As he wrote on the sports website Players' Tribune, "Everyone is going through something that we can't see."[2]

It's not that stereotypes of the unfeeling male don't have some basis. With masculine conventions still policed vigorously, most boys learn to keep their feelings private and to suppress and override them. With the exception of anger, boys often lose touch with how they feel. Cold showers, hazing rituals, bullying, and tests of courage have historically reinforced emotional disconnection. By the time a boy reaches adulthood, being emotionally present will likely be a challenge. A host of negative outcomes are associated with boys' suppressing their feelings, from academic underperformance to health-risk behaviors such as substance use, fighting, and recklessness.

But the notion of separate realms for acting and feeling is mistaken. Particularly in a connected world, relationships are where we live. When a boy is cut off from being aware of his own feelings, he is less able to relate to others. Tucked out of sight and beyond his conscious control, strong feelings are more likely to hijack his behavior. Unconstrained by empathy, he is more capable of hurting others.

If anything, emotional demands are even more complex and challenging for today's youth. San Diego State University psychologist Jean Twenge has tracked an alarming rise in unhappiness among young men and women. She warns of "the most severe mental health crisis for young people in decades,"[3] showing a dramatic spike in loneliness, depression, anxiety, and dissatisfaction with life among iGen'ers (those born between 1995 and 2012) since 2011. Like Kevin Love, many males seem ready to acknowledge that emotional disconnection is a poor life strategy. In a recent survey of younger males in the United Kingdom, a majority reported that anxiety was prevalent and had a negative impact on their work and social lives. Additional data from a survey conducted by the US National Institute of Mental Health (NIMH) confirms that nearly a third of young people suffer from anxiety. The iGen'ers, also called Generation Z, are experiencing an "epidemic of anguish."

Depressive symptoms have also "skyrocketed," reaching all-time highs in 2016 according to Twenge, and a majority of first-year college students now rate their mental health overall as "below average."[4] Though 6 million men suffer from depression each year, symptoms are often confusing and can go undiagnosed. "Men are more likely to report fatigue, irritability, loss of interest in work or hobbies, rather than feelings of sadness or worthlessness," Twenge explains.[5] In addition, suicide, on the rise since 2000, is now the seventh leading cause of death among males, taking the lives of four times more men than women.

Researchers have documented the many ways that boys are handicapped in their emotional development. Psychologist Ronald Levant of the University of Akron has even suggested that alexithymia, or "no words for feelings," typically found in trauma survivors, also characterizes the emotional condition of many males.[6] University of Connecticut psychology professor Dr. James O'Neil, who has spent a career researching men's lives, concluded that "emotional restrictedness" leads to a long list of unhealthy outcomes, including "negative psychological attitudes toward women and gay men, violent attitudes toward women, dangerous risk taking in regard to sex and health issues, substance use and abuse, psychological stress and strain, negative attitudes toward help seeking, delinquent behavior, low self-esteem, hostility and aggression, higher blood pressure levels, depression, anxiety, and marital and family problems."[7]

While these findings are sometimes explained by positing differences in emotional hardwiring between males and females, the fact is that boys and girls begin life with equal capacities for expressing their hearts. It is during childhood that emotional development diverges. Stephanie Shields, a psychologist at Penn State University, argues that it is in the *expression* of emotions, not their *experience* of them, that boys and girls differ. Conditioning accounts for the difference: "The boy learns to match 'boy' emotion to his own behavioral repertoire, the girl matches 'girl' emotion to hers, and both reject the emotional style associated with the other sex as unacceptable for themselves."[8]

University of California at Berkeley sociologist Arlie Hochschild coined the term "feeling rules" to describe how social norms govern human emotion. As children adapt to these rules, the rules themselves become second nature. Boys learn not just "surface acting" but also, more fundamentally, "deep acting,"[9] in which they try to both show a proper emotional demeanor and actually produce it. They must manifest courage and unflappability *and* strive not to be afraid at all. Boys feel disappointed in themselves and ashamed when they experience fear.

The stresses of modern life catch boys' parents in a squeeze: changing times prize emotional intelligence, and boys themselves want to take better care of their minds, but traditional models for socializing boys compromise their emotional literacy. Fortunately, these old-style ideas are being systematically challenged.

Schools, for example, are taking account of changing opportunities and are responding. Programs in social-emotional learning are now standard. In the boys' school where I have long worked, school administrators decided to introduce all of their high school students to a program that encourages peer support and colistening. In workshops on emotional first aid, we talked about life's routine upsets, hurts, and stresses, making a case against simply holding things in. Skills of talking and listening were described, and the boys were asked to choose a partner to try them out.

As they broke into pairs and spread out across the big, open room, most of the boys engaged in the listening exchange exercise with earnest commitment. I was surprised by how readily most of them took on the challenge; my surprise was another reminder how most of us harbor stereotypes, as University of New Hampshire professor Thomas Newkirk put it, about a "masculine distaste for sincerity."[10] But clearly this generation of young men, or at least those in front of me, wanted tools to combat stress and gloom. Looking around the room at the pairs arrayed on bleachers, sitting on the floor, leaning against the wall, and on wrestling mats rolled up on the side, I was also struck by how they needed the permission of an adult to breach the taboo against talking with each other. They could go against masculine taboos on my say-so, but not on their own volition.

Some struggled with the challenge and might have disrupted the exercise. While most managed to have a go despite feeling awkward, these boys shuffled and shifted, on such unfamiliar and forbidding ground that they simply balked. One boy, who grew so antsy he began to distract his neighbors, professed to me, "I don't have anything to talk about." Both Newkirk and psychologist William Pollack, the latter the author of *Real Boys: Rescuing Our Sons from the Myth of Boyhood,* sensitively describe the "double bind" of emotional sharing for males. According to Pollack, "A boy knows that were he to sit down and talk about his disappointing grades, his mother's illness, or his lonely weekends, he would be breaking the Boy Code."[11]

I understood and told the boys as much when we debriefed.

Most men make a habit of deflecting attention away from their interior lives. By the time I began to cocounsel as a young adult, I shared with the boys, I could not remember the last time I had been emotional. In fact, I could not remember a single time that someone had asked me how I felt—not my parents, teachers, coaches, or even my friends. If emotional intelligence consists of grasping feelings with awareness and coding them with language, I had become functionally illiterate. Like some of the boys before me in the room, I had great trepidation about talking with even close friends or my parents about the hard things in my life. I understood boys like the one who had "nothing to talk about." My emotional life was a mystery, and figuring out how to communicate about it was practically beyond me.

Obviously, there is a personal cost to suppressing feelings, as the Man Box research found. Fortunately, the feeling rules governing emotional development are changing. Dr. O'Neil, on the basis of a review of research, issued an optimistic forecast. "A paradigm shift is occurring in America with regard to . . . how US society perceives male emotions," he writes. "More than ever before, men are being allowed to be vulnerable, emotional human beings."[12]

In part, such changes are a matter of practical necessity, as today's world increasingly calls for "soft" skills that foster motivation, perseverance, and self-control. The landmark 1995 book *Emotional Intelligence* by Daniel Goleman, captured the spirit of the times and sparked new scientific interest. Emotional intelligence, defined by the Collaborative for Academic, Social and Emotional Learning (CASEL) as skills in self-awareness, self-management, social awareness, relationships, and responsible decision-making, has been the subject of thousands of studies since.[13] The growth of social-emotional learning (SEL) programs in schools is one direct result. By 2005, 60 percent of schools nationwide offered programs to teach emotional skills.

A 2011 analysis of more than two hundred studies reporting on

SEL programs, reaching 270,000 children, confirmed their effectiveness. The authors concluded: "SEL programming enhances students' connections to school, classroom behavior, and academic achievement."[14] A 2012 survey of teachers found that "Educators know these skills are teachable; want schools to give far more priority to integrating such development into the curriculum, instruction, and school culture; and believe state student learning standards should reflect this priority."[15] From a time when stoicism, flat affect, and grim determination were the emotional ideal, boys hear very different messages about their feelings today.

The Yale Center for Emotional Intelligence has developed an approach "for infusing emotions into the DNA of a school," which is now in 1,200 public, charter, and private schools in the United States and abroad. The program trains school personnel in teaching skills of recognizing, understanding, labeling, expressing, and regulating emotions (RULER) so that they can apply these skills in their teaching. Asked in 2017 about the reception of schools to the program, Marc Brackett, the center's founding director, replied: "It's been overwhelming, honestly. Right now, we have hundreds of public, private, and charter schools asking for training each year."[16]

Helping parents and teachers build emotional literacy into boys' daily lives represents a radical departure from centuries of neglect, suppression, and misconception. In families, parents can encourage their sons to develop their emotional vocabulary simply by listening to them with real interest and patience. In school programs, students learn to acknowledge their feelings and to develop insight into them rather than acting them out. An emphasis on practice is central to these programs. Children learn not only to process what they feel but also to express themselves based on their understanding of the feelings. In their developing minds, the loop between feelings, awareness, and action is strengthened to prevent hijacking by negative emotions that drive knee-jerk reactions.

When that young man said, "I don't have anything to talk

about," he was giving voice to the default position of students whose emotional development has been stunted. Too often, those are male. In their lives overall, boys have far less opportunity to exercise and practice the skills of emotional intelligence. On the Levels of Emotional Awareness Scales (LEAS), a measure designed by Richard Lane of the University of Arizona and Branka Zei Pollermann of the University of Geneva to distinguish different levels of emotional development, scores for females are typically higher than for males.[17] Providing real support for boys to do this work is where the rubber meets the road.

Being a Happy Man

Gender disparities in emotional development reflect how opportunity and outcome are linked. Conditioning boys to the norms of masculinity comes at the expense of their emotional literacy. But the good news is that boys themselves are ready whenever conditions allow.

We designed the peer counseling program at the Haverford School to encourage boys' exercise of emotional skills: listening with empathy, speaking honestly about emotionally difficult subjects, allowing painful emotions to surface and even to flow. With little coaxing, academic geeks, theater majors, and Division 1 football and wrestling recruits practice listening compassionately and describing their own stresses and upsets. As the boys build connection and confidence, they like to address emotionally loaded topics such as relationships with parents, with girls, sex, pornography, and drugs and alcohol. They find the courage to own up to their hardest struggles and even to admit behaviors they worry about or regret.

Counter to stereotypes of the emotionally clueless male, this program validates the hope that boys can fully communicate what they feel. In fact, when they do open up about their difficult feelings, they gloat about a "peer counseling high" from having released pent-up tensions.

One participant explained it:

Before peer counseling, when I would get angry or sad, I would just isolate myself in my room and not want to talk to anyone. But peer counseling showed me that when you talk to someone, it helps you feel a lot better. I was talking to my friend when I broke up with my girlfriend, and normally in that situation, I would just have shut myself up in my room. But thinking about peer counseling, I realized that as you talk about it, things get better. So I decided to speak to my friend, and it really helped me recover emotionally. It just made me feel better.

Opportunities to be real with one another are still an oasis in an overall boyhood dominated by self-denial. One student noted that there is a stark contrast between what the boys do during the meetings and the rest of their lives. Afterward, he reflected, "There is something about being vulnerable and allowing your fellow schoolmates to be vulnerable that is so genuine, I cried later that night. It was all I could think about for days."

Researchers have found that how males "do emotion" becomes more limited as they age. But in our experience in this program, when conditions allow for emotional intimacy, boys are all in, as this boy explains:

The fact that you can talk about anything that you need to in the confines of that, with that confidentiality, I think makes it a safe place. Like, this is not the place to judge somebody else. Kind of like, put yourself in their shoes. And I think that's especially something that makes it a safe environment; like, there's no reaction like "Oh my God, I can't believe you did that!" Or, you know, "I can't believe you feel this way!" It's just like, you know, "I understand what you're going through." And maybe, like, words of encouragement. And I think that's something you don't find everywhere. And, for me, that makes me feel like it's a safe place.

There are many examples over the years of boys who deepen their authenticity in the safety of the program. Tate was a well-liked boy whose warmth and genuine nature had won the hearts of his classmates. Although he was so overweight that he could not participate in sports, he showed up at games and matches to root for his classmates on every team. Shortly after he joined the peer counseling program, I asked him to take a turn in front of everyone, a standard part of each meeting that is useful both for the group and for the individual who gets to tell his story.

Despite how pleasant and generous he was, Tate shared a story that revealed how isolated and alone many boys become when they cannot find anyone to level with. As he began to talk, Tate revealed that his mother had died several years ago. From the looks on the other boys' faces, I realized that no one knew of his loss—he had not found a way to tell his teachers or his friends. As he went on to describe how he went to her graveside, set up a folding chair, and talked to her in times of stress, our understanding of how alone he was grew. He also explained that he did not know his father, never having lived with him, and that he could not burden his elderly grandparents who looked after him. While Tate expressed himself and felt warmly held by his friends, it was hard not to think about all the years since his mother died that he had carried his burdens by himself.

Tate, unfortunately, was not the only boy with deep secrets. In the first meeting of the program each September, we see many boys who are hiding from the world. But just as Tate boldly broke the barrier to tell his story, other boys typically also respond. The reliable recipe for helping boys open their hearts is not mysterious. Boys want what everyone wants: to talk with someone who will listen, understand, and care. They make a connection between getting things off their chests and fighting for the right to be happy.

Near the end of the year, one boy wrote:

> More than anything, my experience in peer counseling has taught me how to be a man; more specifically, how to pursue happiness as a man. There are a lot of misconceptions that permeate through the walls of this school about what a man actually is, but I have learned how to define what being a happy man is for me. I know that happiness means being comfortable showing emotions honestly. I know that happiness means sticking to what is important. I know that happiness comes from taking responsibility for one's actions. I have learned that embracing my weaknesses and accepting my mistakes enriches my life, motivates me to greater heights, teaches me humility, and invites me into the realm of self-love and forgiveness.

In my private clinical practice, I often find that there is a gap between what a boy feels and what those close to him know. Keeping secrets is a normative part of boyhood. But bottling up feelings never works very well, often leaking into behavior. In addition, stored-up feelings get magnified and distorted in the echo chamber of a boy's unrelieved thoughts.

That was the case with Sean, who at sixteen was in trouble just about everywhere: in school, at home with his parents—he was even beginning to draw the attention of the police. When his father called to make an appointment, he had a long list of concerns. Sean was failing in school, defiant at home, and becoming involved in alcohol and possibly drug use despite his parents' warnings about their family history of addiction. He was a very talented athlete, yet his performance on the field was inconsistent, and he had lost his coach's confidence. Everywhere, people were down on him, inclined to chalk up his difficulties to poor choices, bad character, a lack of grit, or worse. He was on his way to becoming a "bad boy."

I was expecting a tough kid, so the young man who entered my office was a surprise. As soon as he crossed the threshold, he began to cry. Throughout that session and the many that followed, Sean readily unloaded the tensions and emotional pain that had backed up on him. He spoke freely about how brokenhearted he was by his estrangement from his parents. In his view, they were quick to blame him, to rage and punish or coldly turn away from him. In reacting to the problems he created, the parents had lost sight of the son they had forgotten lived inside. He felt scared and utterly alone, and seized upon the opportunity of counseling to find release and understanding.

Because Sean was able to clear his mind of these upsets, he began to think more clearly about his choices and ultimately to gain better control over his behavior. At one point, Sean explained that he had always felt the need to get things off his chest. He described the "pressure inside" when he had to hold things in. But as he and his parents fell into a downward spiral, he had not been able to find anyone to tell how he felt. He turned to alcohol and drugs to relieve the pressure.

Sean gained perspective and began to own up to the self-defeating nature of his behavior. Within a short time, he agreed to enter a drug and alcohol treatment program to address the habit of numbing feelings that had gotten out of control. In sessions with his parents, he explained how they could help him. He pulled up his grades and played soccer with more commitment, ultimately earning a scholarship to a top college team.

My surprise at finding Sean to be so self-aware shows how

effectively images of emotionally constricted boys dominate the popular mind. I was ill-prepared for the depth and emotional facility of boys such as Sean and Tate. My own emotional training had planted masculine stereotypes deep in my mind. By the time I happened upon the peer counseling network myself, it had been years since I had been emotional or fully honest with anyone. I had little grasp of how much I had numbed myself in order to overcome difficult feelings and make my way in the world.

For the first year or so, I fumbled blindly for access to deeper feelings. Learning how to feel again came slowly. I had to relearn what originally came naturally. Memory after memory of being shushed, shamed, threatened, or simply ignored came to mind as I fought to recover from how cut off I was. Some years later, when I come across a boy like Sean—one who managed to retain the ability to let down his walls when he needed to—I was duly impressed by the integrity he had preserved.

Reclaiming access to my heart has taken work, discipline, and faith. But I was unhappy with how shut down I had become and felt that something of considerable importance had been lost. The project of reclaiming the integrity of my mind was often painful—the emotional reactions and memories I had stored up were not the good ones—but what happened when I allowed myself to feel was a wide-ranging improvement. Not only did tensions ease, but also I saw the world differently, as I looked out less through a lens of disappointment, bitterness, and fear. Even feelings that were unconscious, taken for granted in habitual pessimism and cynicism, yielded to the power of talking and being listened to. Getting back in touch with what I felt would lead to a more hopeful, reinvigorated outlook.

Most boys, young and still open, have an easier time than I did as an adult. In the school program, our experience has been that every boy comes to notice, express, and regulate his feelings better. The boys exhibit varying levels of emotional openness at the outset, depending on how stressful their lives are and the quality of their relationships. But as they practice in the program, each boy finds his voice—and welcomes the chance. Both Tate and Sean were backed up with difficult feelings they had been unable to offload. Bad decisions compounded their isolation and multiplied negative consequences.

Two emotional states have special relevance for boys, particularly when they do not have an opportunity to bounce back from adversities. Cultural norms reinforce boys' experiences of both shame and anger, confusing and confounding their emotional development.

Experiences of Shame

Shame is an integral part of male development, infecting every boy's self-image. Dr. Judy Chu found among four-to-six-year-olds that an unachievable standard for masculinity was already at play in their lives, setting off a lifelong tension between who a boy is and how he believes he measures up against cultural expectations. "It can begin with being teased for playing a girls' game or for being 'chicken,' and it becomes the companion of every soldier who, facing battle, dreads his own terror and the possibility that his unmanly fear will cause him to act like a coward," psychologist Steven Krugman writes.[18] Shaming boys who do not measure up has been a tradition passed from one generation to the next. He adds: "Normative male socialization relies heavily on the aversive power of shame to shape acceptable male behavior and attitudes and leaves many boys extremely shame sensitive."[19]

Boys are vulnerable to feeling inadequate because they are shamed constantly. The masculine ideal, though unattainable, is not merely abstract; it comes across in daily reminders. The parent who worries about how his son throws a ball, the teacher who invalidates him when frustrated by his misbehavior, the coach seeking to motivate with insults and humiliation, classmates who are quick to call him "gay"—the net effect is to confound each boy's way of thinking about himself. Boys learn early—by age five, according to Chu—that they must dress, talk, and relate in certain ways or face negative sanctions.

Because shame is often delivered by those closest to them, boys are unable to deflect the relentless critique of who they are. Negativity seeps into each boy's self-image so that boys learn to keep their doubts to themselves. As Krugman explains, "Shame arises as the boy surrenders, and hides, his own subjective self."[20] One result is that boys' feelings go underground, hidden even from those closest to them. Learning to operate on top of self-doubt becomes so automatic that it is largely unconscious.

But avoidance goes only so far. Feelings of shame are sometimes impossible to escape. An example was Josh, a very bright, very sensitive thirteen-year-old with attention deficits that made many things hard, including school performance and social life. He grew accustomed to being in the bottom of his class and receiving regular warnings from teachers for restless behavior. He also found it hard to manage the push and pull of life with his classmates. Feeling vulnerable and embarrassed, he was an easy mark for other boys who were bored or showing off. His pent-up frustration led to eruptions, and, of course, that only made matters worse with both his teachers and his peers. His parents' concerns grew. Eventually they arranged for Josh to see me.

From the outset, I saw that in their traditional family arrangement, Josh's father, who was out of the home most of the day, played the role of peacemaker, while his mother was left to be the disciplinarian. In my office, the father could speak soothingly to his son; the mother, however, more backed up with irritation and disappointment, was less sure of herself. The parents were concerned about not just Josh's issues in school but also his tantrums with his mother. Despite how difficult the situation had become, the youngster was deeply connected to his parents and still cared what they thought. More than anything, he wanted to please his mother and make both parents proud.

As he and I explored his misbehavior and meltdowns, it became clear that they occurred when he reached a point of despair and felt that nothing he could do would make his mother happy with him. In response to tensions he felt with her, he either blew up or withdrew. He learned to bury himself in a graphic novel or video game and stubbornly resist efforts to engage him. The parents interpreted his silent treatment as willful resistance and resorted to punishments such as shutting off his electronics—which prevented him from communicating with his few friends over social media. Their relationship with Josh went into a tailspin.

Once he showed me how he loved his family and cared about their expectations, I urged him to let his parents in on the secret. With patient backing, he managed to tell them that he retreated to silence because he felt overcome with shame. I helped his parents understand that what he needed was not blame but assurance that no matter what mistakes he made or setbacks he encountered, his goodness was not up for grabs. They made clear to him that he would not lose them when he messed up.

Ultimately shame must be resolved, or else it dominates a boy's relationships—with himself as well as others. But there are healthy and unhealthy strategies for dealing with shame. Hiding fears and insecurities gives shame a great deal of power, even though hiding may seem like the only course available. But when he is known and accepted, a boy can learn to accept himself as unfinished and imperfect. He can learn to see himself independently of the masculine standard and even develop a liberating critique of the norms themselves. He can come to terms with his vulnerabilities and discover the comfort of people who hold him dear, no matter how he falls short or makes mistakes.

Derek was a shy, bright boy from the inner city on scholarship at a suburban private school. Polite and willing, warm and talented, he typically hung back a bit, taking his cues from what was going on around him, at the expense of being spontaneous. Everyone liked Derek, and he had lots of friends, but his relationships were a bit shallow. He was lots of fun and was typically included in invitations to parties, yet he could be overlooked once there.

Finally, a track coach who noticed Derek's tentativeness and believed he was capable of more took him aside one day and asked him how he was doing. Derek responded to the coach's genuine interest by saying that he knew he was holding himself back. He explained when he had first learned to "keep things to myself." It turns out his father, fighting a poor education and consistent unemployment, had developed anger problems. Derek had witnessed violent arguments between his parents. One time, after his father had gone out, and he and his brother had gone to sleep, Derek awakened to crashing noises and raised voices. Finally, he heard his father stomping upstairs, screaming that he was going to take the children and leave home. As his father barged into the room, his mother caught up and tried to stop him. His father shoved her out the door and down the stairs. Her fall finally shook him back to his senses, and he rushed out of the home, never to return.

Derek and his mother went on with their lives after the incident. But he was in shock and confused by conflicting emotions. As often happens with children, he felt badly that he had not stopped his father and prevented his mother from being hurt. He blamed himself for being so paralyzed with shock and fear that he did nothing. He decided not to tell anyone what he had been through, and once the habit of keeping things to himself was established, it took deeper root. He explained to the coach that he didn't want "anyone's pity." In his new school, stereotypes of families from the city abounded among his sheltered friends and teammates.

Relieved that he had gotten the story out, Derek was ready to address the way shame inhibited him. Together, he and the coach came up with a plan. The coach asked him to commit himself completely: no holding back even when he hit a wall. During practices, the coach yelled at him to reach deeper, try harder. Finally, on one grueling day, Derek collapsed at the finish line in a tantrum of pounding rage and tears. All his upset and frustration at how it had limited him poured out. The coach sat down alongside him on the track, simply listening to what he was feeling and letting him know it was all right.

The combination of Derek's honesty and the coach's instincts allowed him to achieve a breakthrough. They both grasped that emotional stoicism was preventing him from achieving his potential as a runner. Censoring his heart, keeping himself in constant check, saps a boy's vitality.

Feelings of shame can cause a boy to isolate himself in order to still anxious self-criticism. The pattern of male isolation develops early. Normal feelings of wanting to be close with his mother, for example, become suspect when a boy receives messages that he should be tough, independent, and self-sufficient. According to psychologist William Pollack, "This painful separation process by which many very young boys are shamed into withdrawing from their mothers more than they naturally want to, and then are only partially nurtured by their fathers, is a devastating disruption in a boy's emotional life."[21] Mothers of boys everywhere mourn the age when their sons become too embarrassed to hug them publicly, afraid that they will be seen as "mama's boys" or "babies."

Depending on how harsh these messages are, a boy can become defensive in order to mask shameful feelings of dependency and longing. A common strategy is to deny the desires altogether—"I don't need anybody"—or turn to male bonding and hypermasculine behaviors for closeness and connection. For some boys, disconnection fuels anger and rage. The more they are blocked from finding acceptance by others, the more likely they are to turn to the only emotional outlet available.

Angry Boys

Anger is a special example of how emotional rules differ for males and females. Girls are expected to hold in anger—to be "nice"—while boys are often permitted to act it out. As a consequence, boys are more likely to be aggressive and hostile, as well as to steal and engage in other antisocial acts. These emotion rules create a conundrum for those who care for boys. So long as anger is the only permissible way for boys to show emotion—whether fear, hurt, disappointment, loss—how can they strengthen their emotional intelligence? Penn State psychologist Stephanie Shields writes in her book *Speaking from the Heart: Gender and the Social Meaning of Emotion*, "The question of anger is *the* fundamental paradox in the emotional female/unemotional male stereotype. The stereotype of emotionality is female, but the stereotype of anger, a prototypic emotion, is male."[22]

She goes on to say that anger arises "when we believe we have been or might be deprived of something we believe is rightfully ours."[23] Unlike sadness, anger is an action emotion. The angry individual is flush with the impulse to correct an injustice and feels justified to use aggression and power. Higher-status individuals are more likely to experience anger, while people in lower-status positions are more likely to register loss with sadness or guilt.

Anger has been seen as both a trait and as a state. As a trait, some people are thought to be more prone to angry responses than others. These are the boys, for example, who routinely blow a gasket when they are practicing a skill or a sport; their frustration boils over. Or the young man other people tiptoe around because they fear his random explosions. Whatever issue David's parents took on with him—calls from the school about behavior, declining grades, fights with his sister, violations of curfew, and Internet use agreements—inevitably led to David's flying off the handle. His frustration and disappointment predictably boiled over. Chad's anger, on the other hand, blew up only in reaction to a boy whose remarks crossed a line. These two ways that anger manifests among boys come from different places: the freedom to express anger when wronged and a more general entitlement to rage.

Author Megan Boler, a professor at the University of Toronto, also sees two different kinds of anger—moral and defensive—depending on the reaction triggered in the situation. When a boy believes he is the victim of an injustice, feelings of anger arise out of moral indignation and righteousness. But when a boy feels threatened, his angry reactions are more about fear. One young man I saw recently, who had a difficult relationship with his father, reached the point in an argument that he became physically overwrought and began to tremble uncontrollably. It was not hard to see how the intense emotions aroused by the father overwhelmed his self-control. Boler writes: "Two key features seem to underlie defensive anger: fear as a response to change, and a fear of loss. In most cases of fear, it is often easier to react angrily than to feel one's vulnerability."[24]

In his 2017 book *Angry White Men: American Masculinity at the End of an Era*, sociologist Michael Kimmel sees male entitlement as a long-standing historical phenomenon. Displaced by greater gender and racial equality, some men register feelings of "aggrieved entitlement" as they perceive diminished opportunities.[25] Instead of acknowledging fear and loss, these men expressed righteousness and outrage. What was "theirs" had been taken away. I saw similar reactions from boys who were cut or benched on my sons' soccer teams. Rather than see themselves at fault, often they—and sometimes their parents—would complain about coaches who took away "their" playing time.

Calculations of risk often govern how a boy expresses anger. "Will I get into trouble?" "Do I dare face the consequences?" The large gender gap in school misbehavior underscores how much freer boys are to express anger. Defiance and willful opposition are still largely the province of the angry, uncooperative male student. Experts find that, in families, boys receive harsher discipline for similar reasons.

This story about a boy in my practice shows how anger and misbehavior are commonly linked. Lawrence was a middle school student who was hungry nearly all the time. Put in charge of packing his own lunch, including getting his sandwich from the fridge, one morning he forgot, and when he got to the cafeteria, Lawrence discovered that his lunchbox was empty. He had no money and had exhausted his friends' generosity from weeks of begging for their extras. A surge of anger toward his mother rose, prompting an impulse to act. He went through the cafeteria line anyway, helping himself to the food he wanted and darting out of line before he reached the cashier. Only after he was caught and suspended for stealing, had spoken with his mother, and received her punishment did Lawrence recognize how frustration had compromised his judgment.

Boys' anger and the bad behavior that often follows confuses people. For generations, hormonal activity was thought to explain emotional and behavioral differences between boys and girls, though research never supported this view. Boys express angry feelings because they can—and because expressing other feelings is more difficult. Many boys fight when they feel like they can't do what they really want to do: flee a situation or break down emotionally.

One morning during my job at family court, I was summoned by the bailiff to the basement level. As we rode down in the elevator, he explained that I needed to talk to "my" boy. When the elevator door opened, inside the single cell in the middle of the floor was my client, Niles, surly and bruised. The sensitive, sweet boy with an artistic flair who showed up at our weekly sessions had been transformed into a hardened, angry man, barely acknowledging our connection. He had been subdued physically in the lobby after starting a fight with boys from a rival gang he ran into while coming for his weekly appointment. In the scuffle, he had pulled out a pair of nunchakus he had tucked into his pants.

Why, I wondered, would Niles choose violence under the noses of a justice system about to decide his fate? His response to the other boys was less rational than instinctive, I recognized; he did what he felt he had to do. Backed into a corner and heedless of consequences, the flush of anger masked more difficult feelings of fear and shame. Anger was the reaction he could actually express.

What child psychologists Dan Kindlon and Michael Thompson call the "culture of cruelty" ensures that every male gets plenty of practice standing up to bullies and defending himself against public humiliation.[26] The feelings that boys show on the outside often belie what they feel inside. Anxiety and uncertainty, shame and humiliation, haunt many boys' private thoughts. In the public arena, feeling rules mandate that a boy never back down or yield to fears.

Parents as Counselors for Their Sons

Emotional development is a special problem for boyhood. Traditionally, gender differences in emotional outcomes have been explained as a result of biologically based binary differences. But differences that can be observed in boys' and girls' emotional behavior are more likely to be the result of emotional experiences that are governed by gender-based rules. Research confirms that behind their masks is a beating, emotional heart in each boy. Alone, few are able to go against the powerful social norms that box them in.

Parents and caregivers are the most natural champions for boys—their "first responders" and the most natural containers for their upset. To bring your hurt and upset to your caregiver, seeking comfort and understanding, is instinctual, beginning in infancy when experiencing hunger, cold, or loneliness and then extending to other feelings as children grow. Serving as counselors for their children is part of a parent's job description. How can we fulfill this role with our sons?

For starters, we have to recognize how things go awry. Though a boy may expect help with difficult feelings, that's not what many receive. Parents' reactions, sometimes unconscious, can limit their attention, compassion, and ease. Certain topics can be hard to hear. Parents may hesitate to cross boundaries and intrude on their son's "personal business." Boys who do not fit the masculine mold may have few interactions that are not fraught with their parents' own upset. Such worries can even incline parents to urge their son to act more manly. In many different ways, tensions can interfere with their ability to listen.

Cory and his mother came to see me after she'd reached the end of her rope. The tenth grader was crashing in his courses, doing next to nothing. As I discovered when I met with him alone, his lack of motivation and poor performance were related to the fact that Cory was getting high practically every day—his way of dealing with a family still struggling years after his father had left them. His mother was undone at being abandoned by her husband and could scarcely function outside of her job and routine household tasks. Cory was protective and solicitous of her. Getting high became a way to manage anger at his father and worry for his mother.

In his diminished family life after his parents' divorce, Cory chose to keep his growing dependency to himself. He explained to me that he did not want to add to his mother's burdens. He had lost not just his father but also his mother. There was no one left to help him with his stresses.

Somehow he managed to ask his mother to find someone for him to talk to. As he described to me how he was trying to help his mother by keeping things from her, I suggested that helping her do her job as his parent was the help she really needed from him. Cory reluctantly agreed to a joint session to let her in on how he was feeling. In the session, I explored with his mother how hard it must have been for her when her husband and partner had gone but that she was getting stronger. I urged her to let her son know that she was stronger now, that she loved supporting him, and wanted him to let her back into his life. I helped Cory express how alone and afraid he had been feeling, and coached him to rest his head on his mother's shoulder and to absorb the fact that she could bear his weight—that his needing her was not a drain or a burden.

It has surprised me how often, as boys grow into men with deeper voices and bigger muscles, parents forget that they still need care and protection. The myth that a man bears responsibility on his own seeps into relationships with boys as they grow. I usually try to meet with young men and their parents together for some sessions because coaching them in their primary relationships is the best long-term treatment I can offer. With the boy, I coax him to take his emotional needs seriously and to level with his parents. Meanwhile, I remind mothers and fathers that they still have critical roles to play. Though it is not their job to solve his problems, parents can help boys by listening and offering them chances to sort through feelings for their next step.

Be Patient and Stay Confident

The most important qualities boys need in their listeners are patience and confidence. For a host of reasons, many boys have had to man up, training themselves to keep uncertain or upsetting feelings to themselves, allowing only anger to leak out. Reversing course and opening up, though ultimately of great relief, will seem threatening and foreign in the beginning. Some boys may feel that they are regressing to a more dependent stage and that their very manhood is at stake. Parents cannot reassure boys through these worries; the boy himself has to put two and two together, discovering that he is stronger and more resilient when he is less alone.

As he contends with the worry, insecurity, and isolation that come with having to suppress his emotional side, a boy may project his upset onto the parent reaching out to him, who seems to imply that he is doing something wrong. The very act of reaching for the boy who has retreated behind a mask invites him to show what he is really feeling. Parents may catch lots of upsetting feelings as the boy's discomfort comes out into the open. This is the point: using themselves as bait, parents have succeeded in luring the boy to a more honest connection.

What gets tricky is not to take what your son says or how he acts personally. Many parents have rather limited capacities to tolerate disrespect or rejection, particularly when they are stretching out of their comfort zones in the first place. But I ask parents who feel disgruntled or discouraged to think about the situation: Do they really require an overwrought child to exercise self-control and to censor agitated thoughts as a precondition for listening? Can they really expect him to have so much perspective about raw feelings that he can moderate how he talks about them?

Hanging in, keeping calm, and even smiling with warmth and understanding as he criticizes, blames, or rejects them will let the boy know that his parents can handle the truth of what he is feeling. Hidden behind the masks they keep up, boys' stress levels are usually higher than adults suspect. Withdrawal and stoicism hide a fear of what seem like impossible challenges. It falls to parents to offer the larger view that their sons are not alone and that they can figure out their lives (parents' worries notwithstanding).

Build Up Relational Capital

When setting out to listen, parents may find that their timing is off. Their son is not in a place to share and puts them off. No question seems worded quite right, no tone relaxed enough. Sometimes boys' upsets are being so tightly "managed," and their troubles feel so far beyond any help and understanding their parents can offer, that the best they can do is withdraw to ruminate while barely concealing their irritation.

Between avoiding topics they perceive that their parents are not good with, preferring to talk instead to friends or romantic partners or simply shutting down altogether, often there are many roadblocks before boys will actually take advantage of a parent's invitation to open up. Having a foundation of easy enjoyment and fun in their relationships with their sons, built through special time and times just hanging out, is all the more important for this reason. Boys draw on this reserve when they come up against harder feelings.

Sometimes boys can be explicit about needing to talk; other times they just make their way alongside their parent, hoping to be noticed or to find an opening. Under ideal circumstances, parents simply follow their son's lead. An open-ended question such as "How's it going?" or "How was last night?" signals their willingness to listen. But parents should not be put off if the boy chooses not to respond. Other factors may be narrowing his openness and pressing the question may backfire. Sometimes a son will be grateful for his parents' persistence, but sometimes not intruding deepens trust. When the reticent boy finally opens up, he will feel even more in charge of himself and more confident of his relationship with Mom and Dad.

For many parents of teenage boys, the "need to know" can be driven by anxiety more than by real necessity. But parents who take a management-like approach to their sons operate on a misconception that the quality of the relationship is secondary to the boy's performance, safety, or compliance with rules, expectations, or values. Boys typically react to these approaches in one of two ways: some rebel and reactively separate themselves from their parents to gain a measure of independence, while others accept the terms of exchange in the relationship and fail to establish their own lives.

Both my sons played youth soccer, beginning at age four and staying at it through high school and even college. Along the way, from our vantage point on countless sidelines and in bleachers, their mother and I witnessed many boys who faltered and failed to capitalize on their talents. While some found other interests compelling, many turned away because it was their only solution to overbearing soccer moms or dads. Ultimately the parent could not force them to perform, and they could win by losing.

A better way than trying to manage a boy is to offer him the magic of being loved, known, and listened to. This long-game approach may not ease the anxiety underlying a parental impulse to control and dominate, but it has a greater chance of building open communication, particularly with adolescent boys. Sometimes in my practice, I see a boy who tells his parent almost everything. Reliably, behind his connection is his faith that the parent is there for him—not on top of him or rushing in whenever an impulse arises.

Manage Reactions to Anger

Perhaps even more challenging than dealing with boys' propensity to avoid sharing is how parents manage reactions to their anger. Anger, or at least bluster, is common in boys; by adolescence it becomes the only emotion many believe they can get away with showing. But angry males can be frightening. Over the years, many boys have shown up in my office with bandaged or casted hands while there are holes back home in their bedroom walls. Pent up and unable to vent tensions, boys sometimes lash out indiscriminately. A boy's anger, especially as he reaches physical maturity but lacks mature self-regulation, can explode. When parents respond to an angry boy with their own anger or fearful efforts to control him, it is like pouring gasoline on a fire.

Anger is often the first wave in a boy's emotional release—the initial burst of painful energy that precedes more difficult feelings. Usually if the parent reacts calmly and confidently, there will be enough space and safety for the son to peel through this top layer of feeling to more tender emotions of fear, shame, disappointment, and heartache. Depending on how backed up the boy is or how powerfully he hurts, the angry outburst can be big and noisy. It may be hard to see any rational awareness governing his rage. But what a difference it makes when a young man finds room to show how threatened or frustrated he feels. Tense muscles relax, a pit in the stomach is replaced by easy, deep breaths, and instead of the fight-or-flight response taking charge, there is ease, connection, and awareness.

For parents to function as counselors for angry boys, they may need to address their own experiences of having been hurt by angry men in their pasts. Too often, the link between their son's anger and their earlier trauma remains unconscious. Under these circumstances, parents will find themselves propelled by strong feelings to suppress their son or simply to avoid him altogether. But it is a tragic, missed opportunity when parents are limited by unresolved hurts and cannot be emotionally present for their son.

For example, John was a well-adjusted high school boy, musically talented and socially adept. His family adored him, and he ate up their attention. While he respected and was quite close to both parents, his busy father deferred to the mother in most parenting matters. John and she had a special relationship—until he hit adolescence and began to test her moral code. Mother and son came to see me on the recommendation of the dean at school, who saw John becoming wilder and less focused on his responsibilities. In my assessment, I learned that although she had firm policies about substance use and sexual behavior, John's mother was relatively ineffective with him. He either lied or charmed his way around her limits, all the while going further and further in unwise directions. When she stood up to him, John became angry and frustrated—and his mother would relent. When I asked her about the confusing message she was sending her son, she fell into a state of overwhelming anxiety. She felt unable to rein him in.

Over time, what came out was that an alcoholic father had abused her long ago, a period in her life she had gotten as far away from as she could. With the emotional energy of these hurts still alive, her balance was easily undone by triggers such as her son's behavior. She could be plunged into a state of dread. A chronic migraine sufferer, life felt like a day-to-day struggle. As John's limit testing grew more frequent and insistent, she became shriller and more stressed.

Parents who find it hard to stand firm with their sons have often been thrown, consciously or unconsciously, into a replay of past situations in which they truly were powerless. At the most primitive level, avoiding conflict becomes the chief concern, even if their sons are pushing into unhealthy territory. In another scenario equally about powerlessness, parents may lose it themselves, fighting for their own survival and forgetting about being the adult responsible for listening.

Making a connection between past hurts and present reactions can help parents free themselves from a repetitive pattern of ineffective behavior. The painful experience that becomes conscious is on its way to resolution and is less likely to take over the parent's behavior. Though the painful energy of the experience may take some time to work through, parents who have faced up to how they have been hurt are less vulnerable to blindly casting their sons in the role of antagonist.

Staying connected to a boy even as his anger rises creates a space in which he can address mistakes, real or imagined, that have driven him from the relationship. Parents are not perfect, nor do they need to be, and there must be room for the boy to say when he feels let down—or else he may go away. Asking boys to swallow what they feel and be "nice" deprives them of initiative to repair a relationship that has broken down. Where they can, when a parent picks up in a boy's tone or attitude that he is angry, it is always a good idea to ask, as nondefensively as possible, "Have I done something to upset you?" or "What's come between us?" When there has been a real wound, of commission or omission, the parent should apologize. Sometimes it even works to apologize regardless: "I'm sorry I didn't get it right with you." Hopefully, parents have enough ego strength and support that they can afford to take the fall so the connection to them can be restored.

Ideas for Schools

The peer counseling program I have described takes place in a school for a good reason. Such programs provide training in essential skills intended to "prepare boys for life." SEL programs everywhere echo these goals. According to the Collaborative for Academic, Social and Emotional Learning (CASEL), an organization committed to research, practice, and policy, social and emotional development in children is "a fundamental element of academic success." When boys in the peer counseling program evaluate it, they point to skills they have acquired or deepened, including listening to others, opening up about how they feel, and learning to trust someone else. They also appreciate hearing what other boys are going through, coming away more connected to their classmates. Most gain the sense that no matter what they struggle with, they are not alone.

For a teacher in a one-on-one relationship with a student, the conflict between the role as a grade-giving authority and as a confidant must be clarified for the boy to perceive an opportunity to discuss personal matters. Knee-jerk reactions of giving advice, judging, censoring, or one-upping can also cause the boy to keep things to himself. The solution is for the teacher to build a connection on a personal level with each student, drawing from a repertoire of relational gestures—for example, by sharing an interest, identity, or experience in common with a student to deepen connection. Conveying confidence and even humor, expecting that eventually even more resistant boys will come around, is usually also welcome.

Disciplinary consequences evoke boys' emotions. Too often in schools, the behavior code is the priority, positioning educators in disciplinary rather than counseling mode. The rationale I hear is that unbending rules are the best way to teach boys how to live within the lines. Indeed, I have come across many boys who need the hard reality of consequences in order to think twice about their impulses. But lost in a reliance on punishment is help for boys to gain insight and better self-control. When punishment is the dominant approach, boys readily retreat to defensive rationalizations that, though often sheer nonsense, keep them from seeing their own mistakes and changing their behavior

Ted was a quiet boy on most occasions. But one day he got into an argument with a teacher who had caught him using his cell phone in her class. Despite how straightforward the violation was, the boy erupted in his bid for an exception. Feeling as though the teacher was not listening as she handed him a detention, he lost it and began to curse. Fortunately, I was in the school later that day and could fit in time with him. He had been sitting at a desk alone in an office, serving an in-school suspension, since the morning but flared with fresh upset when I asked what happened. I listened, sympathetic for the mess he was in, and before long, Ted broke down and began to cry. As he worked through complicated feelings, he revealed that he was under terrible pressures.

A talented tennis player, at the height of a fierce college recruiting process, he was heartsick by how his mother became more interested in his success on the court than in how he was feeling. He was lonely and overwhelmed and had been responding to an urgent text from his mother when the teacher caught him. He just blew up. Once he told me all that was going on, we were able to make a plan for him to apologize to the teacher, explaining that his outburst had nothing to do with her, and take whatever consequences she imposed. But we agreed also to meet with him and his mother to help them reconnect more honestly. Imposing a limit is often less the end than the beginning of getting to what's going on.

Unfortunately, many adolescent boys are well on their way to emotional disconnection because they haven't found anyone to confide in. In order to suppress complicated feelings, these boys have had to steel themselves against being vulnerable. Discipline and punishment often seem the only recourse with these hardened boys because they are so much more distant and unreachable. But there is another strategy worth trying: teachers and coaches can serve as role models.

In the youth violence prevention program we developed in Philadelphia, named Peaceful Posse by the first cohort of boys, a key component was training neighborhood leaders to work in youth centers, sports programs, and church groups. Our aim was to train adult men to show boys, many of whom had not lived in the same house with a man, how to deal with their emotions. These men set up after-school groups for early-adolescent boys in which every participant, including the leader, talked about experiences that upset him. The effect was to make having emotional struggles normal and talking about feelings more natural. The point was to offer a more human alternative to the way men were depicted in video games, movies, and television shows, as action figures and warriors.

Along the same lines, a male lacrosse coach at a suburban school—a graduate of West Point and a popular math teacher— offered a talk during an assembly. He titled it "Crying," because he perceived that many of the boys he taught and coached were hostage to stereotypes about being male. In his talk, he shared that he had come to see how natural it was for men who feel things deeply to be open about feelings of all sorts, including heartbreak, grief, and sadness. He had decided to show his true feelings to his friends and said he cried openly when he needed to. Though he had to go against cultural norms prohibiting a man from being so open, he felt a responsibility to be honest about the realities of a man's emotional life with younger men for whom he was a role model.

Athletics is another context that provides lots of gut-check opportunities for boys to come to better terms with their emotions. Many coaches, particularly at younger levels, see their roles as not merely to win games and train athletes but also to build character. They understand that their exhortations will likely lead to heart-to-heart talks with boys who encounter limits in their performance. Asking a boy to share how he sees himself in the context of a team or a contest, particularly when he has come up short in some way, opens a window that is usually tightly closed. Having a team count on his contribution brings feelings such as fear or low self-esteem into sharp focus and creates clear incentives for boys to open up about their struggles and feelings. Rowing, running, swimming, and other team sports where a boy's character is revealed in a performance at the edge of his capabilities represent great opportunities for a coach to help him stretch and grow, requiring a shift in how he sees himself and an emotional reckoning. The best way for a boy to become a winner is to find his way through the blocks in his own mind.

⚘

CHAPTER 4

BOYS' LEARNING AND SCHOOLING

A seventh-grade boy gazes longingly out the window of his science class at the athletic field where he'll play soccer after school. Though the teacher is doing her best to reach the students in front of her, as she looks around her classroom, she notices another boy sneaking a peek at his cell phone and a couple of boys talking to each other in the back of the room. There are many competing interests vying for her students' attention.

According to historian Michele Cohen, a "habit of healthy idleness" characterized the academic investment of seventeenth-century male students. In many ways, *idleness* still sums up the way many boys invest themselves in learning—except that the consequences of underachievement are much less healthy. Many boys coast along, unmotivated even by failing marks, and collectively shrug their shoulders when urged to try harder. Many never experience the satisfaction that comes from putting their all into academic challenges.[1] Schooling affords many opportunities to develop grit—the capacity to fight for one's dreams. Too many boys take a pass.

A 2015 article in the *Economist* announcing that "boys are being outclassed by girls" referred to them as "the weaker sex."[2] The article was based on the release of a 2015 Organization of Economic Cooperation and Development (OECD) report profiling academic outcomes of a half million fifteen- and sixteen-year-olds in sixty-five countries. Examining the "new" global gender gap, the report identified a number of gender differences that handicap boys in school:

- Boys play more video games and spend more time on their computers and on the Internet outside of school than girls do.
- They are less likely to read for enjoyment.
- They are less likely to do homework (an hour less per week).
- They are more likely to have negative attitudes toward school (twice as likely to view school as a "waste of time").
- They are more likely to arrive late to school.[3]

But in a knowledge-based global economy, being checked out and unreachable cannot be a sufficient explanation. Visiting schools around the world, meeting boys of all kinds in interviews and classroom observations, I have always been struck by how palpably they hope to succeed. When a boy is educationally disengaged, the traditional explanation that he "doesn't care" can no longer be enough. Not caring is an outcome, not a cause.

Losing Step

Educational underachievement is one of the more obvious losses of boyhood. Worldwide, boys are said to be "in crisis" because of educational underperformance. Both in the United States and internationally, while girls' achievement has soared over the last decades, boys' has plateaued. According to the OECD report, girls outperformed boys by the equivalent average of one full school year. Boys predominated at the bottom levels of achievement and were 50 percent more likely than girls to fail at basic proficiency in math, reading, and science.

Analyzing data for the United States from the past century, sociology professors Thomas DiPrete of Teachers College at Columbia University and Claudia Buchmann of Ohio State University found that a gender gap in achievement has been true since 1900. Differences between boys and girls appear early, prior to kindergarten, and grow through the primary school years. Three factors contribute to these results:

- Girls begin school with an advantage in social and behavioral skills.
- Girls put forth greater effort than boys and get greater returns on their abilities.
- Girls show greater levels of attachment to school and experience more gratification from their performance.[4]

By the end of middle school, so-called soft cognitive skills such as completing homework and coming to classes prepared are so critical for long-term success that eighth-grade marks predict the odds of completing college more accurately than standardized test scores. They also explain boys' growing disadvantage. The educational skills gap between boys and girls is larger than gaps due to poverty or racial hardship.

According to annual surveys, differences in achievement foster different aspirations, exacerbating the gender gap. By eighth grade, boys have lower standards for themselves and put in less effort accordingly. They take fewer rigorous courses and earn poorer grades. Less interested in achievement, they are more willing to take risks such as smoking that reflect less concern for their futures.

Parents with both a son and a daughter often have stories that make these statistics more real. Charlie was a boy with an older sister, Hannah. She was a superstar: organized, self-motivating, sincere with teachers and eager to please them, highly ambitious. Charlie, on the other hand, loved hanging out with friends, playing video games, and joking around. He got along well with people and was always pleasant to teachers, but he just did not get excited about school. His parents could not help comparing his performance with his sister's, commenting at report card time about his poorer attitude, preparation, and investment. He just did not find school rewarding or fun the way his sister seemed to. He and his friends snarked about female friends who worked themselves into a frenzy over school assignments.

Gender differences in achievement are exacerbated when boys are under additional stress. In a recent large-scale study, researchers matched birth certificates and health, disciplinary, academic, and high school graduation records for more than a million boys and girls in Florida born between 1992 and 2002.[5] Among their findings, boys from low-income neighborhoods who attended underresourced public schools were more likely than their sisters to have problems with truancy and behavior in the elementary and middle school years. Furthermore, the boys exhibited higher rates of psychological and cognitive disabilities, performed worse on standardized tests, and were less likely to complete high school but more likely to become involved in the juvenile justice system. According to the paper's authors, these stress factors have a greater effect on boys "not because boys are more affected by family environment per se, but because the neighborhoods and schools in which disadvantaged children are raised are particularly adverse for boys."

Compounding the social stresses of racism and poverty, cultural norms of masculinity make it harder for boys to do well in school. Conditions that interfere with their commitment to learning extend even into the attitudes and behavior of their teachers.

Sociologist Hua-Yu Sebastian Cherng of New York University assessed the quality of high school teachers' relationships with students and confirmed that quality student-teacher relationships predicted higher student expectations and achievement.[6] The study also found that immigrant children and adolescents of color have less access to this important form of social capital.

As the OECD report noted frankly, "Study after study suggests that the best-performing students are 'good' students,"[7] going on to say: "Whether because of socialization or innate differences, boys are more likely than girls, on average, to be disruptive, test boundaries, and be physically active—in other words, to have less self-regulation."[8] In relationships between boys and teachers, stereotypes of all sorts operate to make learning partnerships less likely.

Recently, I visited a high school to offer professional development for teachers. It was May, with graduation right around the corner. As I passed by the college counseling office, where a group of seniors were gathered, I chanced upon a common scene: one girl was jumping up and down, holding her cell phone in one hand and exclaiming excitedly that she'd gotten into her first-choice college. Her boyfriend stood next to her, trying to celebrate with her. But his face showed signs of the conflict he was feeling: he, too, had heard from his first-choice college—which had placed him on the waiting list.

Thomas Mortenson of the Pell Institute for the Study of Opportunity in Higher Education has charted both the rising trends in women's employment, education, leadership, and civic participation and the declining trends for men. He has raised a cry about declines in men's college enrollment, prospects for landing a job, stagnant wages, and upticks in unemployment, incarceration, poverty, and suicide rates.

But alarms about the gender achievement gap have not always been well received. Genuine concern for boys has gotten confounded by a coded backlash against gender equality. Justifiable reactions to entrenched male privilege have made it harder for some

observers to consider how boys are positioned to fail. British sociologist Debbie Epstein and colleagues point out three common beliefs that have taken the conversation in unproductive directions.[10]

First is the "poor boys" meme, casting boys as hapless victims
of harsh conditioning and heartless exploitation. In this view,
schools are places where conditions such as bullying, overcontrol,
and targeted discipline force boys to act like a typical male. But this
view underaccounts for boys' part in the development of their identities. Achieving glory in sports or being big men on campus lures
some to choose short-term popularity over longer-term prospects. It
also discounts how hard teachers and schools work to get all of their
students on track. The subjective experience of the actors in the educational drama is lost in the crush of large social forces.

Second is a "failing schools" theme, in which schools are seen
as organized and staffed to suit girls. Proponents of this view
maintain that efforts to uplift girls have "feminized schools," con-
tributing to boys' discouragement. The problem is that evidence indicates that advances in equality improve school climates in general.
This belief also overlooks the fact that in virtually every school,
many women teachers are boys' favorites.

Finally, a "boys will be boys" belief argues that school cannot
really be a place for boys, given their hormonal aggression, competitiveness, and hyperactivity. Autonomy, adventure, and male-
bonding activities are the only ways to appeal to their instincts. But
this belief is merely a restatement of the "biology is destiny" argument that grossly mischaracterizes the complex relationship between anatomy, experience, and developing minds. Somehow, with
boys, this view nonetheless remains plausible.

More interesting ideas consider both boys' personal agency and
their lives as males. Thomas Newkirk of the University of New
Hampshire suggests that because masculinity is a "more tightly
constructed cultural category, with sharper penalties for deviance,"
boys' unwillingness to invest themselves in school can be viewed as

a form of resistance. Some boys, he wrote, may equate "good studenthood" with being "acquiescent, unmasculine, a denial of who they are and want to be."[11] Along the same lines, British professors Becky Francis, retired from the University of Roehampton, and Christine Skelton of the University College London's Institute of Education assert that attitudes of "rebelliousness, risk, sporting prowess, and heterosexual activity" are urged upon boys by cultural norms.[12] In both arguments, the picture of the boy who must contend with boyhood's opportunity structures is more respectful and more promising.

A Solution

In the new global market for talent and skill, boys who do poorly in school are at a growing disadvantage. But those giving care to boys do not need to resign themselves to such losses as inevitable. New research shows that boys can be reached and turned on, particularly by teachers who understand boyhood and can see through young men's defensive and self-defeating attitudes. In the working relationship established with their teachers or coaches, these boys become more willing to go to the edges of what they know or already can do—and learn something new. Lucky parents have seen what can happen then. Boys who were once defiant or floundering are transformed. They learn to invest themselves and to take pride in their accomplishments.

All children are, as psychiatrist Amy Banks puts it, "wired to connect," and cannot resist an invitation to join in a relationship delivered deftly by a warm and interested teacher. New interest in this dependable aspect of classroom connections holds great promise for breakthroughs in motivating boys. Nearly fifteen years ago, a group of educational scholars drafted the "Manifesto of Relational Pedagogy: Meeting to Learn, Learning to Meet" to raise awareness of the power of what was then a new line of inquiry. They wrote, "A fog of forgetfulness is looming over education. Forgotten in the fog is that education is about human beings. And as schools are places where human beings get together, we have also forgotten that education is primarily about human beings who are in relation with one another."[13]

Educational researchers desperate to turn around lagging achievement are increasingly focusing on the relational dimension. "Positive student-teacher relationships" were affirmed in the 2009 Programme for International Student Assessment , administered to fifteen-year-olds in over seventy countries by the OECD to measure educational progress. And in a 2014 review of nearly one hundred studies, a Dutch research team found that positive and negative teacher-student relationships both have significant effects on achievement. Even highly resistant students respond to teachers who find ways to connect with them. Positive learning relationships are especially beneficial in reaching those—mainly boys—at the bottom of the class.[14] A recent American Psychological Association summary of the positive effects of student-teacher relationships concluded that, with a strong connection, "the student is likely to trust her [or his] teacher more, show more engagement in learning, behave better in class, and achieve higher levels academically."[15]

A strong connection with a teacher can serve as a "secure base," protecting a child from adverse stresses and allowing the teacher to serve as both a role model and an inspiration. In relationships with teachers with whom they feel safe and secure, boys are more motivated to exercise emotional regulation, practicing and improving the executive control of their behavior. Once my research partner, Richard Hawley, and I discovered how central relationships are in boys' learning, we concluded that it is less *how* a boy learns but *for whom* he will learn.

For our research, supported by the IBSC, we collected and analyzed stories of teachers who took a special interest to reach a boy. Once they forged a connection, they leveraged the influence they had earned to deepen the boy's willingness to try his best. Implicit in relational approaches to boys is the understanding that before many boys will try to raise their grades or improve their athletic performance, they first take a measure of the person asking that of them. Their commitment is not won easily, especially if they are being asked to do something new or far from their personal strengths and interests. Why would a boy—or anyone—do that? More to the point: For *whom* would a boy do that? What we found in our studies was that the power of connection to lift boys to new heights is nowhere as clear as it is in school.

Despite how teacher-student relationships are winning attention, more traditional ideas still dominate how educators tend to respond to the "boy crisis." A "learning styles" belief exercises a persistent hold on their imaginations, despite its lack of scientific foundation. In fact, a group of the world's most eminent psychologists, neuroscientists, and educators recently published a letter specifically to challenge this approach, arguing that neither brain structure nor hormones create different learning styles for boys and girls—and that these purported differences should not guide teaching practice. The signers, including Harvard psychologist Steven Pinker, added, "The brain is essential for learning, but learning styles is just one of a number of common neuromyths that do nothing to enhance education."[16]

Unfortunately, a recent poll found that 85 percent of school administrators subscribe to the learning style approach, despite the lack of evidence supporting it. A veritable industry offers training and consultation to schools wishing to adapt their curricula to hardwired learning styles. One of the most serious problems with "boy-friendly" education is its premise that diverse boys—a jock, a science nerd, a boy under significant family stress, another battling street violence and community deterioration—can be treated as a single group. Though I have found in my work with schools that being male certainly shapes a boy's interests and personality, it is unlikely that many boys will respond to appeals based solely on their masculine identities. What teachers know from their lives in the trenches is that to reach any boy, they must build a relationship with him based on who he is as an individual.

The following story, about a bright boy who was caught in a downward cycle of underperformance before an insightful and committed coach broke through to him, illustrates how each teaching relationship requires a very particular understanding of the boy, masterful improvisational skill on the part of the teacher, and great quantities of warmth and resolve. It also shows how powerful and life-changing learning relationships can be.

Kevin was a quick study who was mischievous, high-spirited, always quick to laugh and play. He loved a good joke or prank, sought adventure, and grew up playing games of running, chasing, and hiding. He tolerated school but was bored a great deal of the time and regarded his assignments as dull chores. As he progressed into middle school, and the work demanded more time and attention, he slipped from trying to just getting by. Neither falling grades nor pressure from parents or teachers altered his trajectory or affected his attitude. He could learn readily when he applied himself but rarely did. Though Kevin wasn't failing, few of the habits of successful students—diligence and pride of craft, seeking help when stumped, organization and time management—were being practiced or mastered. In fact, he was developing another set of habits—settling for poor marks, rationalizing failure, covering up and lying to avoid negative consequences—that would hinder his success. His trajectory was not promising for high school and beyond.

His parents tried everything—checking their son's homework, sitting with him at night to complete longer assignments, lecturing him about the importance of education, praising him for his ability, punishing him when he did poorly due to weak effort—but none of their strategies had a lasting effect. Kevin simply responded that he "hated school" and begrudged the time it took away from the things he loved to do.

Teachers, for their part, were also at a loss. Their repertoire for motivating students—talking with them, spending time to establish a rapport, conferencing with parents, suggesting extra help, applying punishments such as detention or low grades—had little lasting impact on how Kevin approached his work. They came to view him as "lazy," a label that accompanied him from one year to the next.

But in seventh grade, it happened that a young math teacher who shared Kevin's interest in soccer and who also loved to laugh and play developed a special affection for him. His classes often digressed into games and stories, joking and rambunctiousness, and yet this educator skillfully led them through the curriculum at the same time. He was having a good time as a teacher and genuinely enjoyed the boys and girls in his classes. His positive emotions radiated to his students, setting the tone for classroom relationships. Things just seemed to work around him. When it came time for fall parent conferences, he explained to Kevin's parents that their son reminded him of himself, with lots of unrealized promise but struggling with the routines and repetitiveness of school.

"What changed things for you?" Kevin's parents asked. The teacher shared that his attitude, not just in school but overall in his life, changed when he was assigned to an English teacher who caught his imagination. He had never really considered that writing could be fun or an act of satisfying creativity, but this English teacher loved good writing and would read examples from his favorite writers with obvious respect and near reverence. He encouraged his students to invest their hearts in whatever they wrote, even for the most routine assignments, as an expression of what they really felt. Kevin's teacher explained that his English teacher helped him discover something about himself that he had not seen clearly and that he was forever grateful.

Paying it forward, the teacher promised to take Kevin on as his special project. He would make time for Kevin in the odd moments of the day, stopping by his desk to chat or check in about his work, laughing with him before the start of class. As their relationship deepened, the teacher began to challenge Kevin to show more of who he really was in his work. All the while, he remarked on what Kevin did well and plainly enjoyed him as a person. During the English Premier League pro soccer season, their favorite teams vied for a top spot in the standings, and they gave each other a hard time about the clubs' ups and downs.

Over the year, Kevin's mother and father saw a steady improvement in his attitude toward school. By June, he had even learned to care about his work, a habit he would carry into the next grades. But it was his discovery about learning itself that was most transformative: when he could get into it, he could explore subjects and have intellectual adventures that thrilled him. The whole unknown world opened to him. In the trusting relationship he forged with his teacher, he learned to go places he could not have imagined on his own. The parents had trouble expressing the extent of their relief and thanks.

Deepening Understanding

Beginning in 2008, Richard Hawley and I partnered with the IBSC to study what was actually working in boys' education. In a series of studies, we collected rich stories and examples from more than forty schools of all types and from 2,500 adolescent males and 2,000 of their teachers, in six different English-speaking countries.[17]

To begin our exploratory study, we simply asked teachers and boys what had been effective in their experiences. While the responses from the boys and teachers overlapped to a remarkable degree, giving us confidence in the features of successful lessons they described, there was one significant divergence. Teachers focused on the craft of the lessons and spoke in technical language about them; but boys discussed the qualities and personalities of the teachers themselves. Even though our directions had specifically asked them not to mention names, boys could not resist identifying the teacher or coach who had changed their lives and describing him or her in great, colorful detail. The difference between how teachers and boys answered us drew our attention to the student-teacher relationship. What was it that boys knew, and why was it so clear to them and less so to the professional educators? In their resounding validation of teachers who inspired and uplifted them, we came to realize that for boys, "relationship is the very medium through which successful teaching and learning is performed."[18]

Once we published our results, we received frequent requests to speak about what we found at conferences and visits to schools. It was critical to help schools support the primacy of their teachers' relational efforts. But we discovered that despite a strong commitment of both teachers and school administrators, it has not been easy for schools or teachers to place relationships at the center of what they do. We found that though teachers generally know boys require a connection in order to engage, they have had little opportunity to give the matter systematic thought. When asked to talk about why they do what they do, they often have a hard time explaining themselves. Their relational pedagogy typically happens at the level of intuition, as if crafted in a black box. Educators, steeped in cultural stereotypes of boys as independent, have trouble knowing what they know.

Boys themselves, on the other hand, are quite clear. In one focus group, in response to our question about teachers they had gotten on well with, one boy began to talk animatedly about how a teacher had "ignited" him. Other boys in the group chimed in. They spoke of this teacher with great warmth and described the atmosphere of his classroom as though it were a sacred space. "It's a class," they said, "where you wouldn't think of acting out." The teacher's presence was not strict or commanding. Rather, they felt they must take the subject seriously because the teacher was so serious about it; the boys spoke of his "passion" and the care he took with them. Patient, committed, concerned, and helpful: this was how he was described. "There is just something about him," one of the boys said. "You would be ashamed not to do your work, your best work."

We realized that to help schools make relationships more central, we needed to map them more specifically. In a follow-up study to our first, we teased out the features of relationships that worked and those that did not. We discovered that the qualities of teachers who connected with students were consistent across different cultures, countries, and types of schools.

Here's the list of teachers' qualities we found worked to overcome boys' resistance and form working partnerships:

- Mastery of their subjects. Positive teacher-student relationships were not simply a matter of establishing mutual affection. Instead, clear knowledge of the field was the foundation for engaging boys in a learning partnership.
- High standards. Boys often cited teachers who maintained clear and even demanding standards of classroom conduct and quality of work as ones in whom they had the most trust.
- Responding to a student's personal interest or talent. A boy's realization that his teacher knew him beyond being, say, a seventh-grade math or English student deepened his connection to the teacher and his willingness to engage with his assignments.

- Sharing a common interest with a student. Likewise, sharing a personal interest—whether athletic, musical, mechanical—was a reliable relationship builder with similar positive effects on performance.
- Sharing a common characteristic with a student. The fact that the teacher shared a common trait with a student—a defining physical feature, background, ethnicity, a wound, a problem overcome—was often a way to connect with him.
- Accommodating a measure of opposition. Teachers who could resist personalizing boys' oppositional behavior and instead responded to it with restraint and even humor not only succeeded with difficult students but also created a promising climate classwide.
- A willingness to reveal vulnerability. Sometimes teachers drew on a personal struggle as a way to humanize themselves for their students. One of the more common ways was to apologize to students when they made a mistake.

When teachers, employing one or another of these strategies, establish a successful partnership with a boy, it can make a tremendous difference. The practical benefits are foremost, of course: when boys acquire skills and mastery of subject matter, they are able to pass required tests. This benefit alone is no small accomplishment, as one young man shared:

I was constantly having trouble in math in middle school, especially algebra. I couldn't get my head around it. The more I tried, the more I just couldn't get it. After a couple of lessons, an extra math instructor came into class, and I asked her how to work out these equations. She went through it slowly, and I started to understand it a bit better.

She wrote in my book how she worked it out, and I started to understand even better. Then with the next couple of problems, I did the same working out she did, and I started to get them right. I felt extra motivated to continue with my work, as I felt great about understanding what we were doing. It made me continue on, and I finished with forty-eight out of fifty on the test. It was from that point that I stopped having problems with math.

But beyond immediate improvements, there are even more important benefits. When boys develop new abilities, their concept of self grows, and they become able to see new possibilities in their lives. Boys spoke of being so turned on by a physics teacher that they imagine becoming scientists or poets at the hand of a passionate English instructor. This young man spoke about being turned on by his history teacher in ways that set him on an unexpected path:

The particular class experience that is most memorable for me is American history. From the moment I walked into that classroom, I was filled with excitement and passion for history. It was like nothing I had ever experienced. My teacher loves history and is so enthusiastic about it that her love instantly transferred to me. I was fascinated and captivated by it. It was the first time I put a genuine effort into anything academic. From this point on, I learned to put work into everything, especially history. This was definitely the changing point in my schooling.

In addition to growing their skills and expanding their ambitions, in a successful relationship with a coach or teacher, boys discover that there is help and that they can expect their needs to be met. They realize that they are not alone, even as they face difficult hurdles. This young man shared a story that happened in a computer class but which carried well beyond that single subject:

> This took place in Computer Studies in tenth grade with the teacher. When we began programming, I had difficulty understanding how it worked and how to do it. However, the teacher was very understanding towards me and helped me through the whole way. She never gave up on me even though I kept on having difficulty, and finally, after many morning and lunch extra-help sessions, a light finally turned on in my mind, and I understood everything. I was able to get a really good score on the big test of that unit, but that is not the point of the story. The thing that is memorable is that she never gave up on me and always believed that I could do it. There is no way that I could've understood this confusing and complex unit without her extensive aid. She went the extra mile to help me.

The depth of appreciation boys expressed for teachers who helped them was often profound. Education philosopher David Hawkins, in his famous essay, "I, Thou, and It," captured this aspect of successful learning partnerships when he wrote: "What is the feeling you have toward a person who does this for you? It needn't be what we call love, but it certainly is what we call respect. You value the other person because he is uniquely useful to you in helping you on with your life."[19]

Failure to Communicate

As appreciative as boys are when they receive help, they can be upset, disappointed, angry, and even bitter when teachers fail to relate to them. Without such connections, boys are more than willing to check out. They believe a teacher is supposed to be willing to guide them. As more than one boy said to us in a group interview, "That's their job. They're supposed to care about us and help us to learn."

In learning relationships suffering some kind of breakdown, boys don't mince words: they describe these teachers as unresponsive, inattentive, disrespectful, poor teachers, or downright mean. One boy commented about a teacher he felt had mistreated him, "I hate him. I'm not doing anything in that class. He can flunk me, they can kick me out—I'm not doing anything." When asked why, given the fact that he was hurting himself more than the teacher, he remained adamant: "I won't do anything for him." Such hardened attitudes were common in boys' stories of relational breakdowns. Feeling let down, boys disconnect righteously and readily.

We asked boys to tell us why they thought things did not go well in relationships with certain teachers. The list of explanations was almost perfectly opposite the list they named in explaining positive relationships. Also striking was how relational their complaints were, consisting of different ways that teachers had let them down or failed to meet their baseline expectation for being helped.

- Teachers who were disrespectful or disparaging. Respect was the fundamental requirement for a learning partnership, in boys' views; its absence was their most common explanation for the relationship's failure. Teachers who displayed negative or critical attitudes risked boys' absolute refusal to relate, no matter what the consequences.
- Teachers who showed little personal enthusiasm for their subject. Boys expected that teachers had mastered their subjects and cared deeply about them. They hoped to be guided by a teacher's personal passion in ways that elevated the class and made it interesting.

- Teachers who were inattentive or indifferent to them. Boys expected not only good teaching but also teachers who were capable of noticing their enthusiasm. They could be quite angry with teachers they perceived as tuned out.
- Teachers who were unresponsive. Similarly, boys expected—needed—teachers who would respond to their struggles to learn with a commitment to help, including a willingness to revise their approach if it wasn't working for a boy's learning style.
- Teachers who were unable to control their classes. In many ways, the frequency of this reported theme reinforced our hopeful finding that boys do, indeed, hope for classes managed by competent teachers in which they can focus and learn.
- Teachers who were uninspiring or boring. Distinct from the teacher's level of passion and involvement with their subject, how teachers taught their lessons mattered a great deal to boys. They hoped to be lifted by their teachers out of the tedium of school routines.
- Teachers who communicated poorly. Sometimes boys did not feel any particular annoyance with teachers; rather, they simply could not understand them or their lessons.

Obviously, we did not think boys' views of relational breakdowns represented the whole story. But their one-sided interpretation was paralleled when we asked teachers the same question: Why had the relationship they described gone badly? Though teachers expressed regret when they were unable to repair the breakdown—often in words that were quite heartrending—like the boys, they nonetheless tended not to blame themselves. In the end, they tended to blame relational breakdowns on a student's personal or family circumstances, psychological problems, learning deficits, or, in some cases, cultural stresses. Teachers and coaches typically maintained that they had done everything that could professionally be expected of them—though in accounts of their successes, they celebrated sustained efforts to overcome these same circumstances—and defensively believed that forces beyond their control explained the failure.

That frequent breakdowns occur in learning relationships is not surprising. After all, both boys and teachers have full lives, with many sources of stress that can impact their ability to pay full attention to their school relationships. It is quite normal in human relationships of all kinds for there to be cycles of connection-disconnection-reconnection, as relational scholars attest. Disconnection is not the problem. The true challenge for relational pedagogy, as the late psychiatrist and author Jean Baker Miller of Wellesley College argued, is "how these roadblocks can be turned into pathways of connection."

Given the frequency of disconnections, small and large, in classroom and school relationships, we wondered how the problem of relational breakdown might be solved. From teachers' perspectives, often we heard the view that it was up to the boy to repair a broken relationship: "I have gone as far as I can with this boy; he has to do his part before I am willing to do more." But when we explored this idea in a focus group with top student leaders at a high school, we learned that even the most empowered students are at a loss when their relationships with teachers or coaches go awry. Feeling intimidated or resentful, boys are not usually in a position to reach across barriers of age and power differences to reestablish a connection. Instead of trying to repair things, more commonly they will write off the course, or the teacher, resolving to endure until the end of the term and sometimes developing a more generally negative attitude.

For practical reasons, then, the responsibility for connecting with a student falls to the teacher, as the adult and professional.

Psychologist Daniel Rogers of Kennesaw State University describes this default role as relationship manager, attributing to it three specific responsibilities:

- to serve as the expert facilitating the student's learning;
- to maintain an overall awareness of the alliance; and
- to monitor and mend strains in the alliance.[20]

In our data, we found that teachers who are successful in establishing and maintaining relationships with students do not expect them to assume equal responsibility for the partnership. They assume that the boy, vulnerable and fully absorbed in trying to master difficult subject matter, is doing the best he can. But being the relationship manager with large numbers of students is a tall, maybe impossible task.

And boys do not make it easy. When male students are offended, frightened, or overwhelmed, their resistance can blow up in ways that put off even the most patient teachers. In confrontations with a belligerent, disruptive, rejecting, or disrespectful boy, many teachers become defensive. Self-protectively, they default to the position that they have done all that can reasonably be expected; it is now time for the boy, despite his disadvantages, to take the next step. Thus, we found that underlying relational breakdowns is a teacher who has switched from managing the relationship to protecting himself. This candid admission from a teacher was an acknowledgment of this all-too-common outcome:

My reason for being unable to establish a decent relationship with this student was that, quite frankly, the prospect was too exhausting—we didn't have much common ground, and I couldn't detect any desire on his part to connect. I knew that he was continuing to struggle with growing family challenges at home, but he wore a

poker face by day. It was very difficult to tell when anything was bothering him. As I reflect on this student, he
was clearly a kid who needed help but didn't want it. He
was interested in being cool, playing sports, and I think,
most importantly, he wanted to come across as a strong
young man. I think asking for help, or accepting it, must
have felt like a sign of weakness. I have to admit I found I
just didn't want to make the effort anymore. He constantly
scowled at me and others, treated his peers with disrespect,
and showed contempt for almost everything. This is a terrible thing for a teacher/coach to admit, but I gave up. So
I'm sure he sensed my dislike for him. I justified this by
saying he showed no respect toward me and clearly disliked
me. I felt I had really tried with him during his first two
years. I couldn't get over my own frustration with him, and
I'm sure he fed off of that. He was difficult to deal with, but
I felt I had done enough to reach him.

By contrast, when teachers do not give up or place the burden
for repairing the relationship on the student, even despite feeling
frustrated or pessimistic, breakthroughs can happen. For example,
Sarah was a math teacher in an all-boys class with a group of athletes who were not taking her seriously enough. They sat at the
back, talking and fooling around. When she corrected them, they
would sometimes mock her or make comments behind her back.
To nip the problem in the bud, she identified Calvin as the group's
leader and took him aside after class one day. She explained that
she saw his leadership potential but worried that he was leading in
a negative, rather than constructive, direction. During the meeting,
he was polite though quiet, and Sarah felt that she had made her
point. But from that day on, Calvin seemed deflated and checked
out: he did little work, barely paid attention in class, and hardly
looked at her when she spoke.

Determining that her "solution" had made the relationship worse, Sarah decided to try a different approach during a fall parent conference. At the start of the meeting, she apologized to the boy and explained to his parents that she had misjudged him, probably embarrassed him, and asked Calvin for another chance. Though he said little in front of his mother and father, Sarah began to notice that he was less shut down in class, turned in his homework on time, and kept apart from the other boys' fooling around—which lowered their volume. In time, she was able to work her way to a more satisfying relationship, even offering him constructive criticism on his work and applauding his improvement over the course of the year.

Sarah's operating premise, like that of all good relationship managers, was this: if one strategy did not work, she would keep trying until she found one that did. What was so striking, in addition to her confidence and persistence, was her flexibility. The problem was for *her* to solve; she never allowed herself to dish responsibility off to the boy or his family.

In considering breakdowns in learning relationships, the human stresses of teaching come to the forefront. Tamara Bibby of the University of London's Institute for Education, captured these stresses when she wrote, "The constant sense of exposure, combined with the constant need for reassurance that one is seen, valued, and can be acknowledged, that one is good enough and therefore deserving of notice (love), makes the classroom a very complex and potentially dangerous place, one that can generate stress for all involved."[21]

Sometimes it is a wonder that despite the occupational challenge of managing a large number of complicated relationships, often under very difficult conditions, idealistic college graduates still flock to the teaching profession. But these new teachers' hopes are not delusional. In talks with veteran educators who have spent decades with young people, there are always stories attesting to the satisfying nature of their work. Challenging as relational teaching can be, it provides sufficient rewards to sustain many for the duration of their careers.

Relational Schools

In another project in my series of studies, a small set of schools worked with me to make relational teaching the centerpiece of their approach. Each school came up with strategies to support teachers and coaches in their relational efforts, knowing that most of them would encounter relational challenges during the school year. Putting precious resources of time and attention behind a school's commitment to reach each individual boy meant that teachers were not left to figure out things on their own.

Pessimism about reaching a student arises when a teacher is under stress, experiencing some threat to his or her professional competence. Pressured in these ways, teachers tend to become defensive. Boston College professor Andy Hargreaves, who has written about the "emotional labor" of teaching, found that feelings of powerlessness are especially unsettling for teachers whose professional identities hinge on being successful with students.[22] In light of how commonly frightened boys balk at efforts to engage them, it is unrealistic for teachers to take their resistance personally. But in practice, a boy's resistance can easily get their goat.

Some basic principles should guide how schools support relational teaching. As I have said, there needs to be philosophical agreement among all that the person managing the relationship is always the teacher, not the student. This is less obvious in the classroom than it might seem in theory. Despite the understandable desire for students to take more responsibility, especially as they get older, waiting for a boy to take initiative in a relationship between an adult teacher and a student is impractical. It is the professional who must solve connection breakdowns.

Likewise, everyone in the school must get behind the idea that, no matter their difficulties, every boy can be reached. Relational teachers tend not to send their difficult students off to special services or disciplinary pullouts. Instead, they work at building influence by finding ways to connect with them, hoping their attention and care can help rally boys who are obviously struggling. Relational teachers regard impasses with students as a sign that they have not yet hit upon a workable approach—and they keep trying until they succeed. While gathering more information on a boy from outside evaluations can add dimension to relational efforts, the overreferral of boys for psycho-educational support services speaks more to teachers' frustration and despair than to need.

This is also where peer support is crucial. No teacher can expect always to be objective. Especially when they become self-protective, teachers may not see their own part in relationship breakdowns. Miriam Raider-Roth reminds teachers that assistance lies very near at hand: "We cannot see our blind spots without our colleagues' gentle and persistent feedback."[23] Many schools have launched professional growth opportunities to provide for reflection and peer coaching. Devoting some of these opportunities to review relational issues makes it more likely that teachers will examine where they are experiencing strain.

In workshops with these relational schools, I have experimented with a model for helping teachers reflect on times when they cannot get on with a student. In a workshop at one school, the dean of the faculty shared a story about a defiant and disruptive boy. He admitted that he had "lost it" in a heated exchange with him. After that, the boy became even more difficult to reach. As he spoke about what happened next—the boy got into trouble, was kicked out of school, and got into even more trouble on the streets—he broke down. The room could not have been quieter as he let on how guilty and sad he still felt years later for having lost this student. What stood out in his story, clear to his colleagues, was his heartfelt commitment to the boy and his grief at coming up short.

Spontaneously, as he collected himself, several other teachers spoke up, to validate his courage and honesty and to offer feedback. One at a time, they spoke about his goodness, their respect for him, and how evident it was that he had tried with all he had to reach the boy before things broke down. They offered ideas for what he might have done differently and what he might try next time, underscoring how a growth mind-set is integral to relational teaching: everyone can improve. Peer support can help teachers who have run out of ideas of their own—even the best of them.

How Parents Fit In

Parents play a critical role in learning. When they are aligned with teachers, their united front steadies shaky, ambivalent boys as they enter into partnerships with their teachers. When they are less aligned, their detachment and negative feelings can be broadcast to the boy and undercut his faith that he is in good hands. The learning alliance must include not just teachers but also the boy and his parents.

This essential parent-teacher partnership can be confusing for many families, our research showed. Parents usually appreciate that they must defer to the teacher's primary role, but many do not know how to play an active part supporting their efforts. The fact that parents or teachers can either reinforce or undermine each other's effectiveness is often unrecognized.

Parents have high expectations of teachers, often unspoken, particularly in the relational realm. They believe that every teacher should have the sensitivity and professional insight to read their son accurately and match their teaching styles to his learning needs. Perhaps the single most important quality they want in a teacher is the ability to connect with their son. They want teachers who can see what they see—to "get" their son. When they happen upon a teacher who connects well with their boy, parents feel they are on the right track. "When he has a teacher whom he connects with somehow, he's just so much more open to learning," one parent remarked.

In meetings with parents, it becomes apparent how much they are looking for help from teachers, and not just in their scholastic efforts. Parents want teachers to take the time to see their sons as multidimensional and to get to know them beyond their academic performance, understanding that they will work harder and achieve better grades when they are accountable to their teachers. With a personal connection, parents believe, teachers can elicit the best from their sons.

Underlying these hopes and expectations are strong emotions. As the other significant adult meaningfully shaping their son's prospects, parents have a great deal riding on the quality of the teacher's connections with him. There is so much of themselves invested in him, and they pray that others will add value beyond what they can provide. When they find a teacher who does help, their relief and gratitude are huge, as this mother explained:

> My son had a remarkable relationship with one of his teachers in the school. It's changed his whole attitude; his belief in himself. It's just amazing how his relationship with other students, his social system, has changed as a result. My greatest concern was that he wouldn't identify things about himself that are special, and what this relationship has done is give him a belief in himself. It actually changed how he interacts with himself, and that's what changes everything. He feels safe to explore whoever he is. I feel that

he has something in his life he can forever look back on and actually use as a marker, so that no matter what happens, this will be something that he can hold on to.

When a relationship with a teacher goes well, it is a blessing. Parents are happy to step aside, let the teacher do his job, and reinforce his or her efforts as best they can at home.

But parents often find letting go is difficult. When the student-teacher relationship is not going to their satisfaction, they are torn. Should they intervene, running the risk of antagonizing the teacher, or remain silent? Some feel they are in a double bind: caught between advocating for their son and partnering with the teacher. In these situations, many parents become passive, tied up with worries. The level of parental stress seems to be tied directly to the quality of their son's relationship with a teacher. "You don't want to upset your son's teacher," commented one parent. "You don't want to put him off, you don't want to offend him, because in the end, it's coming back on your child." Some parents even attempt to take on the role of the teacher at home and to work around deficits in the classroom. But the ones who try this sometimes report that it has a negative impact on their own relationship with their son—not to mention how it fails to address directly the boy's problem with his teacher and leaves him in a default position in the classroom day in and day out.

Parents in these focus groups offered a number of recommendations to help teachers reach their sons:

- Convey confidence. First and foremost, they suggest that teachers conveys confidence in a boy's potential. Confidence offered by the professional is important for the boy's self-image. "You could just see him flourish and grow, particularly when he found that

he had somebody who believed in him," a parent
shared.

- Offer respect. Parents suggest that teachers are more
  likely to develop relationships with their sons when they
  respect them. A boy is more likely to offer respect, they
  said, in return for the respect he perceives from the
  teacher—and will be more willing to work under those
  circumstances. One parent added about a particular
  teacher: "She is not always affectionate. But it is a
  respect thing, his respecting the teacher. He will really
  try to step up for the teacher whom he respects."

- Maintain a sense of humor. Parents recommend a sense
  of humor as well, seeing that a lighter heart facilitates
  their son's willingness to establish a positive
  relationship. With such high stakes attached to school
  performance, a teacher who can help a boy (not to
  mention help his parents) keep things in perspective is
  greatly valued. "He really enjoyed that year and the fun
  in the classroom," a parent remarked.

- Practice good teaching. In their emphasis on teacher-
  student relationships, parents recognized that good
  teaching practices in general are critical—a necessary
  condition for relational success. If boys conclude that a
  teacher is poor at conveying lessons or that he is
  unenthusiastic about the subject, they are more likely
  to reject his efforts even if they like him.

How Parents Can Help Their Sons with School

In my work with families, I see regularly how parental expectations
are woven into a boy's self-concept and aspirations. For this reason,
just as teachers must be on the lookout for any diminished expec-

tations they may harbor about a particular student, parents must also examine what they think their sons are capable of achieving. Do their own experiences with school color how they see their son's potential? How much do "boys will be boys" attitudes seep into their expectations? Do they resign themselves to poor effort or to acting out? Do they take their son's side in a conflict with a teacher and allow him to check out rather than mount an effort to fix the relationship?

In many cases, underlying a boy's school failure is a parent's inability to secure his agreement to do his best. There can be a wide range of reasons—the boy may have developed an aversion based on negative experiences, for example, and be tightly defended, exhausting his parents; or he may have undiagnosed problems that frustrate his best efforts—but generally I see underperformance as a symptom of system failure: boys learn to work first at home and then apply that commitment at school. Schools can train boys to learn and even to work more efficiently, but they usually find it hard to engage a boy who is opposed to trying.

Many parents don't know what to do when their sons give up on learning and often resort to strategies that do not work. Being arbitrary and demanding, trying to command rather than accompany their sons, or approaching them in the opposite way with indifference and a lack of their own personal investment, are equally ineffective at eliciting their sons' effort. Children tend to do what their parents truly believe they should do; when a boy falls short, it is useful to think of his struggle as a challenge for the relationship, not the boy's problem alone.

Once they are sure their baseline expectations are appropriate and clear, parents can then review whether they are fully part of the learning team. They are not able to control the student-teacher partnership but their influence with both partners can be instrumental. As I have seen, their attitude affects how their sons regard their teachers and respond to their assignments. Their support can influence the teacher, who will take note of their emotional investment and be mindful of their involvement. Staying connected to their son's progress, being open to how the teacher sees the boy, and conveying a willingness to support what the teacher is trying to do will help teachers do their best.

As part of being teammates with their son's teachers, parents need to make sure that teachers have all the information they need to be effective. If a teacher seems to be going at things in ways that are not working, parents can coach their son to speak up for himself rather than jump in to communicate for him. This helps him to learn self-advocacy and negotiation. Just as importantly, this strategy steers him back to the teacher and reminds him that it is *his* relationship. The boy gets the message that his parents believe he can resolve tricky problems in his relationships. Only if the boy gives up should the parent take a more active part. Sometimes that may mean inviting him to work out his frustrations or disappointments, and then try again. Parents should never accept their son's simply giving up in a relationship with a teacher, writing off the course or class, because defeats like these can harden into a more general pessimism.

A Focus on the Longer Term

Learning is personal for boys. That was the primary lesson of our research. In the context of relationships with their teachers and coaches, boys respond to the demands and challenges that come with efforts to deepen knowledge and improve skills. Because it is personal, however, the ups and downs of both teachers' and boys' lives affect how well they bring themselves to their partnership and its focus on the work of teaching and learning. Boys can become distracted, and teachers can be preoccupied or worn thin.

When it works well, the team of parents, teachers, and the boy can be a powerful force for growth. Good teamwork between teacher and parents can help boys stay on track, mindful of their futures even as they are going through significant stresses in the present, as this story shows. Toby was a ninth grader when his father was discovered by his mother to be having an affair, and his family came unraveled. Close to both parents, Toby was torn and withdrew from each rather than choose between them. While his father moved out and the legal process dragged on, Toby turned to school friends and his older brothers for support. The family home seemed to echo with memories of the happy family he had counted on.

His mother worried about him and offered counseling support, but he turned down her repeated offers. A series of explosive confrontations with his father, in which Toby expressed how disappointed he was with the character and values his father's behavior demonstrated, elevated her concern. But Toby insisted on doing things his way, expressing a loss of faith in both parents.

What his mother could do was reach out for help. In addition to seeking therapy for her son, she rallied friends and family. For Toby, she arranged to meet with his primary school advisor as well as with the dean, letting them know what was happening and asking them to keep a special eye on her son.

Over the next year, there were many ups and downs. Toby's grades dipped, and he didn't make the cut for the varsity football team. His mother believed that his confidence was suffering from all the upheaval and losses he'd been through. She kept checking in with teachers and coaches, trying not to become a pest but making it clear that she needed to keep the village around her son up to speed. Steadily, she worked her own way through the bumpy stretch of her divorce, struggling to stay in working communication with her ex-husband. But she was worried about Toby and the effects of the family stress on his ability to keep focused on what he had to do.

Toby's homeroom teacher and advisor was someone he truly liked. Not only a good English teacher whose passion for writing was evident, the teacher also happened to coach the cross-country team. When Toby's work deteriorated and his grades slipped, the teacher consulted with his mother and decided to bolster his confidence rather than harp on the grades or the work. He recruited him to run on his team and spent hours through the fall running alongside him, telling stories, cheering him on in races, and simply being a friend.

When Toby became discouraged by his performance in a race, the teacher would remind him of all he had accomplished and encourage him to adopt a longer-term perspective. He shared his own ups and downs as a runner, explaining how he had come to see running as a metaphor for everything else in his life requiring mindful performance even when distractions and difficulties abound. As the months went by, Toby learned from the teacher how to keep his eyes on his goals, beyond the turbulence of his family troubles, and encourage himself rather than implode. His mother, noting the impact of the teacher's mentorship, could not have been more thankful.

CHAPTER 5

ॐ

BROTHERHOOD AND BOYS' CLUBS

By the time they are two years old, children typically see themselves as boys or girls, laying the foundation for their self-concepts. While this binary distinction is loosening as the number of children identifying as transgender has doubled from 2011 to 2016, the child who does not see himself one way or the other is rare. Still, there are many signs that how we think about gender categories is evolving. A 2017 op-ed in the *New York Times* by writer Lisa Selin Davis argued that her daughter, who began to reject feminine norms at age three, was "not gender nonconforming. She is gender *role* nonconforming."[1] Many parents try out gender-neutral approaches to raising children, wanting not to limit the futures their children imagine.

But parents' best efforts to protect their children notwithstanding, gender norms are unavoidable in all present societies and influence everything from clothing and toys to friendship choices. By the age of three, boys and girls largely segregate by sex, an outcome that imposes costly sacrifices but also provides some benefits. Research shows that gender scripts encourage boys to be independent and to roam more freely than girls. A common finding is that boys spend more time outside the home than girls do. Freedom allows them to explore and have adventures, instilling confidence and skills for negotiating public life. But freedom can also leave them isolated from the positive influences of their families and communities.

Boy society makes its own rules. Masculine norms drive these rules and incite boys to do things they would be unlikely to do on their own. Spending time with friends becomes an end in itself and occupies more and more of a boy's attention. Ties with families become thinner as the peer group creates its own world, with activities and experiences that are not usually shared with families or schools. Boys want to impress one another and do what the group values to maintain their position.

Off by themselves from preschool until midadolescence, male friendships are the main way that boys develop relationship skills and explore closeness outside their families. With their friends, boys practice caring, trusting, sharing, giving, and taking. Boys extend to one another virtues that they learn first in their families, such as loyalty.

To Dr. Harry Stack Sullivan, a renowned psychiatrist during the first half of the twentieth century, as their cognitive abilities grow, children learn to offer one another empathy and mutual support. Deeper connections, what he called "chumships," teach children to consider other points of view and commit themselves to their friends' well-being.[2] Having a friend and being a friend reach new levels of significance. From being oriented primarily toward their families and neighbors, young peoples' lives expand as friendship networks develop in school and best friends are made. Their lives take on new dimensions.

NYU psychologist Niobe Way documented a depth of compassion, love, and intimacy in the friendships of adolescent boys, leading her to take issue with notions that there are essential differences between boys' and girls' friendships. Boys' friendships are especially important, she explains, because having someone who knows and accepts them enhances boys' lives.

Unfortunately, these friendships get overwhelmed by a cultural force that boys can neither deflect nor entirely escape. The same boys who spoke to Way so openly about connections with one another reported losing their friends as they got older and also came under greater pressure to make sure no one mistook them for being gay. The mandate to find a girlfriend and to restrict intimacy to that relationship grows as boys enter midadolescence.

Where that can leave young males is cut off from friendships essential to their well-being. Psychologists have been paying more attention in recent years to what has been termed an "epidemic of loneliness" particularly affecting the elderly and adolescents.[3] In the words of writer Hara Estroff Marano, addressing a growing societal concern, "Friendship is a lot like food. We need it to survive. . . . When our need for social relationships is not met, we fall apart mentally and even physically."[4] Chronic loneliness has been shown to trigger the body's stress response, increasing levels of the stress hormone cortisol and suppressing the immune system. On the basis of heightened awareness of its prevalence and dangers, in 2018 British prime minister Theresa May appointed a Minister for Loneliness to orchestrate public health responses in the United Kingdom. Hopefully, the increased attention will lead to ideas for helping boys better resist the forces undermining their friendships.

Ties That Bind

Separated from girls, it is in their trusted friendships that boys share feelings and reactions, discovering the relief that comes with the empathy and understanding of a compassionate peer. Niobe

Way found boys to be quite clear about the importance of their friendships. As one young man explained to her: "You have someone to talk to. Like, you have problems with something, you go talk to him. You know, if you keep all the stuff to yourself, you go crazy. Try to take it out on someone else."[5]

Boys' friendships build important life skills. Learning the difference it makes when someone has your back, how peer connections lessen the anxiety of new challenges and strengthen self-esteem during setbacks, are lessons for a lifetime. As Brett and Kate McKay wrote on their blog *The Art of Manliness*, "Friends are those men you can count on when the chips are down. They'll back you even when the whole world is against you."[6]

In a separate study, Judy Chu observed adolescent boys in relationships with one another and then interviewed them. Her observations confirmed how important it is when a boy finds a friend with whom he can be himself. Examining which boys were better able to resist masculine pressures, she found that some boys yielded more completely to norms, even when they felt demeaned or misrepresented by them, while others were more daring. It was the existence of at least one true friend, someone who knew and accepted them, that differentiated the groups. She wrote, "Boys who felt known and validated in their relationships seemed better supported to resist other people's assumptions, perhaps to the effect of preserving their integrity."[7]

One boy she met with, a disappointment to his parents for not being more "gung-ho masculine," could be comfortable with who he was despite family and school pressures because he had a friend who accepted him. In an interview with Chu, he explained:

"When I was thirteen, I met my closest friend right now, and he really helped me to become who I want to become. . . . Like, he pointed out all the stuff my mom was doing to me that . . . I never realized that it was there. . . . And then he pointed it out to me, and

I was, like, 'Hey yeah, that's wrong.' And we both were, like, 'Hey, why don't we just be who we want to be?'"[8]

Boys' friendships are especially important, Way argues, because in them boys are able to resist the boy code. One boy, George, explained: "With best friends, I don't have to put this mask on and, like, say things that they want to hear. . . . It's not like this thing where, like, oh yeah, I have to say what he likes or thinks."[9] In interviews with her and her team of researchers, boys described how close and caring they could be with one another:

My best friend and I love each other. . . . that's it. . . . you have this thing that is deep, so deep, it's within you, you can't explain it. . . . I guess in life, sometimes two people can really, really understand each other and really have a trust, respect, and love for each other. It just happens. It's human nature.[10]

They said they would "go wacko" or "take it out on someone else" without their friends. From her studies, Way concluded that boys are as intimate with their friends as girls are and are equally emotionally attuned to one another.

In their brief history of male friendship, the McKays trace its evolution: from heroic friendship in ancient Greece, where the ideal of the platonic friend was conceived; to the intense bonds and deep affection common in nineteenth-century America (both Abraham Lincoln and Theodore Roosevelt openly embraced close friendships in their adult years); to the more formal and distant bonds of the twentieth century. Except in traditionally male organizations such as the military, sports teams, and fire and police corps, most males today are more constrained with other men. Concern about appearing homosexual seems responsible for the change. Prior to the turn of the century, males were freer to show affection for one another without a fear of being labeled. But as homosexual relationships were characterized as aberrant, particularly by psychologists, men became more self-conscious.

A fifteen-year-old boy, Kenny, told me recently that other boys in his grade had spread rumors that he was "gay" with another boy. He was upset and confused by the rumors. This was his first experience with such threatening peer policing. It caused him to wonder, "Is there something wrong with me?" He became self-conscious and began to monitor how open he was with other boys. Psychologist Gregory Lehne of Johns Hopkins University captures what he was up against: "Love and close relationships are difficult to maintain in a competitive environment, because to express your weaknesses and admit your problems is to be less than a man."[11]

Though times are changing, the direction of change is unclear. In the Internet era, a wide variety of sexual images and a gay liberation movement that seems ubiquitous has transformed cultural attitudes. Sociologist Eric Anderson of England's University of Winchester has asked, "What happens to the traditional, conservative, orthodox version of masculinity when our culture of homohysteria decreases?"[12] From research with young men in both the United States and the United Kingdom, he suggests that more "inclusive masculinities" will allow males to "act in ways that were once associated with homosexuality," with less threat to their identities as heterosexuals.[13]

But Way thinks that gay liberation might, perversely, mean *more* pressure on boys to establish their heterosexuality. In her view, "gay liberation likely provokes heterosexual men to insist even more ferociously on their manliness in the most stereotypic ways. Conventions of masculinity get reinforced with a new sense of vigor to distinguish those who are 'in' from those who are 'out.'"[14]

Whichever way these cultural changes play out, the friendships of young males will be affected—and with them, boys' overall well-being. Under the present circumstances, boys' loss of connection has harmful consequences. Way suggested the classic term *anomie*—which refers to a state of alienation and meaninglessness resulting usually from social oppression—as an apt description for the depressed, listless state she found among boys in late adolescence. The loss of a good friend is often painful, sometimes devastating, as this boy explained to Way:

"The friend I had, I lost. . . . That was the only person I could trust, and we talked about everything. When I was down, he used to help me feel better. The same I did for him. So I feel pretty lonely and sometimes depressed. Because I don't have no one to go out with, no one to speak [with] on the phone, no one to tell my secrets, no one for me to solve my problems. . . . I think that it will never be the same, you know. I think that when you have a real friend and you lost him, I don't think you find another one like him."[15]

The loneliness and loss he narrates may contribute to a frightening change that is found among older adolescent boys: the suicide rate soars to four times that of girls. Way argues that this is not a coincidence: "In a culture where needing or wanting emotional support or intimacy is the antithesis of manliness, boys during late adolescence suffer the deep alienation that comes with such an equation."[16]

Brotherhood

In her wonderful study of an elementary school playground, sociologist Barrie Thorne observes, "Although girls and boys *are* together and often interact in classrooms, lunchrooms, and on the playground, these contacts less often deepen into friendship or stable alliances, while same-gender interactions are more likely to solidify into more lasting and acknowledged bonds."[17] Boys and girls become "familiar strangers" as they learn to observe gender boundaries in their everyday lives.

There are various theories explaining why boys and girls segregate when given the choice of who to play with, ranging from biologically based temperament and play-style differences, to cultural pressures to disavow the other gender, to more cognitive processes that incline boys to find other boys, and the things that they do, more interesting. But what Thorne's study revealed was how school, as the most important social stage mounted by children, organizes and reinforces gender differences. When a boy finds something interesting about a girls' game or feels a bond with a particular girl, he places himself at a border that is policed by the other children as well as by adults. Teasing and harassment that occur at these borders train boys to follow the masculine scripts—or else.

As a result, girls' and boys' groups evolve in different directions. The conventional belief is that girls bond in pairs, while boys bond with a group. Girls practice relationship skills such as talking and sharing secrets, and boys engage in games and projects. But Thorne's playground observations also revealed ritualized ways that boys and girls interact with one another: games of boys against the girls, chasing and invasion games, teasing. Their play enacts the cultural meme that boys and girls are radically different from each other.

Herded into their separate group, boys come upon a distinctive feature of boyhood: the brotherhood. Just as girls' groups embody and enforce norms that apply distinctly to girls, so there are rules governing brotherhood particular to the culture of boyhood. A boy's standing with his peer group determines how he is treated in his neighborhood and his school. Beyond its survival value, connection to the group is also important for the camaraderie and acceptance it offers. Stories of great adventures, wild times, and lifelong friendships have a hallowed place among males of all cultures. "I have your back!" is a boy's ultimate endorsement.

Brotherhood is built into the major institutions of boyhood: play groups, recess yards, athletic teams, Boy Scouts and boys clubs. In these groups, boys perform for one another and follow rules that are quite distinct from their individual friendships. No boy can escape the peer group, and every boy has to find a place within it. Experiences within the peer group shape how a boy perceives himself and how he conceives of his life.

At its best, brotherhood can enhance a boy's sense of belonging and teach lasting values. On sports teams, for example. Football coach and trainer of coaches Joe Ehrmann believes that being part of a team is to learn how to "be a man for others"—to discover purpose in being part of something bigger than one's own life, and having a responsibility to teammates and coaches who are equally dedicated to you. He explains: "We belong to each other. Full acceptance is the rule. We need each other. A team is a complex organism. We are interdependent; no teammate can function without connection with other teammates. We affect each other. Oneness—a team is One."[18]

Ehrmann developed a philosophy he calls "transformational coaching." Distinguished from the "transactional coach" who cares primarily about winning and losing, the transformational coach "is dedicated to self-understanding and empathy, viewing sports as a virtuous and virtue-giving discipline." His ultimate goal is that players "know three things before they graduate from high school. One, they are loved. Two, they are loved and accepted for who they are, not what they do. Three, they need to know that they have something of significance to offer the world."[19] This example offers a glimpse of the power of the connections forged in brotherhood to build virtue and strengthen character.

There are other important examples. Dr. Way learned that minority boys and boys from blue-collar and impoverished families, with fewer resources in general, have developed brotherhood to a fine art. Among African American males, brotherhood based on common oppression emphasizes values of loyalty and connection. George Washington University's Dr. Lionel Howard, whose research has focused on the role of relationships in African American male development, argues that how well African American males handle the adversities and challenges of their lives depends on the quality of their bonds with other African American males.[20]

Another context where research finds that brotherhood

provides positive experiences is in the single-sex school. Proponents claim that when boys are spared the pressure to demonstrate their differences from girls, they feel freer to try things outside the Man Box: arts, emotional expression, engaged learning, deep friendships. One such school, the Eagle Academy for Young Men, in the Bronx, has achieved a graduation rate for African American boys more than twice the New York City average; 90 percent of its graduates go on to college. In part, school administrators attribute their success to the creation of a peer culture in which boys actively care for one another. Boys, as Dr. Joseph Derrick Nelson of Swarthmore College found in his research, learn what he terms Transformative Brotherhood at such schools:

- to place the needs of others before their own;
- to acknowledge when someone is in need;
- to lend a helping hand;
- to participate fully in collaborative endeavors; and
- to accept peers for all of "who they are."[21]

At its best, brotherhood helps boys to feel understood, supported, and loved, as these different examples show. Drawn to other boys from an early age, as soon as they notice that being male is an important part of who they are, boys' friendships can support their development of critical life skills. Brotherhood can uplift and even save some boys' lives.

Lost in the Crowd

But brotherhood sometimes exerts a more negative influence. When membership is defined by those who are excluded, boys' clubs can become almost cultlike and encourage behavior that lies outside the bounds of civility. Fraternities, sports teams, and other groups emphasizing brotherhood sometimes encourage an extreme version of masculinity that distorts an individual boy's values and judgment.

As early as elementary school, boys' groups can promote antisocial norms, egging on members of these groups to act in ways they would be unlikely to adopt on their own. In Judy Chu's two-year study of three- and four-year-olds, where they had been more indiscriminate about who they played with when they began school, they coalesced into a group that excluded girls. Each boy became more self-conscious about those he played with, the toys he chose, and how he behaved in the public space of school. Their group marked its boundaries with antagonism toward girls.

The peer group both pulls and pushes. Many boys discover as they enter the all-boys space that they have to leave a great deal out. They fight to be themselves against the gravitational pull to conform. Understanding how to help boys retain a sense of who they are in spite of social pressures driving them into hiding is critical for the men they might become. Without a close connection to turn to, boys are more likely to fall into pretense. As writer George Orwell understood, boys can grow into their masks.

Sam was a middle child in a large family. His older brothers were tough acts to follow, academically, athletically, and socially, and had little time for him in their busy lives. Sam's father, when he wasn't working, also seemed caught up in his older sons' athletic activities, one in baseball and the other in lacrosse. Sam had a hard time distinguishing himself in his father's eyes, though he tried many different sports himself. His mother, while kind and sympathetic to him, simply had an easier time relating to his younger sisters.

At Sam's K–8 school, eighth graders were at the top of the heap, and the biggest, toughest, most defiant boys ruled. Unobserved by adults, there were after-school fights in the recess yard reinforcing the prevailing pecking order. Boys who did well in school, who cooperated with the teachers and put effort into their schoolwork, were teased and tormented in countless ways—pushed in lines, tripped in the hallways, razzed in the bathrooms.

Sam, a talented writer, had a relatively easy time with schoolwork and actually liked learning. Teachers made no secret of preferring him over other boys who were more tuned out, rarely participating in class. But as adolescence arrived, Sam discovered that actually caring about school and earning teachers' praise got him into trouble with his peers. He was becoming a target.

By eighth grade, the boy's grades had begun to drop, he received detention notices for minor misbehavior, and he was becoming angry and sullen at home. On occasion he acted defiantly toward his mother and mean toward his younger sisters. His parents noticed that he had switched crowds at school and that he asked to spend overnights at the homes of popular boys on weekends. They felt reassured by this last development and were pleased for Sam, thinking that he was "coming out of his shell," and chalked up the ill temper to puberty and hormones. He evidenced a new interest in girls, but one day his mother found disturbing content on his phone, which she was secretly monitoring. Twice she found lewd and suggestive pictures of girls, passed along by his new friends.

Overall, it became clearer that Sam was in some trouble, and his parents sought counseling for him. In individual sessions during our initial assessment, Sam revealed that the teasing and mocking at school had become overwhelming. He finally concluded he had no choice but to join in with the boys at the top, who rewarded him by including him in their parties and overnights. Sam discovered that he could be quite entertaining—the funny guy—and was willing to take greater risks to secure his place. He never challenged the dominance of the bigger boys and, in fact, discovered one boy in particular whom he liked and who liked him. He began to enjoy the chumminess and security of being included. He had learned to get along by going along.

But Sam also revealed how frightened he felt by the direction things were going and how lonely he was in his family. His parents had little idea of what he was facing. At parties, boys brought alcohol they had stolen from their parents and occasionally even marijuana. Boys and girls had begun hooking up, and there was growing pressure to adopt at least the posture of being cool and indiscriminate. Sam had gotten himself into the social fast lane. At lunchtime, his buddies would tell stories about their weekend exploits; about how far they had gone sexually and which girls they had taken advantage of. The further Sam went to keep up with his friends, the more estranged he felt from his family, as well as from himself. It became harder and harder to imagine ever telling his parents the truth about his life.

Sam was not a hard boy to help back from the edge, fortunately. His parents, responding to the wake-up call, were able to see that they had contributed to their son's shaky position by taking him for granted, being busy, and getting caught up in the hype of their older sons' athletic success. They let him know they were sorry. They found ways to validate him for the qualities that made him different from his star older brothers, including his flair for creative writing. His father initiated time each week to check in with Sam, asking him if he wanted to hang out, and do whatever Sam wanted. Sometimes they went to the diner, sometimes they threw around a lacrosse ball, sometimes they just sat in the basement, where Sam destroyed his father in whatever video game he chose.

For both Sam and his parents, the eighth-grade experience was a lesson in the seductive power of brotherhood and its dangers. Sam could have gotten lost. To the extent that boys take to heart the script they follow in relationships with their buddies, they can lose their grounding and detach from their moral compasses. The voices of their parents can be drowned out by the more immediate and consequential pressures of the group. Sam's story is an instructive lesson about boys' dependence on relational anchors to help them resist peer norms. In his story, we also see the limits of boys' courage. Sam's was a cautionary tale about how boys get overwhelmed and agree to go along with other boys, even when they do not believe in what they are doing.

For boys less fortunate than Sam, without parents to retrieve and hold on to them, norms of brotherhood can become confusing. The anthropologist Peggy Sanday of the University of Pennsylvania has observed that rape is a sociocultural phenomenon, more likely to occur under certain conditions. When extreme versions of masculinity, including hostile attitudes toward women, are promoted in male groups, the group becomes one that is "rape prone."[22] Hypermasculine attitudes and sexual scripts that view women narrowly as objects of male desire make for a dangerous combination under these circumstances. UCLA psychologist Neil Malamuth developed a Likelihood to Rape scale and found, disturbingly, that one-third of college-age men said they might rape a woman "if guaranteed they would not be caught or punished."[23]

But antifemale norms have a harder time gaining traction when a boy is rooted to a home base. Connections protect boys from the full range of excessive, abusive, and destructive behaviors celebrated in hypermasculine cultures. These extreme versions of masculinity have a special appeal to boys whose early socialization in families and peer groups has already made them receptive. As they get older, grow apart from their parents, and make their group their home, earning the "respect" of the group is the main currency of exchange.

Greek life fraternities, more popular than ever with one in six men who attend a four-year college full-time, exemplify conditions where brotherhood gets away from itself. According to public health researchers, 86 percent of young men living in fraternity houses binge on alcohol, twice the rate of other students.[24] Comparing sexual assault rates among fraternity males before they joined and after, one researcher found that men were three times more likely to commit sexual assaults after initiation. In a 2014 *Time* magazine piece, writer Jessica Bennett asked, "What do you expect to happen at a club where women are viewed as outsiders, or commodities, or worse, as prey, and where men make the rules? It should be no surprise they end up re-creating the boys' club—and one that isn't all that great for the boys, either."[25]

Membership in their groups requires an active and ongoing negotiation between who a boy believes himself to be and what his group stands for. Most boys will succumb to the power of the group at times, even becoming lost, like Sam, in surrender to its norms. But, also like Sam, their connections can reinforce core values that help them find their way back from its toxic norms.

Helping boys to exercise courage is a critical skill in raising sons. Strengthening a boy's convictions and emboldening his resistance are counterweights to masculine norms. How the dilemmas posed by brotherhood are resolved can set a trajectory for the rest of a boy's life.

What Parents and Schools Can Do

As a boy engages with his peer group, the most basic thing for parents and teachers to keep in mind is the adage "To have a friend, be a friend." Caring, trusting, sharing, and compromising are relationship skills that all children must develop to be successful in their friendships. As they take their first steps in these relationships, boys draw on the working models developed in attachment relationships with their parents to establish their relational style. In this sense, primary relationships with parents, teachers, and siblings set the stage for what comes next. Boys who are secure in the knowledge that they are cared for will have the confidence they need to extend themselves to others. They will have an easier time being generous, taking turns, and expressing interest in their friends. They will be freer to turn down offers to do things at odds with who they are.

Some research suggests that it is the boy's bond with his mother in particular that strengthens his ability to express warm feelings toward others. Mothers are not only more likely to help their sons resist masculine conventions for emotional restrictiveness. The strength of their relationship as the son enters adolescence is also directly related to how well he carries his emotional facility to his friends. Niobe Way writes, "Boys who reported having an *increasingly* supportive relationship with their mothers from sixth to eighth grades were also likely to report *increasingly* higher levels of resistance to conventions of masculinity in their friendships."[26]

It turns out that the quality of the attachment bond children form with their caretakers is a remarkably powerful predictor of the quality of their subsequent bonds. As I mentioned in chapter 1, attachment researchers found that the twenty-question Adult Attachment Inventory can predict the attachment status of sons and daughters from that of their parents with 85 percent accuracy.[27] While relationship styles can improve in adulthood, overcoming patterns of guardedness, mistrust, domination, and exploitation forged in early hurts can be hard work. For mothers, fathers, and other adults, building solid connections with sons and mentees, and maintaining the quality and depth of these relationships, is an essential preventive strategy to empower boys for later life.

Beyond laying the foundation, here are some specific suggestions for parents and others who want to support boys as they engage in friendships and cope with their peer groups.

Provide Opportunities

Because having good friends is so important for boys' development, families must make space in crowded family and classroom schedules for their sons to spend time with their friends. That has gotten harder and harder as childhood has adapted to the busy work lives of modern families. Between full-time day care and extended time in school, summer camps, and sports and arts programs, children's time is not their own. At least until they reach an age when they are able to get themselves around, boys will need their parents to make time for them to hang out with friends in the weekly routine.

As neighborhoods have become less family friendly, fewer children can simply walk out of their homes to find playmates and friends. The playdate is the alternative, though it is usually beyond the organizational capabilities of younger boys to make arrangements on their own. This is where parents' attention and their ability to listen to their son comes in: any initiative they take to socialize should be encouraged. Even simple expressions such as "I wish I could play with Tommy" represent his first steps to solve the problem of social isolation. Providing scaffolding and logistical support so boys have a fair shot at successfully building connections of their own can mean responding with "Why don't you invite him over this weekend?" and "Would you like me to talk to his mother after you check with him?" Following the boy's lead, rather than directing him, deepens his initiative and independence.

Yet with parents working and schools ramping up test-related expectations of teachers, it is harder for boys to find adults in a position to back up their need to spend time with friends. It is faster and more efficient to engineer the boy's day than to wait for him to notice what he wants and to pick up on his lead. But longer-term skill development is the point. We want boys to learn how to navigate their worlds—parents and well-meaning teachers cannot substitute their skills for those of their sons and students. Rough-and-tumble social jockeying and ever-shifting hierarchies will require a fair measure of resilience, creativity, and grit, skills that are ideally learned in advance of their getting into the deeper waters of adolescence. By early adolescence, when their peer group touts the value of independence from parents and teachers, boys who have not learned to fend for themselves are likely to have a harder time earning respect.

Research on resilience confirms that a boy is better able to stay afloat when he has at least one ally: someone who validates who he is, cares about what he wants, and will stand by him no matter what. While they search for a buddy or two, boys will be fortified by the unconditional acceptance of their teachers, coaches, clergy, and parents. Standing up against the threat of being excluded may not always make sense in particular contexts, but what will matter in the long run is that each boy believes he has some backing, some refuge, and that he is not wholly dependent on forces beyond his control. Balancing personal preferences against fitting in is the trick every boy must learn.

Keep an Eye Out

In Sam's story, as well as in those documented by observers such as psychologist Judy Chu, it is clear that parents and teachers have roles in relation to boys' friendships that are often unrecognized. Particularly while boys are young enough that their social lives are relatively transparent and their challenges are reasonably manageable, parents and teachers can help them gain skills at balancing the demands of the group against their own values and needs. Keeping a close eye on how boys manage these challenges and maintain their balance—intervening to coach those who get lost or overwhelmed—provides a safety net while they develop their own perspectives on who they are and their adeptness at striking the right balance.

The problem is that "kid society" operates by its own rules, out of sight and beyond the control of adult authority. In a study conducted by a student research team at an independent school examining bullying and violence, two key findings underscored the unseen-but-just-beneath-the-surface nature of these rules. Fighting and hazing were reported by one in ten boys; one in three had been bullied, threatened, or intimidated. As to where the incidents had occurred, it was the cafeteria, school yard, gym, and locker room—spaces where adults were less present—that stood out. Boys are expert at finding gaps in adult surveillance.

Not that parents and teachers are so vigilant. In fact, it is stunning how only the squeakiest-wheel interactions are typically noticed. Separated by generational differences in norms, perspective, and understanding, younger and older people pay scant attention to each other and seem truly to live on different planets. As they age, boys look more and more to their friends and to their peer group on important matters of dress, music, relationships, aspirations, and fun, and develop scorn for all things adult. Teenage boys are a separate tribe.

It is the rules of this tribe and their impact on particular boys that adults must keep tabs on. Seeking to be friends and to be included, boys come under pressure to conform to the norms that prevail even when these norms deviate from values held dear in their families. Walking the line between being part of things and holding on to their own beliefs will be trial and error and require a fluid exercise of judgment and courage. There will be lots of chances for each boy to practice standing up against pressures. And, likely, lots of mistakes. When a boy gives in to the irresistible pressures of his group, it will help if he can acknowledge to someone that he is conflicted and uncomfortable in doing so.

When their son joins a peer group, it means lots of opportunities for parents as well—of a different sort. Without micromanaging their son's social life, parents and others who care will want to be mindful of the quality of that social life: Has he built a network of relationships? Are the boys he travels with ethical peers?

Is he able to be himself with at least some of them? Are his friendships committed and durable? Ideally, a trusted connection with his parents will allow the boy to be open about friends, teammates, and other peers. It's great when he can use his parents as sounding boards without fear of being worried about, second-guessed, or superseded.

In Sam's example, both the good and bad news is instructive. His family, while kind and caring, did not notice that he was becoming overwhelmed by the dynamics of the group until his behavior signaled that he was getting into real danger. Once they reached for him with new interest, and he could let them in on the reality of his social life, Sam was able to reset his moral compass. Getting things off his chest and finding his parents understanding strengthened his resolve to right the balance. His grades picked up, and he spent more time with his family. And while he remained friendly with the same crowd at school, his mom and dad's intervention provided him with a pretext to cut back on parties and stop trying to keep up with the fast but shallow pace of the popular group.

The norms of brotherhood, while they vary across different cultures, still reflect a singular, dominant ideal that privileges certain qualities and types of boys, punishing others. Where the self-confidence of girls who are physically bigger than most of their peers has been found to suffer, for boys it is the opposite: bigger, early-maturing boys are regarded more positively than smaller, less athletic, or less stereotypic ones. How boys see themselves in the looking glass of brotherhood will reflect this cultural bias. They will have a hard time not taking its messages, positive and negative, to heart.

Malik was a boy who enjoyed lots of friends through fifth grade. But as adolescence and growth spurts arrived, group dynamics changed in middle school. He found himself overlooked and increasingly excluded. A group of four or five boys began to stand out as the most popular and to seek one another's company exclusively. At lunch, they would save one another seats, while Malik and other boys who had always been friends with them scampered to grab one of the remaining seats at the table. During lunch, these boys talked excitedly to one another and would often turn on the other boys whenever they chimed in, making fun of them to bolster their own standing.

The breaking point came when Malik discovered the boys were planning a birthday party for one of them and that he was not invited. He found out the hard way, because the party had been organized secretly. He texted one of the other boys who hovered around the gang on Friday night, asking if he was doing anything and wanted to hang out, only to get back the message that he could not because he was "going to Evan's party." All the pent-up frustration, humiliation, and futility he was feeling welled up, and with that, Malik broke down.

Fortunately, his mother noticed his face as he read the text and was there to listen. Though she hurt as much as her son, she bit her tongue and simply consoled him without adding her opinions. She was able to remember that it was the long run that mattered, not the immediate hurt her son was feeling. Malik needed to be able to think for himself about how to handle the social life of his school. On his own, he realized that the boys he had been hanging with were not his friends and that he should invest in relationships with another group of boys who, while less "popular," treated one another better.

Encourage Withdrawn or Inhibited Boys

Parents should not worry when boys go through "dry" periods with friends. According to research on early adolescent boys' friendships, conducted by psychologist William Bukowski of Concordia

University in Montreal, slower social times are common.[28] With so much in flux, it would be surprising if a boy's friendships didn't also ebb and flow. To the extent that their friendships are a training ground for long-term relational skills, it is even desirable that boys learn to adapt to changing circumstances and to deal with setbacks, although many parents hope unrealistically that they maintain steady winning streaks.

But once burned, twice shy. Some boys find the peer group too much to contend with and give up trying. Jeb, who was a sixth grader when he first came to see me, quickly showed how confident he was with adults: witty and entertaining, easily trusting, and not afraid to be vulnerable. He was able to be himself, taking it on faith that I would listen with respect and care. This was something he had learned to count on in relationships with his parents and teachers.

His relationships with his classmates were another story. He described the other sixth graders as unpleasant and aversive, his lack of success at finding good friends having tainted his view of what was possible with them. Beloved by his teachers, who appreciated his genuineness, willingness, and humor, Jeb spent weekends alone with his family. Texts from classmates rarely appeared on his phone.

Never getting to enjoy the uplift of fun with friends left Jeb pessimistic and despondent. Yet neither he nor his mother connected the two things. In fact, they tended to attribute the one—few friends—to the other, imagining biologically based depressive tendencies. Jeb also had a learning difference and had spent earlier school years in resource rooms with other special-needs students until he worked his way back to the mainstream. The years he spent apart left him at the margins of his school's peer group and even elicited mean comments from other boys when he would join them in physical education or health classes. Jeb came to believe he was different and unlikely ever to be accepted by other boys. His view of himself suffered.

After getting a full picture of Jeb from his parents, teachers, and some testing during an initial assessment, I realized that he was caught in a developmental crush that would only get tighter. Boys have an innate drive to become their own person, with their own relationships, and must build lives of their own. Jeb had retreated to the safety of his family, and his mother contributed unwittingly to his growing powerlessness by validating this feeling that he was simply different. Perhaps, she wondered, medication was needed? For his part, Jeb was stuck and clueless about breaking out of the downward spiral.

I asked Jeb about his relationships, making sure to add that he was funny, smart, and really interesting to talk to, and that I was sure others would find him so as well. When he complained about the other boys and rationalized his inaction, I suggested we make a goal, and that I would support him until he achieved it: at least one social date every weekend. I helped him make a list of all the boys he might enjoy, allowing him to complain about each boy but not letting him write off the youngster completely. "No one's perfect, Jeb, but you're in the market for a good friend and need to give lots of boys a fair tryout." My confidence in him and my light attitude toward the boys he felt discouraged about seemed to provide enough of a boost that he gave it a try. Of course, he discovered that many of his classmates were happy to spend time with him, and his attitude began to shift. He actually accomplished his goal before long and did not complain of depression again.

I was not unsympathetic with Jeb about how rough and mean the boys in his class were capable of being. He knew that better than I did. But I did know something he did not: while the deck seemed stacked against him, he could change his status one friendship at a time and work his way from the margins to the mainstream, simply by beginning with boys who were more open to him and expanding his connections. Experiencing success, his sense of powerlessness and despair would lift and he would grow in confidence. The funny, warm boy adults saw would show himself more and more with his peers, and, in a cascade, Jeb would discover an important secret about getting along with the mean team: not to volunteer for scapegoating or to accept being a target.

Every boy feels insecure in the peer group—even ringleaders who are riding high. Anyone can suddenly become the target of its ridicule. Many boys who have a healthy sense of themselves naturally find this dynamic threatening. But despite their dumbing down for the group, individual boys respond when someone they feel connected to reminds them who they really are. Every boy's humanity exists within—and generally transcends—the less healthy norms of brotherhood. Helping boys discover how to connect with their peers while holding on to themselves, in spite of group norms, is a fundamentally important way to empower them.

Intervene with Boys Who Get Lost

For boys like Sam, becoming part of the group compensated for feeling twice overlooked. Neither his family nor his classmates ever singled him out for special notice. He worked extra hard to earn the regard of the coolest boys in his class, pretending and posturing for their attention. Sam felt that having a place in the circle of popular boys might compensate for the ways he had come to sell himself short. But as he went along with the group while it went further and further in unhealthy directions, his compromises grew in cost. He actually felt relieved when his parents intervened.

Sam is not an outlier. Many boys who become dominated by the norms of brotherhood wish secretly that someone would come along to help them establish a better balance. Unfortunately, instead of seeing them as victims of an overpowering force, when parents and other adults deal with boys who have gone too far, they tend to react moralistically. Faced with such judgments, boys feel unfairly criticized and held against an unrealistic, outdated standard. Judging a boy who has overcompromised is easy to do from the relative security of adulthood. But such judgments drive boys to distance themselves further from their primary sources of understanding and support, leaving them truly at the mercy of their peers.

For those concerned about a boy's involvement with his peers, this action framework may be helpful:

Level One

For the parent who catches things early and notices that the boy has become withdrawn and somewhat secretive, the first step is to conduct a personal inventory: Is disappointment and disapproval, maybe even disrespect, motivating your concern? Once your motivations are clearer and you are more grounded in compassion and love for your boy, review his strengths to remind yourself of who he really is. That is the child you must reach for. This inventory will also help the parent deliver a more encouraging message and influence what the boy sees of himself in your eyes. Explicitly and thoughtfully validating their son, player, or student is almost always a good idea for any adult wishing to help, especially with boys who may already be receiving negative feedback.

Because the goal is to reconnect and not simply to correct the boy or halt his troubling behavior, there is no hurry; your son will right himself when he is reconnected. It may take time to overcome his skepticism that he is not merely being manipulated, particularly if considerable distance has developed between him and his parents. Special time and listening are reliable go-to strategies to help parents reconnect. By marshaling your attention to focus on your son, listening to him, and noticing how he reacts, you will learn a lot that guides your next step.

At this level, there is nothing special to worry about, no immediate problem to be solved. Restoring connection is the point.

Level Two

Assuming that a dialogue becomes possible as the connection deepens, it may be appropriate to be explicit with your son about the struggle you've observed: "It seems like it got hard for you to show your friends who you really are." These observations should not be expressed as accusations or criticism—making the boy defensive and want to retreat—but should be sympathetic and compassionate in tone. Sharing personal stories along similar lines certainly can help normalize his predicament and reduce the topdown nature of the interaction. The most effective interventions are delivered in a spirit of commitment, respect, and care—especially for someone who is already likely to feel ashamed and powerless.

If the intervention gets some traction and elicits an acknowledgment of a problem, parents, teachers, or coaches are at a decision point: they must make a determination whether the situation calls for taking some action to reengineer the boy's circumstances— a new school or team, for example, or perhaps professional counseling. If the circumstances are clearly over the boy's head, the parent has the only real power to modify the environment so that he has a chance to hold his own. But if the boy is simply finding it hard to fit in without giving up things that are important to him, the adult can offer support and help him brainstorm alternatives.

In both cases, having leveled with someone about the true nature of his struggles, the boy has already taken a decisive turn. Again, it is the long game that matters, and up to the boy to make the change. He can regularly check in to celebrate successes or receive further coaching and encouragement but should not feel he is accountable to some kind of supervisor. The goal, ideally, is that he wants to change for his own sake and not simply to satisfy Mom and Dad.

Level Three

For some boys, attachment to the peer group exercises an especially strong hold. Built on the seductive foundation of acceptance, excitement, and fear, loyalty is a core value of brotherhood. When a boy's other relationships are less secure, he can count on his brothers to stand by him. His friends may seem irreplaceable. Alienated from adults, boys who depend on the group can feel desperate not to lose what they have. Often their experience includes traumatic losses and disconnections in their primary relationships, making them even less willing to risk losing what they have.

Desperate, these boys get swept up in brotherhood's norms. Lacking the moral anchors and inner voices of caring adults who matter to them, they are capable of deluding themselves in a group-think, *Animal House* atmosphere. Alcohol and other mind-altering substances make things worse. Intoxication and wildness become end goals of their own, exacerbating the problem for boys whose moral compasses are already wobbly.

There is a cart-and-horse argument among developmental psychologists: How can a boy be expected to improve his self-regulation if he missed out on formative relationships that cultivate this capacity to begin with? Even more serious, at what point can a boy be considered conscienceless? The good news from neuroscientists, confirmed by advances in understanding the responsiveness of the brain to new experiences in relationships, is that a boy is never unreachable. For every boy whose story sounds completely hopeless, there is another about someone from similar circumstances who turned his life around. The difference is almost always that an adult intervened, managing to get through to him when he was lost and alone. While early experience creates strong models that endure, these models do adapt in changed circumstances.

That's the challenge for the parent or teacher trying to get through to the boy who has lost himself in the brotherhood. Parents not only have to contend with loyalty conflicts and the lure of intoxication but also will encounter less conscious barriers in the way of reaching their sons. In my private practice, I often encounter boys who become dodgy when my efforts to connect trigger mistrust engendered from hard, disappointing experiences. I have learned to be patient, to expect a bumpy road, and to hang in. Ultimately, given the boy's human nature, breaking through is a far more likely outcome than his being able to maintain his detachment. Someone who cares—particularly when he or she does not blame or come off as pushy—is practically irresistible.

With boys who are especially lost and chronically avoidant, it helps when they have less choice in the matter. Scheduled family time together, for example, is a reliable way to work around a boy's counterdependence. Mom, let's say, shows up at her son's bedroom door and holds him to the time, even if it means sitting patiently while he does his best to withhold himself in a test of his parents' resolve. What mothers and fathers can do is take the silence as an opportunity to explain that they just want contact with him, to get to know him better, and are sorry for how they grew apart. "Spending time with you is a priority for me, and I'm going to be with you, no matter what. I don't need you to pretend or even be nice to me. What I am after is to know you as you are." Because trust may be weak, it is important for parents to demonstrate that they are willing to do whatever it takes to restore the relationship.

Physical signals can be important. For example, while the boy huddles protectively apart, you might try moving a bit closer—not fully invading your son's space but also not accepting his rigid boundaries. A toe touch, a playful pillow toss. It can be difficult for the parent not to take the boy's rejection personally, but I have coached many to remember that as tentative as they might feel, the boy is much more leery of trusting them.

Even though he does not have a say in *whether* they spend time together, it is important that what happens *during* this special time is something he can shape. To get the right message across, you must meet him on his terms. Often the point of your time together becomes clearer from something small: when a parent is willing to sit in silence or engage with his or her son in activities that may seem meaningless. I coach parents to expect lots of testing before the boy becomes more open. Finding something he might enjoy communicates a willingness to invest time and attention in what the boy cares about. Being explicit about the agenda—"I just want to connect with you"—also helps, as boys who feel stuck are on the lookout for traps.

Dedication and perspective are definitely handy in winning back boys. All the tricks of parenting come into play, such as being patient and confident, meeting the boy where he is, and not taking rejection personally. Doing regular gut checks, so as not to revert to defensive, pessimistic projections, will be important. As much as the parent may want to blame him for his attitude or behavior, the boy's goodness and promise must be kept in mind. But the thrill of succeeding with your son is worth the struggle and effort.

CHAPTER 6

LOVE, SEX, AND AFFECTION

Young men are fascinated by their new capacities for romance and sexual attraction. In the glare of sexualized media, in fact, this fascination often begins even before puberty. Testing their changing bodies, learning to convert romantic feelings into affectionate exchanges and to establish and maintain intimate relationships—these and many related topics are endlessly absorbing. But although they are primed to explore physical closeness, masculine norms that dominate boys' sexual and relational development hinder them. Just as boys enter school already behind girls in their development of important noncognitive skills, so deficits in their experience with closeness and affection also place them at a disadvantage as they seek intimacy.

The good news is that parents and other caregivers can help boys with these challenges, despite the popular impression that adolescent males try to shut adults out of this part of their lives. A boy's most profound emotional experiences often happen as he reaches for love, and naturally he wants to talk about them when he feels safe. Simply as listeners, parents and mentors can help boys find their way through this confusing time. In addition, a parent's own examples and how well either Dad or Mom maintains closeness with his or her son impacts how the youngster navigates the barriers on the road to healthy, mature sexuality.

Boys today face new threats that have arisen since their parents grew up. Age-old pressures of peer culture and restrictive masculine norms are intensified by social media, online pornography, and a dating culture dominated by myths about casual sexual encounters. Beyond those more gradual developments, though, the onset of the #MeToo movement and new Title IX rules against campus sexual assault at the college level filter down to secondary and middle school dating rules in ways that upend historic romantic patterns—making it even more important that boys figure out who they really are in the areas of love, sex, and affection. As he holds out for something real, a boy can benefit from the active support of an adult who maintains faith in his goodness while being honest about the actual challenges of masculine norms and new dating rules facing him.

The Big Picture

Universal stereotypes of males as sexual predators, deeply etched in popular culture and peer relations, can color how a boy perceives himself. His first exposure to pornography, for example, often comes about with friends. Regardless of how foreign or repugnant a boy might initially find the images posted on these sites, he receives a powerful message from the group about how he *should* react as a boy.

Almost from the cradle, parents respond to cultural fears of spoiling a boy's masculinity by distancing themselves from him. This narrows their opportunities for communication, closeness, and affection. From the time a baby is identified as male, even while still in the womb, he is treated quite differently from girls. Psychologists Ronald Levant, former president of the American Psychological Association, and Wizdom Powell of the University of North Carolina, use words such as "trauma" and "abandonment" to characterize how a boy's attachment is weakened or broken well before he is ready to be independent.[1] His needs for touch, closeness, love, and affection often go unmet during his most formative years. By the time he reaches adolescence and is able to date and to explore sexual intimacy, he may long for close human contact.

It is almost as if boys are typecast for a particular sexual script, and their conditioning prepares them for the part. We know that one boy is different from the next, but his sexual and romantic desires are often obscured by the wholesale image of boys as "slaves to their hormones." The father of a teenage girl in my practice captured a common sentiment as he expressed how he felt about his daughter beginning to date boys: "I'm very concerned. I know what I was like around girls when I was a teenager. I need to protect her from boys who have only one thing on their minds."

Compounding such stereotypes is the peculiar American reluctance to discuss love and sex with adolescents. According to sociologist Amy Schalet of the University of Massachusetts, there is a "profound discomfort in American society not just with teenage sex but with teenage love."[2] Nor are parents the only ones who receive messages to stay out of boys' romantic relationships. Few boys can find *any* responsible adult willing to talk with them about their questions and desires.

In this communal silence, the headline-grabbing bad behaviors of a few young men dominate how boys are thought of as a group. How many movies depict frat boy attitudes and their scoring cultures as if they are just humorous examples of "boys being boys"? How much do advertising images of players and smooth operators influence generations of uncertain and inexperienced teenage boys? As an example, a young man, sensitive, thoughtful, and anxious, told me recently about his first sexual experience. Travis explained that his girlfriend, caught in a pornographic fantasy of her own, asked him for "rough sex" and that he felt obliged to perform accordingly. He only had plotlines from his own pornography viewing and peer group norms to draw on for guidance. I asked him what he himself wanted—he had no idea. The problem is that in today's world, the consequences for not knowing and for allowing the default culture to define him can be life altering.

Perhaps to avoid stereotyped expectations, most boys learn to keep feelings about love, sex, and affection to themselves. But as Dr. Schalet adds, "American boys end up paying a price for a culture that does not support their needs for intimacy."[3] Isolated as they go about this critically important task on the way to becoming responsible adults, boys can get stuck. Pressed on every front to perform, forced into stoic postures that hide feelings of uncertainty and loneliness, and pandered to by a culture that misrepresents their true hearts, boys are whipsawed between incitements to act as sex-crazed beasts and their own desires. Their basic needs become so freighted with cultural baggage that many boys simply cannot think clearly.

The Lonely Online Hunter

Typically, boys first begin sexual activity between ages twelve and fourteen with the onset of puberty, although some may experiment before then. As their bodies change and sexual feelings awaken, most boys begin to masturbate. By age thirteen, nearly half of all boys have masturbated to ejaculation; by age fourteen, the percentage rises to three-quarters, increasing to nearly all boys by age fifteen. In terms of frequency, most teenage males masturbate once daily, some twice. Before he has sex with a partner, the average male will have masturbated around two thousand times.[4]

Between the onset of puberty and full maturity—by age twenty-one—virtually every teenage boy in today's digital age finds his way to pornographic websites. Given the vacuum surrounding the topic of sex, boys find pornography the easiest way to learn about it. Once on these sites, they receive invitations to use the raunchy images and videos to stimulate autoerotic behaviors. Pornography becomes both a cause and an effect. Promoting a mode of sexuality disconnected from emotional sharing, the pornography industry draws in boys who are lonely and curious; once in, many boys become hooked. Feelings of shame, embarrassment, and obsession can make this natural part of their development problematic—and very private.

From this state of isolation, boys' awkward and uncertain efforts sometimes pop into public view. Take TJ, a seventh grader at a boys' school, who was discovered by his Spanish teacher masturbating under his desk. By the time he was referred to me, TJ had received several talking-tos—by the teacher (an ex-nun), the dean, the head of the school, and his parents—and had adopted the familiar hangdog posture of boys who are ashamed. TJ was reluctant to talk about what had happened, certain that I could never appreciate what he might say about the thoughts and feelings driving his bad judgment.

I decided that sharing some information might help. I told TJ about other boys who had been found in similar circumstances. I explained how common confusion about their maturing bodies is among boys and how well things generally turn out, especially when they can tell someone—me, if he wanted—what they are feeling. Only by talking could he expect to get better control over the impulses that got him into trouble.

Eased by this perspective, TJ revealed that he had gotten so caught up in pornography lately that he was relieved to be found out, hoping it could help him stop. Gradually, he was able to talk about how he felt, and how the relationships within his large family offered little real closeness. As he put together the pieces, TJ understood better why things had played out this way. When I saw him months later, running around with friends at recess, his easy laughter confirmed that he had moved on.

The first order of business with a boy whose feelings about sexuality have become confused is to bring him in from the cold and reassure him that his feelings are rooted in healthy and natural impulses. TJ was able to work his way out of the hole he had dug simply by telling someone what was going on, realizing how he had gone off course, and reorienting himself. But any boy trying to be true to himself is deluged by powerful market forces projecting images and ideas targeted at him.

From a neurodevelopmental perspective, researchers suspect that frequent users of pornography may become "arousal addicts" and that their brains are "porno-sized," causing them to associate sex with self-focused gratification and intense stimulation. Among older adolescent males, half masturbate to pornography several times a week; for nearly 15 percent, it is daily. One concern is that these experiences are impersonal and devoid of love and connection. Another is how they affect real-life encounters: boys who watch more pornography summon these images to become aroused in sexual interactions. Stanford University professor and psychologist Philip Zimbardo explained recently, "During our research, a lot of young men told us about how porn had given them a 'twisted' or unrealistic view of what sex and intimacy are supposed to be, and how they found it difficult to get aroused by a real-life partner."[5]

More troubling is that pornography prepares boys poorly for the new age of affirmative consent. On college campuses across the country, recent changes in how sexual consent is defined legally have made sexual encounters even more complicated. In California state colleges and universities, for example, a new law established "affirmative, conscious, and voluntary" consent as the standard. Writer Emily Bazelon, in a *New York Times Magazine* essay titled "Hooking Up at an Affirmative-Consent Campus? It's Complicated," notes that for males at both the secondary and college level, there is "nervousness about accidentally running afoul of consent rules," as a twenty-one-year-old Yale economics student explained to the author. But when boys' attitudes and expectations are shaped by the misogynistic images of pornographic videos, in which women are portrayed as sex toys, and themes of domination, exploitation, and even abuse predominate, they are being set up to run afoul of these standards.

Another boy's story illustrates more extreme consequences that can occur when isolation is made worse by feelings of fear and shame. Stan was an excellent student, quiet and shy, though he was a decent basketball player and enjoyed hanging with his teammates on weekend nights. Just before dawn one morning, his family was awoken by a pounding on the front door and a repeated ringing of the doorbell. When his stepfather answered, a horde of FBI agents and state police barged into the house with a search warrant. They explained that someone in the home had been downloading and distributing child pornography. With the flashing lights of their cars in the driveway signaling their presence to neighbors, the strike force confiscated computers and mobile devices, and ransacked the house.

It turned out that Stan had been accessing pornographic images from Internet file-sharing sites that were monitored by the FBI, and he was now in deep trouble. To make matters worse, the images were of boys his age. Sam's exploration of his sexual orientation was outed to his parents and the world.

I saw Stan under an agreement worked out by the family with the prosecutors, required in the end to attest that he was not a predatory risk. Through our sessions, Stan explored his feelings of attraction and very limited sexual history. He determined ultimately that he was gay and succeeded in letting his parents know. Prior to the raid, he had grown more and more distant from his family, particularly as he realized the nature of his sexual attractions, and became more secretive. In his isolation from family and friends, he came to think something was wrong with him and could not imagine how he could ever be himself. It took the harrowing experience of the home invasion and his parents standing by him to imagine a better future.

Stan's experience, like TJ's, illustrates how loneliness and natural developmental pressures can distort a young man's judgment. Both boys viewed Internet pornography as an easier way to explore their sexual feelings than in actual peer relationships; in the privacy of their bedrooms, they became even more cut off. Sound judgment was compromised. In TJ's case, he actually thought it might be okay to masturbate in a public place.

As for Stan, the story is complicated by what psychologist Michael Sadowski calls the silencing of gay and queer youth and the rise in risky behaviors that often results. Despite political advocacy on their behalf, these boys are still pushed to the margins of their schools and communities. They "know—in some deep and personal way—what silence both sounds and feels like."[6] Gay youths abuse substances and become depressed more commonly than heterosexual peers do; they commit suicide at rates nearly four times higher. Stan felt unable to be himself with his buddies, worried about his parents' reactions, and withdrew into very private explorations that were compelling, confusing, and shameful. His only source of comfort was found on pornography sites that made the exploitation of young people seem normal—until the FBI crashed this fantasy.

While young men identifying as gay may still be socially marginalized, rigid boundaries in how sexual identity is defined seem to be easing. Research by Cornell University psychologist Ritch Savin-Williams found that although most males describe themselves as heterosexual, more identify as "mostly straight" than either gay or bisexual combined. National surveys show that 6 percent of teenage males indicate that "mostly opposite sex" describes the direction of their sexual attractions—nearly a million young men who admit to some measure of fluidity. Understanding sexuality as falling along a spectrum instead of into a fixed category is more true of millennials and iGen'ers than previous generations. In a national survey that included the question "Thinking about sexuality, which of the following comes closer to your view?" a majority chose the option "Sexuality is a scale—it is possible to be somewhere in the middle."[7]

But as much as things are changing, many features of boyhood—such as the pornography industry—promote stereotypic, even exaggerated, images of male sexuality. Much online pornography contains degrading and violent images reflecting hostile attitudes toward women. These images affect a boy's capacity to relate in healthy ways toward his female peers. In the view of *New York Times* pundit Ross Douthat, pornography contributes to the conflicted personalities of young men in the #MeToo time: "A breed at once entitled and resentful, angry and unmotivated, 'woke' and caddish, shaped by unprecedented possibilities for sexual gratification and frustrated that real women are less available and more complicated than the version on their screen."[8]

Exemplifying this frustration, making it their cause célèbre, is the group who call themselves incels: younger men who cast themselves as "involuntarily celibate" and tend to blame women and feminism for their sad plight. According to the CDC, as many as 27 percent of males aged fifteen to twenty-four may be involuntarily without a romantic partner.[9] One researcher estimated the number at 4.7 million men in 2012. These males have come to national and even international attention in recent years after a series of mass murderers attributed their anger and loneliness to being overlooked by women.

An abundance of research has established a link between misogynistic attitudes and aggressive sexual behaviors. A research team from the International Center for Research on Women and Promundo-US, both headquartered in Washington, DC, conducted a global survey from 2008 to 2010. Among the findings in their report, factors influencing sexual violence included attitudes of male sexual entitlement, defined by Dr. Leana Allen Bouffard of Iowa State University as "a belief that men's needs or desires take precedence over women's needs."[10] In their Man Box study, researchers from Promundo found that nearly one in three young men had made sexually harassing comments to a woman or girl in the previous month. The men most likely to harass were those who held the strongest belief in "toxic norms of masculinity" and who, as a group, were ten times more likely to harass females than the men who least subscribed to these norms.[11]

Of course, a great deal of Internet pornography is premised on just such ideas, pandering to teenage boys who are already self-absorbed. Popular media tend to follow the script that men have strong, uncontrollable sexual needs that women must serve.

Shawn's story illustrates some of these concerns. A talented African American boy who was a natural leader in his neighborhood middle school in Philadelphia, an excellent student and an outstanding football player, Shawn was also the apple of his parents' eye. Both his mother and father had come from humble circumstances and had attended urban public schools that were overcrowded, underresourced, and often dangerous. They jumped at the scholarship offer extended by the head football coach at a private high school, even though their son would be a racial and economic minority there. At the school, Shawn quickly made friends and was liked by teachers, coaches, and fellow students.

But as he commuted to school each day, leaving behind his neighborhood friends, Shawn found himself in limbo—not fully part of the social life of the boys he went to school with while increasingly disconnected from the buddies back home. He spent more time alone and turned more and more to the virtual world of social media and the Internet for connection. He discovered online pornography and found himself both fascinated and strangely affected. How he looked at girls and how he thought about sex were filtered through the comments and pictures shared among his friends on Snapchat, Facebook, and Instagram. At school, other boys on the football team talked frequently about the pornography sites they visited and the things they'd tried with girls.

As Shawn met up with girls on weekends, he imagined them performing the acts he watched on the videos. He overrode his own reservations and insisted that the girls act like those in the videos. Shawn noticed himself becoming desensitized in both body and soul. Attracting girls to go out with was not a problem, but it became more difficult for him to think about anything but his own sexual gratification. Surrounded by other boys who mimicked the same attitudes, he practically gave up on love and settled for the pleasures of hooking up or watching pornography. It was hard for him to imagine something more moving and meaningful.

At a certain point, Shawn realized that he was caught in a downward spiral. He had a good relationship with one of the younger coaches on the football team and went to him, asking to talk. Despite being embarrassed, he knew he needed help and didn't want to tell his parents or teachers. The coach responded wisely: he normalized Shawn's struggle, letting him know that he understood how pornography can be addicting, and consulted with the school counselor about options. The fortunate combination of a strong foundation in his family's love and a trusted coach enabled Shawn to be honest with himself about losing his way.

What the teenager hoped to reclaim was an understanding that sex should be more than a feeling of release. The disconnected and gratification-oriented experiences reported by boys like Shawn tragically stunt their understanding of sexuality as a means to connect and to love. Even though research affirms that boys, like girls, hope for romantic relationships, too many get overcome by these forces. Between their peer group norms and media representations, boys have almost nowhere to look for healthier views.

The Hope Behind the Hookup

Boys' sexual development sometimes seems like a perfect storm of converging forces. They are deprived of physical closeness before they are teenagers, regaled by stereotypes of themselves as hormonally driven sexual animals, first introduced to sex through pornography, and then encouraged by the scoring culture of brotherhood to view girls as objects of conquest. These views combine to separate sex from romance, objectify both the boys' own and their partners' bodies, override tender feelings, and reduce sexual intimacy to arousal and satiation. Particularly for boys prone to stimulation seeking, sex becomes another high.

A mixed blessing of the sexual revolution that began in the 1960s was the hookup culture. Sexual liberation popularized the use of contraception, pushed back the age of marriage, and freed women and girls to explore sexuality. At the same time, the average age of puberty onset dropped, creating a time gap between when young people can reproduce but are not ready to settle down, according to Kathleen Bogle of La Salle University.[12] One result was that hooking up—"brief uncommitted sexual encounters among individuals who are not romantic partners or dating each other"—became the cultural norm, replacing dating relationships as the most common adolescent sexual experience.[13] By college age, between 60 percent and 80 percent of young people have had some sort of casual sexual encounter. One study of sexually active twelve-to-twenty-one-year-olds reported that 70 percent had uncommitted sex within the last year—at parties, in homes and cars, or elsewhere.[14]

To explain the male part in the hookup culture, social scientists have proposed a hybrid of biological and social theories. Males are programmed by evolution to be "on the hunt" for diverse and frequent sexual partners. They are less threatened by risks such as pregnancy and intimate violence, and are therefore less choosy than females.

This image of the promiscuous and relationship-averse male, however, turns out to be an exaggeration. In a study led by Dr. Justin Garcia of the Kinsey Institute at Indiana University, 63 percent of males (compared with 83 percent of females) preferred "a traditional romantic relationship as opposed to an uncommitted sexual relationship."[15] In another study, nearly half of the males hoped that their sexual encounters would lead to a romantic relationship, and they reported that they had "tried to discuss the possibility of starting a relationship with their hookup partner."[16] Contrary to how they are portrayed, young males are not so sold on no-strings sex. One study found that 72 percent of males—compared with 78 percent of females—reported feelings of regret following casual sexual encounters.[17]

Still, the cultural cliché of the commitment-phobic male on the make persists. To explore *which* young men are more likely to prefer uncommitted sex, a fascinating study conducted by researchers Jennifer Shukusky and T. Joel Wade compared boys' and girls' romantic relationships with the relationships they have with their parents to determine how Mom and Dad influenced their sexual attitudes. The researchers hypothesized that a young person who had a less positive relationship with his or her opposite-sex parent would be more likely to engage in hookups. As it turned out, they found that this relationship proved particularly influential for young men. Those with weaker attachments to their mothers tended to avoid attachments with females later in life. In fact, as Shukusky and Wade concluded, "[T]he quality of the opposite-sex parent-child relationship was the strongest predictor" of their agreement with the hookup culture.[18]

While it makes sense that a mother can exert a powerful influence on her son's dating attitudes, many boys, not to mention their mothers, do not realize that. For example, Brett was a high schooler who had lots of experience with girls. Tall, athletic, cool, with floppy blond hair in a Justin Bieber cut, Brett fit the part of the ladies' man. Yet in a peer counseling group, he spoke of a dilemma with his girlfriend. The relationship consisted mainly of their hooking up, and though he knew there should be more, he was stuck. The more sex he had, the more he wanted, to a point that he thought about hooking up nearly all the time. Brett was afraid to bring up the concern to his girlfriend for fear of losing her, and he didn't want to end their relationship and start over with someone else.

I asked him if he would consider using his mother as a mentor in trying to reach for a relationship that was more satisfying and meaningful. She was thrilled by the idea of helping Brett in this important way, having missed their former connection. Though they both felt awkward, he was surprised to discover how understanding and helpful his mother could be. The teenager gradually brought his preoccupation with sex under control. He finally was able to talk to his girlfriend about wanting more in the relationship—it turned out that she did too.

One way for family members, school staff, and others to strengthen a young man's resistance to exploitative values and heartless sexuality is to take his romantic needs seriously. He can be guided to embrace his pursuit of love as a family value. Without being intrusive or trivializing their affection, parents can invite a boy to acknowledge the feelings he has for his partner. His sexual attractions should be accepted as natural and healthy. He just needs a safe place to talk about these feelings.

Myths and Misdirection

Unfortunately, many boys must make their own way though the confusing myths propagated by popular media. As Justin Garcia and his team at the Kinsey Institute wrote, "Sexual scripts in popular entertainment media are exaggerated examples of behaviors that are taken to an extreme for the purposes of media sensationalism and activation of core guttural interests."[19] One such myth is "Everybody's doing it." But, in fact, teenage sexual activity is actually declining: a research team led by psychologist Jean Twenge examined large national surveys of American adolescents, totaling 8.4 million youths aged thirteen to nineteen, and found dramatic change. Among ninth graders, the number who said they were sexually active dropped from 54 percent in 1991 to 41 percent in 2015. She wrote: "18-year-olds now look like 15-year-olds once did."[20]

Despite these cultural shifts, myths of male hypersexuality persist. Many boys feel compelled by stereotypes to perform instead of relate. The phenomenon of sexting—"the creation and transmission of sexual images by minors"—shows the gap between cultural mythology and real boys.[21]

Widespread beliefs about the explosion of sexting is misleading, according to the University of New Hampshire's Crimes Against Children Research Center. Flawed research designs, inconsistent terminology, and difficulty comparing studies has allowed the media to inflate how many boys send sexual images of themselves: 18 percent—compared with 22 percent of girls—according to a survey conducted by the National Campaign to Prevent Teen and Unplanned Pregnancy.[22] In a study of twelve-to-seventeen-year-olds carried out by the highly regarded Pew Internet and American Life Project, only 4 percent of teens said they had sent sexually suggestive photos or videos of themselves, while only 15 percent said they had received sexts.[23] Though its prevalence seems in flux—another recent large-scale analysis of thirty-nine studies conducted between 2009 and 2016 found that 15 percent of teens were sexting, with older teens more likely to send and receive than younger ones—it is clear that fewer boys send or receive sexual images than media attention suggests. By contrast, 53 percent of adults report sexting.[24]

Though only one in seven teens actually exchange these images, 40 percent of students maintained they knew friends who had sexted, and 27 percent said that sexting happens "all the time." A research team from the University of New Hampshire's Crimes Against Children Center wrote, "While sexting does seem to occur among a notable minority of adolescents, there is little reliable evidence that the problem is as far-reaching as many media reports have suggested."[25]

Such exaggerations take their toll in boys' sexual development. Once these young men leave home, they may submit to what they believe everyone else thinks, making them more vulnerable to the worst sexual stereotypes. A recent American Association for Universities (AAU) campus climate report, based on a survey conducted by the research company Westat, indicated that at top colleges, as many as a third of underclass women had been assaulted by underclassmen.[26] Sexual aggression has become so common, according to Peggy Orenstein, author of numerous books about girls, that "for many high school and college women I met, enduring a certain level of manhandling was the ticket to a social life. . . . All had, over time, been forced to develop strategies to disengage without offending an unwanted partner—they were, to a girl, deeply concerned with preserving boys' feelings and dignity even if the reverse was not true."[27]

Plainly some boys lose sight of themselves, not to mention their partners. Two delusions seem to underlie these outcomes: that males are "entitled" to sex and that it is appropriate for them to exploit women. The root of these attitudes stems not just from peer culture but also from childhood experiences. In some families, attitudes of hypermasculinity, even male supremacy, are woven into boys' socialization. The parents who reserve harsher, more physical discipline for their sons and who ridicule their displays of emotion and need for connection unwittingly teach them to reject and even resent all things feminine. Fathers who belittle or control boys' mothers model an old-style male fallacy that shapes how their sons conceive of relationships with females. Too many boys grow up in households in which hostile and derogatory attitudes toward women are the rule, and these condition their teen and adult relationships.[28]

Despite the headlines, though, only a minority of males is infected by the germ of sexual exploitation. Boys are not somehow predisposed—by hormones, conditioning, or culture—to sexual aggression. Only about 6 percent of male students become sexual perpetrators in college. Sociologist Michael Kimmel identified campus conditions increasing the likelihood of sexual aggression, including: motive (a sense of entitlement and contempt for women), opportunity (sexualized spaces such as fraternity parties and off-campus housing), and support (a code of silence among teammates and fraternity brothers, and university policies that are ambiguous). His findings actually validate the fundamental integrity of most young men, who are not subjected to conditions that subvert their humanity.[29]

To mitigate the impact of harmful masculine norms, adults must strengthen our commitment to helping boys find love and closeness. The peril and promise of a boy's sexual development reside in his relationships. Whether he finds the courage to stand against degrading peer norms and the integrity to resist masculine clichés depends on his connection to himself—which is strengthened and realized in relationships with others. The starting point for helping a young man reveal his romantic feelings is pretty basic. Some years ago, a set of Philadelphia-area boys' and girls' schools organized an opportunity that students called Gender Awareness Workshops. A colleague and I were asked to lead the workshops. About a hundred high school teens would show up on a Saturday morning, their excitement and trepidation electric. We began the day by selecting one boy and one girl and inviting them, in front of the others, to talk about "What is it like to be a boy?" and "What is it like to be a girl?"

I chose a popular guy to go first, so that his example would encourage the rest of the group. As Brad sat facing the other boys and girls, some he knew well and others he had not met before, I was struck by the rapt attention in the room. I asked him an easy opening question, I thought: "What do you like about being a boy?" But from the start, he struggled to find words. He fumbled, blushed, and sweated under everyone's eyes. Though his discomfort and awkwardness were painful to witness, the group's compassion was evident in warm smiles. The otherwise squirmy and chattering adolescents were transfixed as Brad showed how tongue-tied and reticent even popular boys are as they try to overcome the gender divide.

The workshops offered a number of important insights. As difficult as that experience was for him, Brad actually modeled a resolute commitment to learning to be more open with others. Over the rest of the day, both boys and girls followed his example and relished the opportunity to practice talking about themselves. We realized they wanted to do this work and yet could not manage it on their own. The reason was simple: boys and girls are dying to know about each other's lives, beyond the pretense of heavily scripted party and social media stereotypes. High interest at the schools kept the workshops going for several years.

A New Paradigm

Because conditioning restricts boys' opportunities for closeness as they grow older, their uncertainty and inexperience are pronounced when they attempt to forge romantic connections. A team of researchers from Ohio's Bowling Green State University found that instead of the confident, dominant image portrayed in popular media, boys in their studies reported significantly lower levels of confidence and greater "'communications awkwardness' in romantic relationships."[30] Since more than 80 percent of American teenagers have a romantic experience prior to age eighteen, support for boys looking for a romantic attachment cannot occur too soon.

The following story exemplifies what can happen for a boy when a romantic experience goes well. Will was nearly as tall and strong as a professional linebacker. His potential as a top athlete was already noticed in middle school by coaches and encouraged by his father, himself a star college athlete. But then Will's father died of a heart attack, and the teen's world collapsed. His mother became depressed, and Will found himself unable to put his heart into football. He was in shock at how empty his life felt with both his father gone and his mother sad and preoccupied. He dragged himself through his life until one day he could not. He became immobilized, unable to get out of bed and attend school. Will took a medical leave for a year, continuing his education at an alternative school while he figured out a way forward.

Will had met Annie at a party. He was attracted by her kindness and stirred by her interest in him. They enjoyed talking with each other and continued texting regularly. She learned about his father and conveyed concern in ways that encouraged Will to share more difficult feelings. He discovered that he didn't have to put up a front with her; that he could be as down as he felt. Annie not only wanted to know how he was doing, but also she wasn't bothered by his grief or overwhelming sadness. She offered him understanding and acceptance. First in texts and then with nightly calls, he grew more and more attached to her. They spent hours connecting after they did their homework.

I met Will upon his return to school, when he joined the peer counseling group and shared the story of his three-year relationship with Annie. He did not mince words about her impact on him: she had saved his life. Her support and care helped him through his darkest hours. As he spoke, what was most apparent was his commitment to her and his deep gratitude for her care. He acknowledged that they had become sexual partners, but insisted that the important thing about the relationship was how deeply they cared about each other. He loved her and was buoyed by her love in return. His respect for her was palpable.

Will's story resonated with everyone in the group. The tenderness he felt, his protective attitude toward their relationship, and his open acknowledgment of being in love touched a nerve in the other boys. Some were envious; others, empathic. But all recognized how lucky Will was. His relationship with Annie had lifted him up from his loss and given his life new meaning and purpose.

What made Will's story especially compelling was how ably he modeled respect and vulnerability. Such a big guy, a classic masculine prototype, yet when he talked about Annie, what came across was the emotional equality they had established in their relationship. Will showed few signs of chivalry or of believing he needed to protect his "weaker" partner. What researchers Peter Glick and Susan T. Fiske have characterized as "benevolent sexism"—correlated closely with a more hostile form that tends to appear when a woman does not conform to traditional role expectations—did not seem to distort Will's regard for his partner.[31] What his example underscored was how a young man benefits from seeing his partner as an equal.

Though this story is a special example of teenage attachment, a more general observation can be made from how Will's class-mates reacted to it: boys are equal to girls in the capacity to commit their hearts. Just as the truth about boys and sex is quite different from widespread stereotypes, there is a glaring gap between how they are portrayed and how they actually behave in romantic attachments. What Will experienced represented what many other boys also feel, though some have a harder time putting their desires into practice.

When a boy is grounded in a strong attachment to a parent, his quest to find a romantic partner is more likely to be wholesome and straightforward. In one example, Gregory was raised primarily by his mother, with whom he was close; his father had left the marriage for someone else, moved to another state, and was not in touch often. Though Greg sometimes missed having a dad in his life, he could tell that he was a top priority of his mother's. Living in middle-class circumstances on her paycheck as a parochial school teacher, they enjoyed a comfortable if not lavish life. Greg appreciated the easy give-and-take of their relationship; he looked out for her, learning handyman skills at an early age and making a point to thank her for all of her efforts on his behalf, while she stayed close to him even into adolescence. Greg talked to his mom about everything that went on in his life, including when he had his first girlfriend.

As he grew fonder of the girl, their closeness evolved to cuddling, to kissing, holding hands, and then to more intimate touching. Greg seemed perfectly unselfconscious about it all, lying with his girlfriend on the couch in the family room while watching television with his mother, who sat in a chair just a few feet away. She explained during a session without her son at my office that though she often felt awkward, she realized that his unguardedness signified a healthy attitude toward his sexuality. She even took pride that he hid neither his feelings of love nor his interest in closeness. Instead, he was eager to bring his girlfriend into his life at home. He made finding love seem remarkably natural, and she was reassured that, despite her own marital troubles, he could commit his heart to another.

In the din of sensationalized stereotypes about boys, stories like Greg's, demonstrating their sweet innocence, are not heard very often. Even less common are examples of parents like Greg's mother. But this is an area of development so critically important to a boy's ultimate happiness. When a young man's experiences of romantic connection are rooted in a strong, open relationship with at least one adult influence—whose primary job is not to direct but to witness, accompany, and validate—he is more likely to stay on a healthy track. Helping boys resist the myths of masculinity has to be part of the job description for their parents and mentors.

Mothers face special challenges with their sons. Greg's mother believed the cultural trope that a woman could not possibly relate to the sexuality of a developing male. The best she could do was get out of his way and pray that she had not spoiled his masculinity with too much doting or fussing. Let hormones take over, encourage boys to be boys! But something did not seem right about these stereotypic messages: she believed she knew her son. Fortunately, their special bond, forged when the father split the family, enabled Greg to show her that she was right.

Wanting to engage with boys in this part of their lives, a parent or a mentor can first gently aim to break through the silence surrounding it. To boys who are sensitive to potential embarrassment or resistant to attempts to interfere, judge, or control their choices, parents have to realize their changed role. The point is not their need for information but their interest *in him*. All through the day, every day—at breakfast, on the way to school, watching television in the evening, or visiting his bedroom to say good night—they can avail themselves of opportunities to build a relationship that can strengthen a boy's core values during the course of his sexual development.

If distance has already set into the relationship, a parent cannot begin with such a touchy subject but must build up relational capital first. This can be the fun part: watching a boy begin to open up when he realizes that his parent is genuinely interested in what interests him and simply wants to know and enjoy him. One mother of three boys told me that she found an easy way in with her sons: she gives them back rubs at night, after days that almost always include bruising sports practices and burdensome schoolwork. During this relaxed, warm time, her sons find it natural to spill out whatever is on their minds. She has a policy that she will not refer later to whatever they share, deciding that if they want, they will bring up the subject again.

Once a boy has discovered—or rediscovered—the value of sharing his life with a parent or mentor, and has learned that opening up will not lead to unwanted advice, criticism, or control, the relationship can tolerate more pointed questions. The adage "If it ain't broke, don't fix it" should prevail, but vigilant parents may notice an issue they want to discuss further. As a rule, teenage boys are highly sensitive to parents seeking to assuage their own anxieties, but an invitation to share how they think about their lives can convey interest more centered on them.

A useful way to approach intervening with boys whose explorations of sexuality may have become confused or stuck is to focus less on correcting behavior than on the power of listening to help them self-correct.

- A parent must first establish a strong enough
  connection that a son is able to talk about intimate
  experiences. Sharing their own stories, commenting on
  current news or popular events, and asking easy
  questions are all ways to take the first step to engaging
  the boy. Trying to tackle more difficult subjects without

the boy's willing participation will lead only to resistance or superficial compliance.

- When the boy signals that he feels safe enough to talk about himself, a parent's second step is to sensitively introduce the particular topic of concern, being careful not to lecture or criticize. The goal is not to tell a boy what to think but to improve his ability to think for himself. Questions such as these can help ease the way for communication: "Have you found someone you care about?" "How does it change things when you become physically close?" "What do you think about pornography?"

- Many parents worry that they might intrude on the boy's privacy. But they *are* intruding, purposefully. The point is that they are *needed* by their son, even if they don't often hear "Thank you for your interest in me." Of course, the questions have to be free of criticism, shaming, or prurient curiosity. A teenage boy will resent parents' pressing him to please them.

- The time and place may determine how such questions are received. Parents need to appreciate that a great deal goes on in a boy's life. They must pick a moment when he is relatively at ease and able to consider an invitation to share and to reflect. The mother who gave back rubs discovered that her sons came to count on these occasions to share their burdens with her. Other parents report that driving to and from school, throwing a ball around, and playing video games provide natural contexts that allow boys to relax and open up.

- The final step is to listen as the boy responds to the question or prompt. If he sounds a defensive note, it is a sign that the parent's tone, or the underlying emotion conveyed in the question, has backed him into a corner. Parents can remind their son that they have faith in him and assure him that they are not being critical. The goal is for the boy to download what he thinks and where he feels hung up with someone who knows his heart and his cherished values. Parents do not need to solve the problem, even if they ache for their son's struggle; attempting to do so can reinforce the boy's own feelings of helplessness. Given support and an opportunity to vent, many boys become better able to stand up against peer and cultural pressures.

When parents or mentors understand both their role and its limits, it can result in a boy who understands what he wants and who can pursue a course that pays off. Take fourteen-year-old Mishka, for instance. He was the type of boy who skated through life: a decent student but who did not really apply himself; an athlete with natural gifts but who tended to fold under pressure; a boy who was more concerned with being popular than with having real friends. With girls, he was more invested in his standing with other guys than in genuinely expressing affection. As he ran through a string of girlfriends, he never got beyond the most superficial level of attachment.

The youth minister at his church finally noticed the pattern and decided to speak to him about it. At a weekend retreat, he pulled Mishka aside and said: "You are such a warm, interesting boy, and yet you don't ever give girls a chance to get to know you. Are you afraid of something?" When he told me the story later, the minister was still touched by Mishka's response. The teenager's eyes filled up, and he eventually admitted, "I don't know how to." Taking the answer as an invitation to probe further, the minister gently asked him how he had come to mistrust himself. Mishka shared that he was not sure about anything to do with his sexuality. He felt ashamed and uncertain, and was working overtime to keep his feelings masked behind a show of confidence and status-seeking, superficial attachments.

In the end, the minister coached him, over the course of several years, to recognize his own goodness, to trust his heart—and ultimately also his parents—and to explore his sexual feelings with more openness. Mishka found a girl he respected enough to be honest with. His feelings for her grew as they drew closer, and he discovered even deeper feelings, including feelings of attraction. His fear and lack of experience had distorted his ability to understand himself.

One warning sign to parents and mentors that a boy might require help is an overreliance on pornography. But being able to distinguish mere curiosity from compulsion can be difficult for parents, especially if the subject of sex is rarely discussed.

What parents can look for is a pattern of use that may signal addiction: declining performance in school and activities; withdrawal; lots of time sequestered alone in his room, often with the door closed or locked; irritability and even hostility when boundaries are broached. In this case, the concern is less about the amount of use than the effect it has on overall functioning.

When mothers and fathers do notice problems, they should trust their gut and intervene—but not blame or condemn. Validating his loneliness and longing, his feeling of discouragement or shyness around romance, demonstrates the parent's willingness to join him in the challenging trenches of adolescence. A boy who finds understanding and absorbs his parent's confidence can be empowered to unburden himself about how he got stuck. Then he can be free to try another way.

The story of Ari and his mother, Ruth, illustrates both the challenges and possibilities when a parent resolves to help her son develop healthy sexuality. Ruth sought me out with an urgent question. While surreptitiously monitoring her son's phone and computer, she'd discovered a growing number of explicit exchanges with girls in his school, crude boasts with other boys, and pornographic references to sex acts. The final straw was an exchange with an adult woman who worked in the mother's bakery and whose own dating life was troubled. In the texts she intercepted, the woman encouraged Ari to describe sex acts he would like to perform with her.

Ruth was at a loss. Her question "Is this normal?" expressed the self-doubt she felt as a single mother raising an adolescent son. My first piece of advice was to assure her that she could trust herself. There were no secrets known only to men about raising a good son. At the least, she needed to confront her employee as well as set a firm limit with Ari about how he was expressing his sexuality. The message she conveyed was that his love and his body were precious. His longing was not to be exploited, even if others treated theirs with less respect.

Boys can become stranded in other ways besides in their use of pornography. Another common trap is seeking only to score. Random hookups are not necessarily signs of a problem. Both boys and girls act upon their natural curiosity and willingness to explore sexual desire without the baggage of a commitment. But parents should notice if his experiences are always short-term, shallow, and aimed at sexual gratification. He may be avoiding intimacy for some reason. He may have become unwilling or unable to commit his heart out of fear that he has nothing interesting to offer to a partner. Deeper and more satisfying experiences, developing a language for feelings, and an ability to care are all parts of a boy's sexual development.

To support a young man who has gotten stuck this way requires intervening with compassion, understanding, and confidence. The adult should keep in mind how easy it is for boys to feel ashamed and either to clam up or, worse, defend their compulsive behavior. Many boys are grateful to a concerned adult who creates the conditions in which he can acknowledge what he is doing. Sometimes all that is needed is to ask or to offer an observation. Sometimes the boy's isolation and shame can be lightened if the adult shares an experience of his or her own—most of us have plenty from which to pick.

Tom and Tommy spent lots of father-son time together, so when Tommy hit adolescence, their relationship already had a strong foundation. Tom enjoyed his son's new maturity and interest in broader topics. Tom also modeled a deep companionship with his wife, and Tommy transitioned from playing video games with his buddies right into a committed relationship of his own early in eighth grade. But his girlfriend found his dependence on the relationship suffocating, and she broke off with him for another classmate, plunging him into unexpected levels of anger and hurt.

Fortunately, father and son shared many long drives to soccer matches. One day Tom asked Tommy how he was dealing with the breakup. Tommy talked about how much he wanted a close partner, admiring what Tom had with his mother, and despaired of finding it himself. Tom decided to demystify how he had achieved the steadiness of his marital relationship. He shared some of the rejections and disappointments he experienced along the way. In their back-and-forth discussion, Tom assured his son that he would figure it out. Finding a partner was not a race. What mattered at this stage was for him to learn more about himself and his own values—including how to bounce back from disappointments.

No matter whether the adult is a father, mother, or mentor, these examples illustrate the power of a solid connection to strengthen a boy's resistance to the distorted norms and pressures that can prevent him from achieving a fulfilling relationship. By virtue of overwhelming circumstances, Will developed a clear understanding that he needed someone to care about him and to offer genuine emotional support. Shawn was also able to lean on another, a coach, to halt his slide into compulsive, dehumanized sexuality. With some prodding, Brett, too, discovered how he could leverage connection to elevate his game. Ari's mother and Tommy's father both drew on their strong relationships with their sons to assist them with difficult challenges that might have taken them down.

Finding love and romantic partnership is a developmental task that boys must undertake. As they enter this fraught stage, full of distorted male stereotypes and misleading temptations, it is no surprise that they may become confused and at times completely lost. Because an adolescent wants to think for himself, the most reliable contribution those wanting to help can make is to know him and love him. The protective assets of connection and listening can strengthen a boy's commitment to love and closeness. Knowing that someone is in his corner, he becomes confident that he can find the right way to his own heart.

CHAPTER 7

BOYS AND THEIR BODIES—
SPORTS AND HEALTH

How boys relate to their bodies is shaped by what they have learned about being male. Self-preservation is a fundamental *human* instinct, the foundation for a person's integrity. But this instinct is compromised by social norms that encourage boys to endure pain, sacrifice their health for impersonal goals, and act as if they are indestructible machines. Many boys heed the call to use their bodies in mindlessly forceful ways, to their detriment.

A child's identity begins with his body. As boys learn to be "boys," cultural messages for how they should dress, eat, exercise, take risks, sleep, care for themselves, and so forth take deep effect. Many—perhaps most—parents believe that male biology drives masculine behavior and that the many differences observed between boys and girls, especially in the physical realm, result from these biological causes. But after decades of research on sex differences—"one of the most researched topics" in psychology, sociology, and political science, according to Australian sociologist Raewyn Connell—no such defining differences have been found.[1] Psychologist Janet Hyde of the University of Wisconsin analyzed more than five thousand studies involving 7 million research participants and determined that most of the gender differences reported in the studies were small or nil.[2] On the basis of this evidence, Connell offered, "The main finding, from about eighty years of research, is a massive psychological *similarity* between women and men."[3]

Despite this fundamental similarity, from the time children are identified as male or female, their bodies are used as a basis to differentiate them. The system of gender overall, in fact, depends on bodies, beginning with a set of assumptions about what different types of bodies represent. On the basis of these representations, meaning, identity, and ways of relating to children are built into wide-scale practices that are perpetuated from one generation to the next.

But children are more than mere recipients of these meanings and practices. Newer research shows that neither the model of the body as machine, driven by biological mandates, nor the body as canvas, onto which society paints gender, does justice to the highly interactive way that individual children shape their identities. Connell offers the example of stiletto heels, which, though often painful, remain popular with young women who flirt with fashion standards and enjoy the way they look. In another study of a male bodybuilder, Connell describes the young man's efforts to sculpt himself into a symbol of male perfection to show how boys "take up" gender norms and shape their bodies accordingly.[4]

What parents and others who care for boys discover is how much this interactive process can discount and flat-out disregard health considerations. It falls to those who care for boys to keep an eye out and intervene when necessary.

Taking Care of Themselves

At the risk of being morbid, the fact that men and boys have higher death rates across all fifteen leading causes of death (not including Alzheimer's disease) than women and girls do is a necessary starting point. What should we make of this fact? How does conventional masculinity exercise such an unhealthy influence?

There are many examples of the mismatch between masculine norms and the needs of boys' bodies. In service to an ideal as "the stronger sex"—robust, tough, and self-reliant—boys adopt attitudes and behaviors that have a negative impact on their health. The psychologist Will Courtenay uses the example of skin cancer to make the point. According to the CDC, males have a skin cancer death rate twice that of women. Yet males are significantly less likely to use sunscreen than females. Making sure boys apply sunscreen would seem a logical response. But instead, young men heed the louder, more pressing, more immediate call to demonstrate toughness. As Courtenay writes, "Masculine men are unconcerned about health matters; masculine men are invulnerable to disease; the application of lotions to the body is a feminine pastime; masculine men don't 'pamper' or 'fuss' over their bodies."[5]

Another example is young males' use of seat belts. According to the National Highway Traffic Safety Administration, which in 2018 launched a special summer campaign aimed at males, there were 10,418 unrestrained passengers killed in 2016; of these, 44 percent were males aged eighteen through thirty-four. Of total road fatalities, NHTSA estimates that 2,500 lives could have been saved by seat belts.[6]

An indifferent attitude toward their bodies does not originate with boys. Taking another example, that of male-specific cancers and preventive vaccination, young men's choices reflect the attitudes of their families and medical providers. The CDC estimates that 70 percent of oral and throat cancers contracted by males are caused by human papillomavirus (HPV), which, at nearly thirteen thousand cases annually, equals the incidence of cervical cancer in women. Exposure to HPV is now virtually unavoidable for sexually active adolescents, with 80 percent of people exposed at some point in their lives and 20 percent to 30 percent of teens infected at any point in time.[7] Vaccination can make a big difference. In a 2016 study, it was found that in the ten years since the first vaccination was introduced, HPV infection rates fell by up to 90 percent in countries with mandated immunization programs such as Australia.[8]

In the United States, however, 60 percent of adolescents start the vaccination series, a jump from 30 percent a decade ago. Male vaccination rates lag behind female for several reasons. When first introduced by the pharmaceutical giant Merck & Co., marketing for the vaccine was aimed at girls, as virtually all diagnoses of cervical cancer can be attributed to HPV. When researchers studied parents' choice to opt their sons out of vaccination, the most common reason given was that their health care providers never suggested it. In fact, while the vaccine was recommended for girls beginning in 2006, it was not until 2011 that it was also recommended for boys. There was a general belief that it was not necessary for boys, in addition to worry that it would encourage their sexual promiscuity.[9] As a result, 2016 data revealed that while vaccination coverage increased from 7.8 percent in 2011 to 27 percent in 2016 among males, it still lagged behind females, at 48 percent.[10]

In their neglecting to apply sunscreen or avoid critical vaccines, we can see the complex interaction between masculine norms, caregivers, and the young men who engage in a wide range of behaviors that increase their risk of disease, injury, and death. Yes, boys themselves play a part, but would they make such unwise choices in the absence of cultural cues to do so? A recent review led

by Columbia University Medical Center adolescent medicine spe-
cialist David Bell concluded, "Compared with females, adolescent
males have higher mortality, less engagement with primary care,
and high levels of unmet needs."[11] The review confirmed that the
stronger the adherence to masculine norms, the more likely a young
man was to follow poor health practices. Boys use more substances,
such as alcohol and tobacco, drive more recklessly, and engage in
higher-risk sex and in other kinds of dangerous activities more frequently than girls.

The age group with the greatest gender health gap is fifteen-to-
twenty-four-year-olds: 75 percent of deaths in this group are male.
Males are three times more likely than females to die from injuries
sustained in motor vehicles or on bicycles, in sports, in falls, or as
a result of spinal cord and traumatic brain injuries. Males are also
four times more likely to commit suicide than females. In 2014 the
suicide rate for all children aged ten to fourteen surpassed their
death rate from traffic accidents, doubling in the five years from
2009. Of the total suicides in that age group, two-thirds were boys.
According to the CDC, the rise can be attributed in part to a new
social media culture in which public shaming is both more widespread and more profound.[12]

But the fact that boys are encouraged to use less sunscreen or
make unwise health choices is only half the story. Even after entering the health care system, their care is influenced by attitudes
related to gender. The diagnosis and treatment of attentional defi-
ciencies and hyperactivity in children has resulted in twice the
number of boys than girls being placed on stimulant medications—
particularly if they're from lower-income families. There has been
a twentyfold increase in prescriptions for ADD over the last thirty
years, with the CDC reporting steady growth from 7.8 percent of
boys in 2003, to 9.5 percent in 2007, and to 11.0 percent in 2011.
According to psychologist L. Alan Sroufe, this approach to attentional differences, based on the belief in an "inborn defect" de-

tected on brain scans, is flawed. He argues, "However brain functioning is measured, these studies tell us nothing about whether the observed anomalies were present at birth or whether they resulted from trauma, chronic stress, or other early-childhood experiences."[13]

Accounting for some stress is how boys are encouraged to think of their bodies in instrumental rather than connected ways. According to cultural scripts, male bodies are tools—means to an end. In rough play, unbridled competition, and constant military games, boys tend to follow the cue that it is not their bodies, or the persons inside them, but the roles they play that matter. Risk taking, personal care, and accident and death rates reflect how faithfully boys play their part: 70 percent of premature deaths among males are attributable to behavior patterns established when they are teenagers, according to the World Health Organization.[14]

From the start in my first job as a counselor, I saw many boys whose behavior placed them at risk. Timmy, for example, was a study in how a boy might be sweet and innocent generally but become reckless and fierce on the streets of his urban neighborhood. He was eleven years old when I met him and he lived with his grandmother in a working-class row house neighborhood. He attended the parochial school right across a narrow street. He was referred to me in my role as school counselor by the principal, who was concerned about the lack of male role models in his life and worried about his being drawn to the streets. When I spent time with Timmy, he was innocent, open, and sweet. He loved watching animal shows on television.

Over the several years before he left for trade school in ninth grade, Timmy began to hang out in the nearby park at night and spend time at the nearby recreation center's basketball courts and baseball fields. Allied with the boys he hung with, fights with gangs from other playgrounds became more frequent and more violent. I asked him if he wasn't afraid in the fights, and he said, without bravado, that he was not. He said his nickname was Marblehead, a play on his family name that conveyed how well he could take a blow. "I never feel anything," he explained. In football and street hockey games, he said, "I love to hit." I asked him what he meant, and he explained that he felt a "release" when he tackled or checked another player. Timmy had found a sanctioned outlet for his anger.

Masculine socialization trains boys to disconnect from their bodies, regarding them mainly as something to be operated in sports, at work, and even in sexual encounters. What is important is that they work and not get in the way. So, in service to end goals, many boys become disconnected from themselves to the point that pain simply fails to register.

At Play in Sports

Sports historians track the growing popularity of organized sports and athletic training to the late-nineteenth-century fear that boys were becoming "soft." Gender boundaries were being blurred as family and work roles changed, and so there was more emphasis on male physical superiority. Sports exploded in popularity. "A massive, nationwide health and athletics craze was in full swing as men compulsively attempted to develop manly physiques as a way of demonstrating that they possessed the interior virtues of manhood," Michael Kimmel wrote in his cultural history *Manhood in America*.[15]

Playing sports taps a deeply pleasurable nerve. Sports are empowering for players who discover new skills and develop new capacities, often to the cheers of coaches, teammates, and fans. Boyish play represents a delightful contrast to the pressures of school, work, and social life. Sports give play to deep, instinctual drives and provide profound visceral pleasures. As sports sociologist David Whitson explains, "The experience of force and skill coming together, however briefly, in the long home run, the perfectly hit golf shot, the crosscourt backhand, or 'flow' in a cross-country run, is a great part of what makes sport so popular."[16]

Beyond the sheer joy of moving and attempting feats of strength and skill, the bonds of teamwork are another pleasure found in sports. Opportunities to share deep emotions openly explain why young men often cling to sports as long as they can. In fact, many find sports more compelling than academic or work challenges. Some young men commit their lives to sports, only reluctantly squaring themselves with other responsibilities of adulthood. Intended as a training ground for manhood, sports can actually prolong boyishness. For some star high school or college athletes, it never gets better.

But as engaging as sports can be, they were designed as a training ground for traditional masculinity. Among boys in neighborhoods and schools, playing a sport can establish and reinforce the masculine pecking order. When being "the best" confers special status, pursuit of sports success can dominate boys' lives.

Even today, despite the rise of women's athletics, sports remain a bastion for traditional masculine values. Playing "through pain" and sacrificing "for the team" are deeply written into sports training for boys. Sports sociologist Don Sabo of D'Youville College in Buffalo speaks of a "pain principle" in which a player's willingness to "suck it up" is a measure of his masculinity. Players themselves as well as coaches and other teammates create cultures of denial about the real costs and consequences of playing despite injuries. Teaching boys to repress vulnerable feelings, reduce success to winning, inflict injury on others as a legitimate part of the game, stoically endure their own injuries, and generally exercise power to dominate opponents are all ways sports instill the norms of traditional masculinity.[17]

The passage of Title IX in 1972, a law intended to end gender discrimination in education, revolutionized women's sports. In 1972 only 7 percent of high school athletes were female; by 2012, the number had risen to 41 percent. In 1972 only 2 percent of college athletic budgets went to female sports; in 2010, girls received 48 percent of scholarship money and 40 percent of athletic budgets. As they use their bodies in sports, girls benefit in many ways. The academic performance of athletes improves relative to nonathletic peers, including in science. Female athletes are more likely to graduate high school, have higher grades, and score higher on standardized tests; 82 percent of female business executives played sports.[18]

But while some things change, some stay the same. At the college level, male team sports—basketball and football, in particular—consume disproportionate shares of athletic dollars. The costs of Division 1 football alone exceed the total for all women's sports. As legal analysts Joanna Grossman and Deborah Brake observe, "The more masculine it is, the more money gets poured into it, the more fans it has, and the more it reinforces traditional norms of masculinity."[19]

In schools where male superiority is featured in big-budget sports, athletes can find things confusing. There is the "toxic jock" syndrome, for instance, referring to how some boys overidentify with the role of athlete and lose their humanity. Peer hazing, sexual entitlement, high-risk behavior—all grow out of a locker room culture that fosters feelings of entitlement. Athletes on these teams are at higher risk for criminal behavior across a number of categories. David Whitson has argued that the world of male sports "remains a bastion of reaction, in which traditional masculinity is celebrated and other kinds of masculinity are disparaged and deterred."[20]

I have counseled many aspiring male athletes. Some have come for help to achieve more optimal performance; some because their behavior off the field has created problems. Bill was a young man whose sports dreams became the focus of both his and his parents' lives—until the dream ended suddenly.

He became enamored with soccer in grade school and was highly motivated to achieve from the start. An athletic boy, large for his age, Bill tried out and won a spot on a top regional travel team. The team trained hard and often; family weekends were taken up with tournaments and play days in all parts of the tristate area. As the team rose through the age brackets, the coach became more intense about practice, specialization, and commitment. No matter the season or the weather, the boys would be outside practicing foot drills and tactics.

Bill had played other sports when he was younger—baseball, lacrosse—but as his team reached for success, he gave each up to meet the growing demands of his coach, who made it clear that no player was irreplaceable. Playing time was the coach's way to reward boys willing to give their all. Bill had success, and his parents fed off the big dreams brewing on the sidelines, dreaming of college scholarships and more. Unwittingly, they sent the message that soccer was their main interest in their son. Where at first it had been lots of fun, soccer became a highly pressured performance. Play became both more competitive and more physically brutal. The team regularly practiced heading balls regardless of concerns about concussions. Injuries were a fact of life; every boy experienced some sort of injury—pulled muscles, turned ankles, knee ligament tears—sometimes career ending.

But Bill still loved the game itself. Moments of creativity and teamwork on the field, the payoff for all the hard work in practice, kept him coming back. In high school, the team began competing in regional showcase tournaments, where the sidelines were lined with college coaches scouting for prospects. Though National Collegiate Athletic Association (NCAA) rules limit the money available to teams, each boy imagined that he might be one of the few to win the golden ring.

In a tough, physical, high-stakes game in the state tournament, the referee took a permissive stance, and the number of fouls increased. Finally, as Bill defended the net, the attacking player kicked with all his might at Bill's leg stretching to poke the ball out of the box, fracturing his tibia. Bill was not only out for the remainder of the season; with pins inserted into his leg, he was never again as fast or fearless.

Sports accidents and injuries happen. But as gender equity impacts the culture of athletics, the question arises about how norms related to injury prevention and training might be affected. Eric Anderson of the University of Winchester has reported a "softening" of traditional masculinity among athletes. Commenting on a 2009 study that tracked declining participation in risky team sports such as ice hockey and soccer, he posits: "If men are no longer required to align to orthodox notions of masculinity, then they may be less inclined to partake in activities that may be harmful to their health."[21] In a tally of youth participation in different sports from 2009 to 2014, football and wrestling were the big losers.[22] Even in rugby-crazed Australia, studies show a steady decline in participation.[23]

Though high-profile competitive sports may avoid critical scrutiny for the time being, how physical education is delivered in schools has received fresh attention. Despite being identified as an important predictor of adult fitness, childhood fitness is undercut by the resistance of many boys to phys ed and sports, which they regard as prime spaces for bullying. Canadian scholars Michael Atkinson and Michael Kehler have identified a growing "anti-gym/exercise ideology" and an "antijock" movement stemming from the way locker room culture, competitive athletics, and teacher complicity have all compromised the effectiveness of exercise programs mandated in schools. They write, "It is no surprise, then, why the boys learn to fear and loathe collective participation in physical education."[24]

Locker rooms are especially hot spots for peer maltreatment. Unusual spaces in schools for their distance from adult control, locker rooms tend to be dominated by boys who bully and police other boys. In the United States and other parts of the world, physical education, the design and supervision of boys' locker rooms, and sports programs more generally are being rethought, as the traditional one-size-fits-all approach has both left out many boys and played an enabling part in perpetuating harmful norms.

In addition to these general trends, there are several health issues that deserve the special attention of parents and others who care for boys.

Sports Concussions

Despite the popularity of the pain principle in boys' sports, there is growing concern that head injuries, more common in certain sports than others, take it too far. There is a new acknowledgment that contact sports produce—and have *always* produced—shockingly high rates of brain injury. According to the CDC, "A concussion is a type of traumatic brain injury—or TBI—caused by a bump, blow, or jolt to the head or by a hit to the body that causes the head and brain to snap quickly back and forth. This fast movement can cause the brain to bounce around or twist in the skull, creating chemical changes in the brain and sometimes stretching and damaging brain cells."[25]

High schoolers between the ages of fifteen and eighteen experience 46 percent of concussions. According to researchers at the University of California, San Francisco, concussion rates rose 60 percent between 2007 and 2014—most significantly among adolescents—with 55 percent of diagnoses being male. According to the American Academy of Pediatrics, nearly 2 million youth under the age of eighteen are concussed annually. One in five high school athletes will suffer a concussion during their sports seasons, and a third will sustain more than one in the same year.[26]

Football accounts for more than half of all sports-related concussions. Hockey, soccer, wrestling, and lacrosse also produce relatively high rates. The prevalence of high school concussions peaks between September and October every year, during the height of football and soccer seasons.[27] In football, "some players on the field experience a head impact on every play,"[28] according to Michigan State sports medicine researcher John W. Powell. In a frightening study, acceleration monitors were installed in the helmets of seven- and eight-year-old youth football players, and an average of 107 head impacts per player were registered. When accelerations reach threshold velocity, studies show "white matter damage" that can last as long as a year. Advances in preventive technology notwith-standing, there is still no concussion-proof helmet.[29]

In fact, there is recent evidence that damage to brain tissue is cumulative and that even nonconcussive impacts have an effect. In a study conducted by neuroradiologists at the Wake Forest School of Medicine, twenty-five boys aged eight to thirteen wore special helmets that tracked impact for a season; they were given MRI scans at both the beginning and the end of the season. The findings: the more impacts to the head, the more damage to insulated neurons called white matter, which are critical to communication between different regions of the brain.[30] Chronic traumatic enceph-alopathy (CTE), an incurable degenerative brain disorder, is be-lieved to be set in motion by repeated blows to the head that are often below the threshold for a concussion diagnosis.

Parents of boys who want to play contact sports struggle with what to do. Andrew was one such boy, a ten-year-old who was compact, muscular beyond his age, and already conditioned by years of playing multiple sports to minimize physical pain and risk. With both a father and mother who had played high school and college sports, an older brother who played on an elite team for the top local soccer club, and an uncle who worked for an NFL team, athletics was a prominent part of his family's culture. Andrew loved to play and to play hard, even in backyard games with his brother. Playing in the snow, building forts would turn into ice and snowball wars; pickup basketball games in the driveway involved lots of elbows and reckless fouls. Roughhousing with his father could devolve into determined efforts to punch or knee him. Andrew was incredibly competitive.

A bold, fearless athlete, Andrew was positioned by his soccer coach as a central defender, the guy willing to do whatever it takes to break up an attack as the last man before his team's goal. Though short, he was still a force to be reckoned with for his speed and aggressive tackles. Naturally, though, he longed to play football, the quintessential masculine sport among his friends, and lobbied his parents relentlessly to switch from soccer. Andrew's mother and father had done their research and were concerned about the potential for injury, particularly for children whose brains were still developing. They knew their son and recognized that he would play football with the same abandon and competitiveness he brought everywhere else. They told him, "Not before you are twelve," eliciting his frustration and cries that they were being unfair. His best friend played on a team, and Andrew had to listen to him report on his season while he was held back by his parents' qualms.

When this family came to see me, Andrew's frustration and complaints were part of a package of concerns. I could see how deeply and successfully they had built their relationships with their son and perceived the issue to be his trusting their judgment and allowing them to parent him, even to the point of accepting limits he did not like or fully comprehend. Privately, his parents and I discussed their concerns about how football and its dangers might feed the same pattern of carelessness and disregard for his body that they already worried about, having taken numerous trips to the ER after reckless stunts. They held the line with Andrew, and he grumbled but ultimately accepted that his parents were looking out for him.

Andrew was like many boys who win in the contest for masculine rewards. Validated, held up as exemplars of valor and success, these boys can have a hard time balancing priorities and need an ally to help them keep track. Against the intoxicating effects of peer and adult attention, only Andrew's connection and respect for his parents kept him from being swept away. He had already demonstrated that risk-taking could trump consideration of his well-being. His parents had to step in.

Boys' sports are at a critical point. Four states—California, Illinois, Maryland, and New York—are considering legislation that would restrict or ban contact football under fourteen years of age. Traditionalists have responded with alarm, perceiving a threat not just to football but also to contact sports in general. Meanwhile, rule changes, limited-contact practices, and new blocking and tackling techniques are being implemented widely in an effort to address the medical concerns. But in the view of researchers at the Concussion Legacy Foundation, an advocacy organization dedicated to ending CTE, "no tackle is ever safe enough for a developing child."[31]

Just as parents have to weigh how their sons participate, schools and youth organizations also have a lot to think about. The head injury phenomenon, for example, is unresolved. Second-impact syndrome, which occurs when an athlete returns to active play before an earlier head injury has healed, raises serious questions. Recent studies have found reduced cognitive performance, prolonged recovery, and an increased likelihood of subsequent concussions from repeated head injuries. While knowledge advances, sideline calls to determine when an athlete is ready to return to play remain subjective.[32]

Body Insecurities

Eating disorders have long been regarded as a problem for girls and women, particularly when unrealizable standards of beauty are internalized in tireless self-criticism. But new research has found that boys, too, suffer from distorted body self-perceptions. Where for girls the concern is being thinner, for boys it is the opposite.

Sometimes called "bigorexia," muscle dysmorphia is the opposite of anorexia nervosa. Harvard Medical School researcher and pediatrician Alison Field maintains that the prevalence of this problem is about 18 percent,[33] or about one in five boys. For those young men who experience this version of body discomfort, the goal is practically unattainable: to be both more muscular and leaner. Even overweight boys may perceive themselves through a distorted lens as they strive to fit the masculine ideal of six-pack abdominal muscles. Perfectionistic or anxious boys are at special risk to obsess about their weight and muscle.

At a time when the average young male consumes an average of seven hours of media per day, boys are more susceptible than ever to the brawny action figures and superheroes that are featured. Marketers and toy manufacturers have honed their message to this audience. According to psychologist Raymond Lemberg, television and video game characters have lost fat and added muscle over the last decade or two, setting an impossible standard for the male body. "Only 1 percent or 2 percent actually have that body type. We're presenting men in a way that is unnatural," he adds.[34]

Many boys respond to these new ideals by turning to vitamin and nutrient supplements and more frequent, more intense workouts. Research suggests that as traditional ways to establish masculinity have diminished, the cultural emphasis on displaying muscularity has become even more important. In a 2012 study, more than a third of middle and high school males used protein powders or shakes to build muscle. A smaller percentage, between 3 percent and 12 percent, admit to using steroids.[35] It is the young men most constrained by the Man Box who are most likely to get carried away in pursuit of the "perfect" male body.

The term "Adonis complex," coined by three pediatricians to describe this male body image problem, draws on Greek mythology and its story of the half-man/half-god figure as the ultimate in masculine beauty. The term conveys the impossibility of the new masculine standard, boys' feelings of inadequacy trying to measure up against this standard, and the lengths some go to—including compulsive exercise, dietary supplements, and steroid use—in pursuit of perfection.[36]

Adding muscle and cutting fat are not the only body image issues affecting boys. Pornography viewing has driven "penis shame" to new levels. In a study conducted by a team of researchers from King's College in London, a ten-question scale measured "a man's fear of being alone or rejected because of his penis size, his terror that others will laugh at him, and his anxieties about being naked around women and men."[37] The researchers found that 30 percent of their respondents were dissatisfied with their genitals; those men who identified as gay or bisexual were more likely than heterosexual males to report penis anxiety.

Drug and Alcohol Use

According to a federal survey of drug use and health, adolescent males abuse substances at higher rates than girls do. Boys' use of alcohol is higher than any other group. In a 2013 report, 40 percent of high school males admitted to using alcohol in the last month, with nearly 25 percent consuming more than five drinks. In addition, 25 percent of boys reported marijuana use in the last month, 10 percent used inhalants, and 10 percent also used ecstasy. Many boys begin drinking or using drugs as preteens. Nearly 25 percent drink alcohol and 10 percent smoke marijuana by age thirteen.[38]

There have been many theories to explain gender differences in substance use, including the effect of male hormones on the willingness to take risks; slower maturing of the areas of the forebrain that regulate behavior in males; and role modeling by sports stars, entertainment icons, and other important masculine figures. But advertising by beverage companies clearly plays a part. Beer company ads have created a masculine brand—relaxed, fun loving, romantic, sexually attractive—that influences boys' self-concepts and their aspirations. A 2012 study published by the American Academy of Pediatrics followed four thousand teenagers from grades seven through ten. The boys in the study drank "significantly more alcohol" than girls, experienced more negative consequences from their use, and showed signs that their drinking was influenced by beer ads. Early adolescents who said they liked alcohol ads were more likely to drink and to have more serious alcohol-related problems.[39]

Two reviews of research on the effects of advertising on adolescent alcohol use, one in 2009 and the other in 2016, found decisive evidence that exposure to these ads influenced teen drinking behavior. As the authors of the more recent review explained, "Significant associations between exposure to, awareness of, engagement with, and receptivity to alcohol marketing at baseline and initiation of alcohol use, initiation of binge drinking, drinking in the previous thirty days, and/or alcohol problems at follow-up were all found in the studies."[40]

School programs that teach youths to view media with a discerning eye—media literacy—have been found to help teenagers decode the messages of alcohol advertising, as have legal restrictions on both the content and placement of ads. Helping teenage boys ask questions—"What is this ad actually encouraging?" "Whose interests is it promoting?" "How is it biased?"—helps to protect them against sophisticated efforts to manipulate their attitudes and behaviors. But many who work with adolescents fear a losing battle. A 2004 report by the national Committee on Developing a Strategy to Reduce and Prevent Underage Drinking ended with this thought-provoking comment: "The committee reached the fundamental conclusion that underage youth drinking cannot be successfully addressed by focusing on youth alone. Youth drink within the context of a society in which alcohol use is normative behavior and images about alcohol are pervasive."[41]

The movement to legalize marijuana also shows a link between social trends and boys' substance use. Studies of adolescent use in Washington, which legalized recreational marijuana for adults, found increased use among eighth and tenth graders since legalization, consistent with declines in the perceived harmfulness of the drug. By contrast, in states that did not legalize recreational use, marijuana use decreased during the same period. According to the Colorado organization pushing for tighter regulations, SMART Colorado, in a federal survey assessing marijuana use among twelve-to-seventeen-year-olds, Colorado ranked first. Just 48 percent of students viewed marijuana use as risky.[42]

My professional experience, both in adolescent chemical dependency treatment and in schools trying to establish effective prevention programs, leads me to concur with others who hold that efforts to control teen substance use in a context where they receive very mixed messages will be unsuccessful. But this conclusion means that adults who care about boys have a more critical role than ever helping them to make healthy decisions.

I spent a stint as a team leader in an inpatient program for adolescents with both substance abuse and emotional issues. The boys and girls were admitted for a variety of reasons. Sometimes their parents had simply reached the end of their tolerance for uncontrollable, dishonest, or defiant behavior. Sometimes schools required treatment as a disciplinary consequence. And sometimes the juvenile justice system made the referral. What impressed me was the dramatic change evident in some teenagers between the time of their admission and their discharge. Feral and out of control at the start, completely unimpressed by adult authority, when they left, they looked like young people again. Even their faces had changed, becoming more relaxed, lighter, and more open. After realizing they could not bend, break, or work around the rules and discovering adults they could trust, something eased.

Ben was one who stood out. He was very privileged, gifted as an athlete, a student, and a leader. He was captain of his school wrestling team and student body president as a senior. He was also in deep trouble with substances, spending increasing amounts of time high or drunk. His behavior was closing in on him, coming to the attention of the school and the community. While initially inclined to chalk up their son's problems to boyish hijinks, his parents and the school were forced to take notice as troubles mounted. A professional assessment revealed that the parents were impaired themselves and that family life was dominated by the mother's mental illness and the father's functional alcoholism. Ben was in charge of his life and had little insight into just how lonely he actually felt. When the school finally intervened, he was sent to the treatment program where I was responsible for his care.

Working in a model that cast addiction as a disease, the program guided Ben in first assessing the extent of his dependency and then educating him about recovery from it. In individual and group therapy, he grew more honest about how frightening it was that he had been so able to evade accountability—and that to a great degree he was on his own. In group education sessions, he heard hair-raising stories about how other teens' lives had been sabotaged by the desperate need to get a buzz on. He talked about the losses he experienced in his family and found other members of his new extended family who reassured him that they would step in. Before he returned home, he made a commitment to continue talking to a sponsor so that he would be less likely to fool himself.

Like many adolescent boys, Ben defended his right to party. He could rationalize his behavior by referring to his parents, his friends, his own pumped-up sense of entitlement. But the truth he could finally acknowledge was that life was scary and unsustainable without someone looking out for him. When I share stories like his with parents, schools, and other organizations that serve young people, my point is that intoxication is just one of the ways boys can get lost when they are unmoored. A relationship with someone who matters is a life-saving compass guiding boys through their tight passage to manhood.

Self-Harm

In their 2011 book *The Tender Cut: Inside the Hidden World of Self-Injury*, professors of sociology Patricia Adler of the University of Colorado and Peter Adler of the University of Denver describe the teenage phenomenon of "cutting, burning, branding, and bone breaking."[43] In their research, the married couple examined the gendered dimensions of self-harm. While viewed traditionally as a behavior more common among females, self-harm rates underrepresent males whose behavior may not show up in emergency room admissions. Many believe boys' self-injury rates are rising, in part because, as the Adlers observe, "the behavior is extremely contagious." According to a 2016 British National Health Service report, self-harm among boys and younger men is at a four-year high based just on ER visits.[44]

According to one youth advocate, "Boys do cut themselves, but not necessarily as much as girls. What they will do is get into fights all the time, put themselves in dangerous situations, get themselves beaten up." When cutting or burning themselves, males are more likely to make deeper cuts and burns and to be less secretive about it than girls are. Brotherhood rituals that include branding or "blood brother" bonding endorse the view that suffering pain is part of being male.[45]

Many of the young men I see who are gripped by upset, anger, and self-contempt, and who lack other avenues of expression, develop patterns of self-destructiveness. One of them was Andres, a high schooler referred to me after his track coach noticed a tangle of cuts on his arms when he took off his sweats. The coach took him aside to ask about the cuts, and Andres confessed to his self-harm.

When the coach let his parents know, Andres was unable to tell his mother and father why he did it but accepted their offer of help.

I tried to make it possible for Andres to explore what he was feeling when the compulsion to hurt himself came up. Until the feelings driving him to cut himself were more conscious, I thought, he was unlikely to be able to exercise any control over them. To bring his self-destructive energy under his mind's control, he needed to notice the feelings while someone paid attention to him, allowing him to reexperience and explore the upset driving the compulsion. After building an alliance and assuring him of his confidentiality, I asked him to tell me about a recent time he had cut, making sure to include what he felt before, during, and after. It turned out that he experienced a sense of relief after he hurt himself—a relief specific to the anger and guilt surrounding the loss of his best friend in an accident several years earlier. When Andres cut himself, he felt both closer to his friend and relieved of survivor's guilt. When he made this connection and could express the underlying grief more directly, the teenager experienced substantial relief—without the self-harm.

At the extreme end of the self-harm spectrum is suicide, among the top three causes of adolescent mortality. In the United States, boys are four times more likely to commit suicide than girls are. In 2017 there were 4,600 suicide deaths among youths aged ten to twenty-four, an average of twelve per day. Of these, 81 percent were male. As boys proceed through adolescence, there is a growing trend toward suicide: from ages ten to fourteen, twice as many boys commit suicide as girls do; at ages fifteen to nineteen, the rate jumps to four times as many. In addition to completed suicides, there were 575,000 attempts. The rate is particularly high for gay and bisexual males: 30 percent, according to the American Academy of Pediatrics.[46]

Unfortunately, many boys I have seen have entertained suicidal thoughts; some have even followed through on those thoughts in attempts. Dennis was one such boy. He came to see me after telling his school counselor that he had uncontrollable thoughts of killing himself. He'd begun to contemplate how he might do it but became scared. There was lots to unpack as I attempted to ease the tension and hopelessness he was feeling: an ugly, ongoing divorce between his parents, accompanied by his mother's meltdown and their inability to keep him out of the middle; a history of being bullied in middle school when he struggled with being overweight; and paralysis when it came to approaching girls he liked. Now a high school senior facing the challenge of getting on with his life, he could not see how he could ever be happy.

My immediate goal was to help Dennis find his fighting spirit and reestablish a sense that he could improve things. Meanwhile, I lent him my own confidence that he could have a good life even if his parents remained stuck and bitter. I explained that I would advocate for him with them and insist that they offer him their love and support no matter what. I assured him that he was worth my advocacy and helped him recall that, once upon a time, he knew that himself. Gradually, as he disentangled himself from the conflicts in his family and the insecurities of life with his peer group, Dennis rediscovered his self-confidence.

A smart boy, he was accepted to many of the colleges he applied to. He chose the one farthest from his home, eager to start a new chapter, but taking with him a more confident sense that his parents would be on his side no matter what developed in their relationship with each other.

Embodying Integrity

How can we help boys take care of themselves when the sacrifice of their bodies is extolled and valorized? For males to acknowledge what it actually feels like to be in a fight, to push themselves to unreasonable levels of exhaustion, or to be injured goes against the cultural grain. Taking such an approach can elicit parents' own fears of making their boy "soft." But what modern research teaches about skill development, endurance training, and exercising bravery actually points to an opposite conclusion. As coach Joe Ehrmann reports, boys with access to their feelings are better able to relax into the "zone" and perform at their peak. At their best, a "band of brothers" teaches boys to value each member as integral to the group, to look out for each other, and to leave no one behind.

Helping younger males distinguish between the positive and negative aspects of athleticism can help them untangle their feelings about their own masculinity. In light of what researchers have learned about messages to boys about masculinity, it is likely that boys who have disconnected from their bodies—who numb themselves to pain, push past limits, or play through injury—have learned that they are expected to perform this way. For too many, courage is understood as unwise self-sacrifice.

A better, more accurate message is that the body is at the center of who they are as human beings. How they treat it—staying connected to what they feel and being thrilled by what they can do—will ground their lives in the most fundamental reality. In many ways, encountering the limits of their skill and endurance in sports teaches boys a growth mind-set. They learn how to coax the best from themselves by accepting and then steadily extending those limits. Life, they come to understand, is less about conquering their bodies by suppressing weakness than it is about cultivating new capacities.

Sports sociologist Don Sabo, a former football player turned advocate for boys' health, recommends that parents and others offer boys a countercultural message: "Be a buddy to your body." He urges trainers, coaches, and parents to help boys register their pain rather than glorify it. On the sidelines of athletic contests, there are many opportunities to assist boys when they are hurting, yet too often messages to "Suck it up!" or "Stop whining!" are what an injured boy will hear.[47]

Old-school masculine training trades on the premise that optimal performance comes from dominating the body's pain and limits. Coach Ehrmann and sports sociologist Sabo, on the other hand, place the character-building purpose of sports at the center of their work. Ehrmann begins by reminding boys to value their integrity and to love one another. His message helps his players trust their instincts when it comes to their limits. Rewarding boys when they take care of themselves, rather than merely exhorting them to try harder, reinforces the skill of self-regulation.

To counteract their own lingering investment in traditional masculine views, I offer parents a straightforward guideline for when a boy is in pain: never brush aside his complaints or allow him to minimize the discomfort. Instead, they should always show interest and express concern, regardless of whether the injury is apparent. At first, parents should not be surprised if he becomes uncomfortable. He may even feel ashamed for needing their attention, imagining he is weak or that his toughness is in question. But a mother and father's sympathizing with him because he is hurting, asking him to talk about it, and being patient no matter what he says, allows a boy to believe the opportunity is real to consider how he really feels. He will also get the message that he need not suffer silently on his own.

An implicit casualty of teaching boys that their bodies are "things" to be built up and even sacrificed for the sake of winning, is the virtue of integrity. Learning to objectify their bodies as though they are machines, boys become less committed to keeping themselves whole. They become willing to rationalize, overlook, and numb themselves to injuries and losses. Once they learn to treat themselves in this instrumental and objectifying way, boys are less able to feel empathy for others' pain and suffering. It becomes easier to inflict pain.

❦

CHAPTER 8

VIOLENCE, BULLYING, AND VULNERABILITY

When I was fourteen, entering a large urban boys' high school as a ninth grader, I realized quickly I was out of my depth. Through middle school, life with my friends had gotten steadily more complicated. We spent more time with one another, away from our parents. Dances and parties happened more frequently, bringing together larger groups of teenagers. Some of my friends began to hang out at a local bowling alley where there were pool tables and older boys who smoked and were more streetwise. As our social worlds expanded, some of my friends began to walk with a swagger and broadcast tough-guy postures. It was as if there were something in the air.

When we got to high school, the changes were magnified. Suddenly there were gangs, after-school fights, smoking in the bathroom, drug and alcohol use, and a well-defined hierarchy in which bigger and meaner guys ruled. There was the new phenomenon of the mob, when groups of boys spontaneously circled around two boys fighting, jeering and egging them on. During that first year of high school, whenever we grew bored in algebra class, a classmate and I started playing a game. Wearing hard leather-soled shoes, we devised a version of "chicken," in which we alternately kicked each other in the shin, daring the other to stop or risk further escalation. All through that year, we carried colorful bruises and scabbed-over cuts on our legs. On Mondays at lunch, the guys at our lunch table recounted fights over the weekend that pitted one gang, the Yard (named for the school yard where they met), against another, First State (the name of the bowling alley in my hometown, Wilmington, Delaware).

In the spring of that year, as one of the monthly school dances let out and everyone headed to cars or to meet their rides, the electric charge of a fight surged, and a throng rushed to one of the gym exits. Peering through the large crowd that had gathered, I could make out some of the guys from my lunch table. One of them, an older boy who people said was crazy, was hauling off and kicking another boy who had fallen to the ground. It turned out the boy on the ground, a very quiet fellow I knew only by name, was in some of my classes. He died that night from head trauma suffered in the fight.

Though that was not the last time I witnessed terrible male violence, that night I learned something about myself and my vulnerability. Without really comprehending what I was feeling, I asked my parents to transfer me to another school for the next year. Like every boy, I had begun imagining what I would do if I found myself in a violent situation like those occurring around me and became certain I wanted to reduce the chances I might wind up in that position.

The years since have blurred my memory of my dog-eat-dog adolescence. The new school lessened the more immediate threat but did not diminish the background noise of young men looking for trouble. I would witness many more fights and be hassled myself at times. It all receded into dim memory once I crossed over to adulthood and found it handy to distance myself from the violence of my boyhood. But just as unsafe risk-taking and poor health choices define how boys relate to their bodies, so the use and experience of violence is integral to boys' peer relations.

Boys are disproportionately affected as both victims and perpetrators of violence. In the 2011 National Survey of Children's Exposure to Violence conducted by a team from the University of New Hampshire, by age seventeen, seven of ten youths overall experienced assaults, mostly at the hands of other youths. More than 60 percent of those surveyed had been victimized during the previous year. More than half revealed multiple experiences of violence, with 15 percent reporting six or more experiences. Boys had higher rates of assault overall (45 percent compared with 37 percent for girls) and reported greater rates of injury from assault. Physical intimidation rates (one in four before age seventeen) and relational aggression rates (one in three in the last year and one in two by age seventeen) for boys show how ubiquitous violence is in their lives.[1]

Boys are more likely than girls to have been in a physical fight in the past year. In a 2017 study from ChildTrends, a nonprofit research center based in Bethesda, Maryland, 28 percent of fourteen-to-eighteen-year-old boys overall affirmed having been in at least one fight in the preceding twelve months. The figure ranged from 27 percent for white and Hispanic teens to 39 percent for blacks. Boys are also more likely to have been victims in their homes.

Among homicide victims aged ten to twenty-four, 86 percent in 2014 were male. Homicide has become the leading cause of death for African American youths.[2] On a global scale, out of the four hundred thousand people murdered around the world each year, 80 percent are male, and more than 97 percent of their killers are also male. Gary Barker, a doctor of child and adolescent development, and head of the organization Promundo, has an explanation for this huge gender disparity: "It takes a huge effort to turn boys and men into killers. . . . Extreme trauma, humiliation, shaming, social isolation, and intense indoctrination are nearly always part of the making of men who kill."[3]

To the Canadian activist and scholar Michael Kaufman, three types of male violence are mutually reinforcing: violence against women, violence against other men, and violence against themselves. This triad reflects a pattern of socializing boys that is characterized by high levels of domination and control, internalized as a template for relating to the world, toward others, and toward themselves. As they absorb this lesson, boys strive to dominate and control others. To Kaufman, the boy does not so much learn these dynamics as they become a part of him—a patterned set of reactions. Tensions that build up as the boy submits to this reality, suppressing his true emotions to pull it off, find an outlet in violence.[4]

The link between masculinity and violence was the subject of a 2018 report issued by Promundo-US. Despite vast efforts and resources dedicated to preventing violence, the authors offer, "There has been a relatively limited effort to bring a discussion of masculinity into these various fields of violence prevention."[5] To extend the conversation, they identify general cultural processes that make male violence more likely—such as restricting boys' emotional range, normalizing how they police one another, and expecting boys to prove their manhood. Eight forms of violence are then reviewed, first to show how males are disproportionately represented and then to make an explicit connection between the dominant norms of boyhood and how they manifest in each form. The eight forms are:

- intimate partner violence,
- physical violence directed against children in families,
- child sexual abuse,
- bullying,
- homicide and violent crime,

- nonpartner sexual violence,
- suicide, and
- conflict/war.

Writer Myriam Miedzian examined these same questions about cultural norms and male violence years earlier when she interviewed more than 130 experts from fields as diverse as psychology, sociology, anthropology, political theory, biology, law, public administration, and communications for a comprehensive examination of the roots of violence. What she found also indicted traditional masculine socialization: "Many of the values of the masculine mystique, such as toughness, dominance, repression of empathy, extreme competitiveness, play a major role in criminal and domestic violence."[6]

In 1994 the American Psychological Association formed a Commission on Violence and Youth to "bring psychological expertise to bear on the problems that have been emerging as increasing numbers of young people have become victims, witnesses, or perpetrators of interpersonal violence." One of its most sobering findings was the insight that patterns of violence, once established in childhood, endure well into adulthood. The authors of the report wrote, "An individual's relative level of aggression among agemates shows remarkable continuity and predictability over time." In fact, researchers concluded that patterns of aggression become even more set with age.[7]

Despite concerns about patterns of violence learned in childhood, research suggests that the kind of "war play" so common among groups of boys may contribute to boys' violence. Early childhood educator Diane Levin of Wheelock College, responding to schools that were seeing more violent play among male students, drew a connection between an uptick in play fighting and a decision by the Federal Communications Commission (FCC) to ease advertising regulations in 1984. Following this change, there was a flood of advertising targeted at boys, built around special products such as a pumped-up G.I. Joe and images of violence that help make the sale.[8]

As researchers sought to explain the epidemic of violence in the closing decades of the twentieth century, Stanford University psychologist Albert Bandura took a strong stand against fashionable ideas such as "superpredators," or "bad eggs," pronouncing, "People are not born with preformed repertoires of aggressive behavior. They must learn them."[9] Boys become violent, according to his social learning model, by observing these behaviors in others, experiencing violence themselves, and not finding examples of healthy self-regulation in their homes, communities, or schools. Researchers identified three particular pathways leading to violence: (1) the overt pathway, which traces a consistent sequence of aggression between ages eight and twelve, fighting from age twelve to fourteen, and culminating in more severe violence thereafter; (2) the early authority conflict pathway, which focuses on open defiance and stubbornness; and (3) the covert pathway, which includes more delinquent behaviors.[10]

Subsequent research has shown that simply witnessing violence can have a psychological impact on young minds. According to a 2016 ChildTrends report, "Children who are exposed to violence are more likely to suffer from attachment problems, regressive behavior, anxiety, depression, and to have aggression and conduct problems."[11] Even community violence that children do not see directly has been found to adversely impact their brain development.

Sadly, mass shootings have become regular stories on nightly news. In a tally of these events from 1982 through 2017, a team from *Mother Jones* magazine counted eighty-eight—all but three perpetrated by a male. Psychologist James Garbarino of Loyola University in Chicago makes the point that although most parents do not have a son who will become violent, their son "has peers who are angry and sad—and capable of lethal violence." Every child goes to school with boys primed to react with violence. This is particularly true for minority males, for whom homicide is the leading cause of death.[12]

New York University psychiatrist James Gilligan, from a career working with incarcerated males, believes male violence springs from an underlying sense that life is unbearable. Violent men are not monsters, he contends, but become nearly unrecognizable as "death of self" and their loss of empathic connections degrade their humanity. When he first began his work, he was struck by the typical explanation when men acted violently: "Because he dissed me." Their need for respect drove them to lash out. Gilligan explained, "The basic psychological motive, or cause, of violent behavior is the wish to ward off or eliminate the feeling of shame and humiliation—a feeling that is painful and can even be intolerable and overwhelming—and replace it with its opposite: the feeling of pride."[13]

In his enlightening study of urban life, sociologist Elijah Anderson also found respect at the heart of the code of the streets. He writes, "There is a general sense that very little respect is to be had, and therefore everyone competes to get what affirmation he can from what is available."[14] To psychologists Dan Kindlon and Michael Thompson, the narrowing of boys' emotional lives makes a violent response to interpersonal challenges more likely. As they are toughened in their peer culture and forced to suppress softer feelings, boys are permitted only reactions of "anger, aggression, and emotional withdrawal."[15]

I was recently listening to a young man's feelings of anger and hurt on discovering that a good friend had hooked up with his ex-girlfriend after their breakup. Feeling betrayed and made a fool of, Peter's face flushed, his muscles tensed, and harsh words burst forth as he told me the story. I asked him what he wanted to do, since he expected to see the other fellow at a school gathering that night. He said he wanted to punch him out. In Gilligan's view, violence is an understandable, if perverse, effort to recover from hurt by shaming the one who caused your hurt. "The most powerful way to shame anyone is by means of violence," he wrote.[16] Such reactions to hurt and shame are common to males and females; what is particular to males such as Peter are the levels of violence they can imagine as a result of their masculine experience.

Life on the Streets

In major US cities, the last several decades of the twentieth century saw a marked deterioration in civic life. For children in these cities, especially in less resourced neighborhoods, such conditions have meant an increase in exposure to community violence. As Elijah Anderson wrote, "Of all the problems besetting the poor inner-city black community, none is more pressing than that of interpersonal violence and aggression. This phenomenon wreaks havoc daily on the lives of community residents. . . . Simply living in such an environment places young people at special risk of falling victim to aggressive behavior."[17] It was concerns about the impact of their exposure to violence that led the Philadelphia chapter of the organization Physicians for Social Responsibility to develop a program for early-adolescent boys. We conducted needs assessment research in one target community and found that 74 percent of the youths there had witnessed a violent act and 48 percent had been hurt directly by some form of violence; 81 percent had known someone hurt by gun violence; 75 percent had known someone hurt by another form of violence.

Our team was particularly concerned about the impact of these stresses on a growing boy's sense of self. We understood from the relatively new field of traumatic stress studies that hardwired, primitive emotional states—fight, flight, freeze—are evoked by such threats. When intense fear compromises cognition, impairing the ability to process the experience, an individual may be left carrying reactions that do not resolve by themselves.

The intervention we designed was intended to provide opportunities for younger teen boys to restore confidence in themselves and their worlds. The curriculum emphasized positive opportunities for connection and relationship, emotional expression—especially to debrief experiences of violence—and new peer group norms encouraging alternatives to the street code. Group support for a boy's personal voice was intended to be at the heart of the program's healing work, because recovery from traumatic experience requires not only telling stories but also reaffirming oneself.

The threat and experience of fighting were prominent themes in research we conducted for the program. As Drew, fourteen years old, said, even though he might "try to stay away from people that like to fight," the truth was that "you never going to avoid, like, you can try to avoid a fight, but you're going to fight during your life. . . . You got to fight your own battles so you know how to defend yourself." Each of the boys we interviewed had many stories supporting this view.

Lorenzo for example:

We were walking home one day from school; these two other kids were fighting. So we was all laughing at the one boy that got beat up. And he just pointed to me and said, 'If you got something to say, say it to my face.' And I was, like, 'Get out of my face because I don't want to fight you.' And he just swung and missed and that's when we started fighting.

Violence prevention programs hold that less fighting is a measure of success. But a more complicated picture is closer to reality. Boys explain that they need to fight sometimes just to maintain a modicum of safety and personal dignity. The motives and objectives for fighting can range from playful exuberance, to contests for dominance, to the preventive assertion of toughness in order to secure safety, to, finally, sheer meanness and hurt. From her observations in an urban school, Assistant Professor Ann Arnett Ferguson of Smith College concluded, "Fighting is the emblematic ritual performance of male power. Participation in this ritual for boys and for men is not an expression of deviant, antisocial behavior but is profoundly normative, a thoroughly social performance."[18]

Yet, despite the pressure to fight, we found that many boys go to great lengths to avoid fighting. Jacob, for example, whose family life revolved around his minister father's position in the community, seemed committed to following his father's example: "There's, like, some people who, like, are bad and stuff. But I don't play with them." Still, peer violence was practically unavoidable. He described a group of boys he would encounter on the way to and from school:

JACOB: They curse a lot, and they, like, throw rocks at people.
MICHAEL: Have you ever had anybody throw a rock at you?
JACOB: Yeah. They missed; they have bad aim. . . . I try to stay away from them; like, when I see them in the alley, I just turn the other way.

Where Jacob would try to "turn the other way" and Calvin would "only fight when I have to," Miguel seemed miraculously to avoid fights, perhaps due to an especially clear motivation: "When I grew older, I would hate to get hurt. I don't know why. As soon as I got older. . . . I was scared to do many things 'cause I wanted to be safe, and I didn't want to get hurt or anything. And that's how I am pretty much now."

What we learned from the boys is that fighting is situational and fraught with conflicting needs and pressures. Juan tried to hold to an identity as "a person who doesn't like to fight." But there were practical limits:

Basically, I don't get in trouble unless you push me too far. If you push me too far into a corner where there's no other way to go except to you, I'll do it. There was this fifth grader who kept bullying me . . . came up to me, and I just punched him, and he fell to the ground. Then I just kept on going. . . . The teachers were trying to pull me away. I pushed the teachers away from me and jumped on the boy again. . . . He was bleeding. His eyebrow was cut, his nose was bleeding, his mouth was bleeding.

More severe responses to violence were found in boys who had fewer options and could respond with less flexibility. Boys like Terrence, for instance, who claimed to have been in about seventy-five fights by age twelve, and who told this story that involved a weapon:

Boy just came up to me. . . . I didn't like the boy, but I mind my own business. So then he came up to me, and he was going, "You know that stuff that you talking about?" And I was, like, "Get out of my face." So then he pushed me . . . He pulled a knife on me, so then I was, like, "This ain't over." . . . I was like, "Well, I know he's got a knife, so I'm going to get a kitchen knife." . . . If he pulled his knife out on me, I'd pull my knife out on him . . . stab him.

Brian was the young man we interviewed who was most comfortable with street fighting. He told stories of fighting over girls, being involved in gang fights, nighttime drug trafficking, school riots. Asked if he had ever been shot at, he answered, "No, but a dude pulled a gun out on me." Asked whether he had ever used a gun himself, he said no but explained that he "always carries a knife with me."

MICHAEL: Why do you carry a knife now?
BRIAN: Just in case I get jumped or something.

MICHAEL: So, what have you done with a knife?

BRIAN: Well, I pull it out on people. Like . . . I don't like fighting, man, 'cause when I fight I, well, I don't love no fight, but I know if I lose I keep on fighting. . . . That's why I don't like fighting. . . . So I'm, like, "I don't want to fight, man," but when they get closer, I just pull my knife out. They just leave me alone.

From such comments, we understood that while boys living in violent neighborhoods are often frightened of fighting, they have learned to ward off threats by engaging in violence as necessary. All of the boys, gentle or tough, those who confessed to being "weak" and those who carried knives to scare off assailants, drew from the resources they had available to survive. A team of researchers from the University of Pennsylvania, studying the impact of violence on the development of urban youths, found that it is "not only a normal part of identity development among some youth living in high-risk environments, but is also necessary for psychological survival."[19] Psychologist Howard Stevenson, also at the University of Pennsylvania, has stated that the public pose of bravado is a natural response to feeling "hypervulnerable."[20]

Our program gave us a finer-grained, contextual, more discerning understanding of boys' responses to chronic violence. In particular, we learned how they cling to those who love and accept them. It was connections that helped them aim for something beyond the code of the streets.

The Biggest and Baddest

Bullying has a special place in boys' lives. Defined as an intentional pattern of harassment, abuse, and violence, bullying can involve electronic, written, verbal, or physical interactions. Overall, 13 percent of children aged two through seventeen experienced physical bullying, and 36 percent were teased or emotionally bullied during the 2013–14 school year. Not only are boys bullied twice as often as girls, but bullying aimed at boys has a more distinctively physical dimension.[21]

School is ground zero for bullying. According to a study by the Kaiser Family Foundation, a leading health policy organization, 80 percent of twelve-to-eighteen-year-olds who reported that they were bullied said it happened at school. Nearly one in ten students reported being in a fight on school grounds in the last year, where a survival-of-the-fittest ethos can infect the culture. Bigger, meaner, and more aggressive boys dominate in these dynamics.[22]

Research on the effects of being bullied found that 6 percent of students do not attend school on one or more days because they feel unsafe. Students learn to avoid particular places in schools—unsupervised hot spots such as locker rooms—or certain activities, like changing classes. Boys who are bullied have lower self-esteem and fewer friends, and are perceived as quiet or different. Public shaming of boys often involves antigay slurs. The most common reaction to being bullied is to fight. Beyond injuries that may result from bullying and its aftermath, victims are at higher risk for psychosomatic complaints, depression, anxiety, sleep disturbances, and increased academic problems.[23]

Two British teachers, Jonathan Salisbury and David Jackson, describe high school culture in their book *Challenging Macho Values: Practical Ways of Working with Adolescent Boys*: "For many students, everyday life in schools, clubs, and colleges is a violent experience. Along the corridors at break, in classrooms, in the toilets, behind the bike sheds—all of these places can turn out to be threatening and scary." To their mind, school bullying represents the "push and pull and striving of boys wanting to become more masculine." Salisbury and Jackson add, "There is a link between power and vulnerability in boys' lives—about how they try to get their own way to counter their fears about their anxiety, dependency, and a sense of their own weakness."[24]

Unfortunately, bullying can lead to long-term problems such as delinquency, relational and employment difficulties, and substance abuse. On the victim's side, not to fight back when threatened often places a boy at even greater risk. Researchers have found that where a culture of bullying exists, Darwinian rules apply: If a boy appears weak, others will try to victimize him. If he shows himself to be strong, he is more likely to be safe.

What to Do About Boys' Violence

Boyhood immerses boys in violence. Whether overt in the form of fighting and bullying or more implicit and in the background, threat and force are always present. Underlying almost every interaction boys have with one another is a real possibility that he might be found to be "out" of the Man Box, the group, or the club; in violation of acceptable ways for being male; and at risk for being targeted. Ultimately, the constant potential for shame, threat, censoring, and violence become part of a boy's unconscious orientation to life. How he thinks about himself, what is acceptable and worthy and what is not, develops from experiences of boyhood. A boy who fears being shamed for being out of the box is quick to police other boys for the same crime.

Against the steady drone of male violence and intimidation, acts of open hostility, aggression, and hurtfulness represent flare-ups—the boiling over from a constant simmer. Social scientist Brett Stoudt of City University of New York conducted an in-depth study of boys at a high school. He found that most of the youngsters faced constant put-downs, had to submit to being measured and found wanting, and were resigned to the existence of social hierarchies reinforced by no-holds-barred competition and overt threats. He concluded, "Violence might be considered the most visible and infrequent end of a continuum that also includes the normalized forms of male violence occurring inside schools every day."[25]

Antiviolence programs are typically targeted to help specific at-risk populations. But so long as boyhood involves the everyday policing of who is "in" and "out," violence will inevitably erupt somewhere, somehow, infecting almost everyone. Researchers such as Stoudt confirm what any parent of a middle school boy knows firsthand: underlying the eruption of more extreme acts of violence are the thousand cuts each boy endures in boyhood. As the Promundo report argues, "Masculine norms shape the likelihood of men and boys experiencing or perpetrating violence."[26]

The good news is that most boys grow out of violent and antisocial tendencies. Despite how common it is for them to act aggressively—one study found that 35 percent of boys engaged in some aggressive offense in the prior year—for most it becomes less and less frequent. But the bad news is that, for some, aggression does not taper off. A small percentage, around 5 percent, virtually all male, are responsible for half of all serious violent acts.[27]

For communities and governments responding to the surge in male violence, it has been helpful to think of the situation as a public health epidemic. The circumstances feel so dire that a medical model seems appropriate. There are three levels to this model: primary, secondary, and tertiary.

Community, School, and Family: Primary Prevention

In 2016 the CDC published *A Comprehensive Technical Package for the Prevention of Youth Violence and Associated Risk Behaviors*, which linked overt acts of violence with exposure to chronic stress. The brief recommended an approach that addresses both risk factors and protective factors. There are a host of programs intended to pull boys off the streets, especially during critical after-school hours, when most neighborhood violence occurs. The programs are located in churches, neighborhood nonprofits, and national organizations such as Boy Scouts and Boys & Girls Clubs of America. Though they offer activities, mentoring, skill building, and educational uplift and engagement, their main thrust is healthy relationships. As the CDC reported, "Relationships with caring adults, in addition to parents or caregivers, can influence young peoples' behavioral choices and reduce their risk for involvement in crime and violence."[28]

Social-emotional learning (SEL) has become so popular in schools for its value in the primary prevention of violence. Cultivating self-management and relationship-management skills, programs target self-esteem, social problem-solving, assertiveness, emotional literacy, and so forth, all shown to reduce antisocial behaviors. Building interpersonal competencies, it is believed, prevents boys from reverting to aggressive strategies when they become frustrated or get into conflict. One such program, Steps to Respect, reports a 30 percent reduction in bullying and victimization after the second year.[29]

Healthy classroom norms generally make it is less likely that a boy believes he can get away with pushing another boy around. Schoolwide programs in peer mediation and conflict resolution also assist boys toward better peer relationships by directing rising levels of tension and aggression into routine, verbal interactions. Some young men, those whose use of intimidation and violence has become habitual, have progressed beyond the reach of these skill-building efforts. Because they are caught up deeply in the alternative reward systems of their peer group, they are less influenced by prosocial norms. For these boys, it is important to set firm limits and to communicate expectations and consequences for violations clearly: a strong dose of reality. In combination with skill-building programs, strong policies against violence and bullying help promote positive norms and prevent random acts of spontaneous violence.

One school I worked with had a long tradition of peer hazing. It was part of the culture of the school, and generations of young men had endured it. The "rat" system of the school was seen as an important perk for older boys and a necessary rite of passage for "new boys." Boys were empowered by the system to teach one another critical lessons about manhood, including respect for hierarchy and for enduring harsh treatment. The school, however, realized eventually that this tradition of peer maltreatment was hurting its reputation. Families began voting with their feet, and admissions and retention rates dropped. The school sought to get a better understanding of the extent of the problem and to find solutions. Eventually administrators banned all acts of hazing and reinforced the policy with greater vigilance and stricter consequences. They meant business. Nonetheless, it took constant reinforcement over years to end boy-on-boy harassment. New students arrived expecting the right to dominate younger boys as a cherished "tradition."

Antibullying programs are also delivered in schools, the primary sites for bullying. But some approaches to addressing the issue work better than others. In a 2013 summary of research on different approaches to bullying programs, the research organization ChildTrends offered three takeaways. First, programs that targeted parents, instructing them on how best to speak to their children about bullying, were broadly successful. Second, a whole-school approach that includes training for staff in how to integrate the program's core messages into classes and curricula throughout the year also worked well. Combining parent and school programs strengthened each approach. Third, social-emotional learning programs, including ones that target specific skills such as empathy and decision-making, showed results that were less clear-cut. Equipping boys with better social-emotional tools is unlikely to produce wholesale change unless masculine norms, built into school cultures, are also addressed.

When school staff members challenge bullying, it sends an important message to boys about moral safety even if acts of bullying persist. When a teacher or school administrator backs up policy with actual enforcement, boys feel they are being looked out for. The most effective antibullying interventions begin with a holistic cultural review for mixed messages and any inadvertent tolerance for peer maltreatment. When they are effective at controlling bullying, schools can be oases of moral accountability in deteriorating communities.

Another context where bullying arises is at summer camp. Child therapist Bob Ditter offers a three-pronged approach for camp directors and counselors in the online journal *Camps*, of the American Camp Association. For the victim, he recommends social engineering of positive peer experiences, empowering the boy to assert himself more effectively, and helping him do a better job of reading and responding to social cues. For the bully, his strategy combines a no-nonsense limit on further verbal or physical abuse with coaching the boy to direct his frustrations in more constructive directions. Finally, for the sake of the community, it is important for bystanders to reach out to victims and welcome them back from their disconnected state.[30]

No matter what community groups and schools do, however, it is unlikely they can completely overcome patterns that boys learn in their families, particularly if they continue to be exposed to harmful conditions of domestic violence, neglect, or exaggerated versions of masculinity. According to CDC researchers, "Family environments that are unstable, stressful, lack structure and supervision, have poor relationships and communication between family members, use harsh or limited discipline with children are risk factors for youth violence."[31] Helping parents to meet their son's relational needs, particularly as they regulate and discipline him, is an important violence prevention strategy.

One common concern that I hear from parents is that their son is mean to a younger brother or sister. In light of how a boy's self-concept can be harmfully affected by his mistreatment of others, when parents observe a boy being unkind to a younger sibling, it is time to intervene. Bullying and meanness among children may signify that they perceive a need to compete for scarce resources of attention and care. When a boy overrides cultural norms for "big brothers"—that they look out for their younger sisters and brothers—it tells us that something is overwhelming him.

In a meeting of peer counseling leaders, Da'sean talked about his relationship with his younger brother. He said that his brother is the most important person in his life; someone he has taken a special interest in nurturing and guiding. As he spoke, his eyes filled up—I could see the depth of his commitment and realized that Da'sean benefits as much as his brother does from their relationship. He can tell every day that he makes a big difference.

But in another family, David's troubled relationship with his mother left him feeling rejected, angry, desperate, and flailing. He convinced himself that his sister was "stupid" and "annoying" to rationalize targeting her with his simmering resentment. In legitimizing his mistreatment of his sister, who quite innocently adored him and longed for him to return her love, David flipped from feeling like a victim to feeling powerful as an oppressor. But being hard on his sister did not make him feel better about himself. What's more, it didn't resolve anything in his relationship with his mother and jeopardized his sister's safety in the family. When I said I knew how disappointed he was in himself for being so impatient and cruel, he acknowledged feeling ashamed of himself.

Ideas for Boys Who Are at Risk:
Secondary Interventions

Secondary-level interventions are for boys showing early signs of aggressiveness, misbehavior, and violence. These are the youngsters most at risk for enduring patterns of aggression unless purposeful action interrupts and alters their developmental trajectories. The advantage of secondary interventions is that they are efficient, tailored to a group known to need help, and often effective. Youth diversion programs, for example, identify early-stage offenders in the juvenile justice system and assign them to mentoring and group counseling programs. In schools, more educational programs focus on skills such as moral reasoning and conflict and anger management. At the secondary level, programs can be for individuals and groups, depending on the need. One school-based example offered intensive behavioral monitoring, with an emphasis on positive feedback for appropriate conduct, to a group of seventh graders who were identified by prior disciplinary records. The treatment group showed positive, lasting change even five years later.

But over the years, some intervention models have been shown to be ineffective. In the youth diversion field, for example, many designs have been unable to direct boys from the criminal path they have begun traveling. According to researchers, the failure of such programs is due more to sloppy design and vagueness about goals and methods than the power of theoretically sharp, targeted interventions to produce results. One interesting research study assigned youths in the study to six different treatment groups, including two groups that received no actual intervention. Youths in the groups receiving treatment responded significantly better than those who received no help, and each of the different treatment models produced positive changes in the attitudes and behaviors of participants. Offering special attention and support to boys who are headed down the wrong path, particularly by bolstering their self-regulation and interpersonal skills, makes a difference.

Family-based interventions for boys who are identified as having problems have also been popular. Helping parents to employ effective discipline, offer appropriate emotional support, and create routines that provide safety and security gets at the root of the maladaptive interpersonal patterns that trip up boys. Some youngsters' repertoire of aggressive and hurtful behaviors gets established early, before they are very far along in school, based on unhealthy interactions with their parents. Child rearing and disciplinary practices persisting in family cultures, despite each generation's vow not to repeat the mistakes of its parents, may require outside intervention. Myths about what boys need and how they should be managed are simply passed along regardless of whether they make much sense.

As the report by the American Psychological Association's Commission on Violence and Youth concluded about secondary-level interventions, "Because the cognitive patterns that underlie violent behavior appear to be learned early in childhood, are habitual in nature and, yet, are potentially modifiable through direct intervention, treatment programs that change these cognitive patterns should lead to relatively enduring changes in violent behavior."[32]

Treating Boys Who Are Aggressive and Violent: Tertiary Interventions

Tertiary intervention means treatment, often delivered one to one. When I worked at the Family Court of Delaware in the Presentence Investigation Department, advising judges on boys who had already been found delinquent, we assessed whether a boy might change the direction of his life. Discussing with the boys how they got where they were and what they felt about the direction they were headed involved lots of listening and offering gentle feedback about their interpretations. Depending on how wholeheartedly boys engaged in these sessions, the judges could exercise sentencing discretion for those who showed signs of being ready to change.

The difference between early intervention programs for boys caught up in maladaptive behaviors and approaches for those who are more deeply in trouble is fuzzy. Usually the judgment of the evaluator determines how the boy is classified, but that is strongly influenced by how the misbehavior is viewed. For example, early in my career, a fifth-grade teacher at a Catholic school in Philadelphia asked to meet to discuss a boy in her class. When I went to her classroom after school and sat alongside her desk, she proceeded to describe the boy to me.

I had learned that to understand why a teacher's attention cues on a particular child, I needed to learn what it was that disturbed her and stood out from other children's behavior. As this particular teacher described Pete, whom she was obviously fond of, she began to well up and quietly cry. I asked what was so troubling, and she replied that she saw this boy—so full of life and capable of leadership—beginning to head in a dangerous direction. "I don't want him to become a Kensington man," she said finally, referring to the working-class neighborhood she had grown up in, where she had seen lots of family and friends get lost in drinking, violence, and macho identities.

She was right about Pete, who was being swept by neighborhood norms onto street corners and into gangs with older boys. Once I accepted the referral from the teacher, I saw my role as trying to build a counterweight to the allure of the streets—a relationship in which I could validate Pete's sense of who he really was and influence how honest he was about the shortcomings of his current choices. Pete was enthralled by the rewards offered by his peer group: popularity, excitement, belonging, fun, adventure. As our work progressed, though, I was able to help him reflect on where it was all headed and how that lined up with his personal ambitions. My plan was to reinforce those dreams for his life so that he could keep the temptations of the moment in perspective.

Studying young men who have been violent, the psychologist James Garbarino of Loyola University Chicago describes them as "lost boys" who have become unmoored from their empathic connections. To recover their humanity, he recommends locating anchors in their lives: "These values and relationships . . . protect them from the influences of social toxicity, negative peer groups, mass media violence, and the crass materialism of our culture." Among the different anchors are "adults who commit themselves unconditionally to meeting the developmental needs of kids."[33]

A boy who behaves violently has lapsed from a mindful state to a reactive one. He is flooded with internal feelings, causing him to erupt. Justifying angry behavior with a stream of rationalizations, the boy feels righteous about disconnecting from the humanity of the other person. But the sturdier a boy's anchors are, and the more he is connected to the perspective of someone who doesn't share his rationalizations, the less inclined he will be to lash out. Parents and educators in relationships with the boy can call him out when he rationalizes hurtful or self-centered behavior.

At the broader level of boyhood, adults need to challenge family, school, and community cultures that glorify hypermasculinity. They do it most powerfully by example. A father who dramatizes his hurt feelings in an angry, selfish outburst at another's expense reinforces the message that with power comes the prerogative to take out upset feelings on others. Boys can see that both acting out and "acting in"—taking out negative feelings on others or on oneself, respectively—are less effective ways to resolve them than expressing them directly and fully. It is only when they find no opportunity to be honest and vulnerable that boys default to hurting others because they themselves are hurting.

Even in a rush of hurt feelings, boys can be expected to exercise control over knee-jerk reactions. A man, particularly one a boy respects, handling hurt in a courageous and vulnerable way presents a model for how a real man owns up to his feelings, including being scared, disappointed, or hurt. The image can last a lifetime. Teachers and coaches, for their part, model important lessons in emotional intelligence if they lose their tempers in the classroom or on the sidelines but come back to a boy with an apology. For boys trying to resist cultural norms that encourage male violence, such images are money in the bank.

CHAPTER 9

ॐ

BOYS' TOYS IN A DIGITAL AGE

One evening at dinner, a friend told me about his twenty-three-year-old son, Alex, who is trying to make it as a screenwriter in Los Angeles. Striving for that big break, Alex writes all day every day, working with as much discipline as he can muster. His days are broken into chunks of high-quality focus separated by brief times for recreation. During these twenty-to-thirty-minute breaks, he signs in to his favorite computer game and plays with great intensity before bowing out and getting back to work. From the time he was a preteen, video games have been a central part of Alex's life. He and his older brother, living in different parts of the same state, are on a gaming team together and even attend an annual weekend tournament.

What stood out as my friend described his son's life was the central place of gaming in his routine. Alex limits his social life in general, the father explained, but he clears his mind and connects with his brother and other "friends" in the virtual world of gaming. He has learned to regulate his time and still have something of a social life by withdrawing into the world of Internet connectivity. That Alex and his brother are male, share a common online passion, and live overextended, productive lives is not incidental. The technological revolution of the last couple of decades has taken old trends in male development and added new wrinkles.

At a recent parents' workshop, I shared stories of typical but challenging parenting moments: a boy being bullied, another retreating from his family and experimenting with risky behaviors, and several others. One scenario had to do with a boy's use of social media, which proved to be the hottest issue of the day. Boys addicted to their phones, computers, and video games; boys who socialize only online; boys using Instagram, Facebook, Twitter, or other sites in ways that shock their parents—these topics stir up heated and anxious discussion. Several parents lectured the group about the dangers of unrestricted screen time; others shared family policies such as confiscating cell phones during meals. Boys' behavior on their devices was plainly causing parents lots of concern.

According to a 2015 Pew survey, almost half of parents worry that their children spend too much time online.[1] But this worry is more acute for parents of boys. In 2004, according to one study of gaming, "Female players were less likely to be video game players, played for fewer hours, and did not seek out game-play situations for social interactions as much as male players did."[2] Another study found 300 percent more male than female gaming time.[3] As recently as 2014, researchers discovered that males spent an average of thirteen more hours per week playing games (forty-three hours to thirty hours).[4] This gender skew has created the male gamer stereotype, despite the fact that girls' game time has been rapidly increasing.

In a circular feedback loop, the male gamer stereotype has impacted not only who identifies with gaming but also the way that games are designed. One researcher distinguished games as "hardcore" or "casual," where dark or violent plots attract more males, while games such as Candy Crush Saga attract more female users. Not only do hard-core games lack female characters in general but also, when they are included, these characters are hypersexualized and stereotyped. Criticism of gender bias in games generated the #Gamergate debate, in which young men ranted on YouTube that "video games are created by men for men."[5]

This belief persists in spite of evidence that the gaming space has become more equitable. In a 2015 Pew Research Center survey, equal numbers of men and women said they play video games. But the survey also found that males were twice as likely to call themselves gamers, and 60 percent said they believed that people who played video games are more likely to be male.[6]

There are some indications that younger-generation players may see things differently: several surveys since 2014 have found that teenage males do not endorse the male gamer stereotype. Rosalind Wiseman, author of *Queen Bees & Wannabes* and *Masterminds and Wingmen*, conducted a study of 1,400 middle and high school students in 2014 to explore whether industry myths contribute to the perpetuation of traditional gender representations. Her team found three surprises. First, boys in her study rejected the portrayal of female characters as sex objects. Second, the gender of the game's protagonist did not influence boys' choice of which character to play. And finally, girls played all sorts of games, including first-person shooter and sports games.[7]

Nonetheless, the feedback loop encompassing toy design, marketing, and consumer demand reinforces traditional beliefs. In 2016 a White House conference titled "Breaking Down Gender Stereotypes in Media and Toys So That Our Children Can Explore, Learn, and Dream Without Limits" was convened. The reason for the conference, according to the invitation, was this: "We know that children's interests, ambitions, and skills can be shaped early on by the media they consume and the toys they play with—and this doesn't just affect their development, it affects the strength of our economy for decades to come." On a panel opening the conference, I offered that it is not boys who create the boyhoods they inhabit. Toy and media companies contribute to the architecture of boyhood.

Toys and media are being pitched to families in more gendered ways than ever, unfortunately. Even as men and women have become more equal today, marketing on the basis that they are fundamentally different has become the rule. Researchers comparing Disney websites and Sears catalogues note that color coding is the norm much more so than fifty years ago. Boys are slated for action toys and hero costumes; girls, for princess outfits and more passive toys. In 2012 psychologist Christia Spears Brown of the University of Kentucky noted that the company making Lego decided to expand their appeal to girls. For the girl version, it created pink and purple Lego kits with templates for kitchens, hair salons, and shopping malls.[8]

At the White House conference, representatives of the toy industry argued that marketing research leads them to hone their pitches in these ways. They point to a number of important surveys showing that the belief in fundamental gender differences has grown since the 1970s. But the leap from these findings to a belief that parents prefer more gender-coded products has been disputed. Sociologist Elizabeth Sweet of San Jose State University is emphatic: "The reliance on gender categorization comes from the top: I found no evidence that the trends of the last forty years are the result of consumer demand."[9]

Product designs and marketing pitches that play on conventional gender stereotypes, even if they do not actually match the beliefs of their target audiences, add volume to the voices promoting these stereotypes. Beginning well before birth, parents typically express an eagerness to know the sex of their child. Once the baby is delivered, their "obsession with gender" heightens, according to Brown. A baby's first outfits are often color coded; his or her onesies stenciled with clever, gendered slogans. "From the beginning," Spears writes, "gender consciousness drives every purchase we make. Even the gender-neutral toys that both boys and girls enjoy, like bikes, come in two versions: one pastel version, usually pink or purple, and one bright version, usually red or blue."[10]

It does not escape children's notice that the important adults in their lives seem obsessed with gender. Play is how they practice their parts in the prescribed gender script. In play, girls are much more likely to cross gender boundaries. The consequences for boys who play outside the lines are more severe. Understanding boys' toys, their design, marketing, and impact, is vital. But the issue is complicated.

Technology and Boys' Development

In the 1960s, Canadian cultural theorist Marshall McLuhan extended the idea of a "looking glass self-concept" to the field of media studies. His famous notion "The medium is the message," described how thinking and relating are influenced not just by the content of books, television, and now social media, but also by the form of the communication itself.[11] When we consider the present generation of digital natives, whose use of video games and social media has "dramatically transformed the way that kids perceive reality," it is easier to appreciate the heightened concern I observed among parents at the workshop. With 92 percent of teenagers going online daily—and 24 percent "almost constantly"—today's young people virtually *live* in cyberspace.[12]

In particular, according to Lee Rainie and Janna Anderson of the Pew Research Center, what distinguishes the digital generation from prior generations is its connectivity to mobile devices. Nowadays when I come into my waiting room to greet my next client, he is typically bent over his smartphone in the middle of a game, madly texting, or both. When boys tell me they have "talked" with someone, they mean they have exchanged texts; when they speak of "friends," they often mean people known only by their screen names. According to a recent Pew report, 57 percent of teenagers have made a friend online.[13]

Parents are not alone in their anxious desire to understand how technology affects their son's growth. A host of books have been published on the subject recently. Unfortunately, they offer wildly different opinions. The technology writer Steven Johnson, author of *Everything Bad Is Good for You: How Today's Popular Culture Is Actually Making Us Smarter,* takes the optimistic view that digital media have been designed "explicitly to train the cognitive muscles of the brain." Appealing to the brain's reward systems, games elicit prolonged absorption as players practice executive-level skills of seeking, deciding, prioritizing, collaborating, multi-tasking, and so on. Where new technologies do not encourage deep understanding, the complexity of the worlds they create cultivates different ways of knowing and connecting.[14]

But others have reached darker conclusions. Stanford psychologist Philip Zimbardo has decried a current "demise of guys" caused largely by the addictive hold gaming and porn exercise over boys. Pointing to growing levels of withdrawal and social isolation, he blames the neurological outcome produced by too much exposure to high-stimulation content, which he refers to as "arousal addiction," for holding back boys. He cites the fact that children spend more time online than in school to suggest a link between excessive porn use and gaming and educational malaise, obesity, heightened social anxiety, and an overreliance on stimulants and street drugs.[15]

Harvard psychologist Howard Gardner offers a more benign take on the "app generation." Gardner and coinvestigator Katie Davis conducted a research study from 2008 to 2012 during which they interviewed educators and teens in both the United States and Bermuda on the use of technology. They concluded that those coming of age since the advent of digital media have been transformed by these technologies: their "thought processes, personalities, imaginations, and behaviors" have been "reconfigured." Gardner and Davis closely examined three developmental domains—identity, intimacy, and imagination—to describe these changes. In terms of how members of the app generation think of themselves, for example, the study's authors found them more "externally oriented," creating new opportunities but presenting new challenges.[16]

On the positive side, Gardner and Davis believe that broad exposure makes the digital generation more cosmopolitan and tolerant of differences, and offers abundant opportunities for individual self-expression. But as they fashion selves in front of wider and more attentive audiences than ever, there is a corresponding pressure for young people to play things safe and prematurely close off identity options. Creating personal identities before an audience encourages packaging of the self over personal exploration and can lead to narcissist self-absorption. On the impact of digital media on relationships, creativity, and imagination, Gardner and Davis conclude with a caution about "app consciousness, an app worldview: the idea that there are defined ways to achieve whatever we want achieve."[17]

Both the content and contours of boys' lives are influenced by the cyberworld they inhabit. Time is an example: the ever-connected nature of communication is "uniquely suited for the overworked and overscheduled life it makes possible," according to Professor Sherry Turkle of the Initiative on Technology and Self at the Massachusetts Institute of Technology (MIT). Relationships are "oversimplified," she adds, and traditional notions of separation and individuation in child development are upended. One young client of mine, for example, anxious and fearful of being alone, has a girlfriend he connects with on FaceTime; some nights they sleep with their camera images on for hours.[18]

The magnitude of technology's impact on development is impressive. Turkle studies the "inner history of devices" and traces an evolution, from the 1980s through the 1990s, to a new phenomenon: the tethered self. Devices become extensions of the teenager's self; the means of expression melded more seamlessly with his or her mind than parents can fathom. As young people fit their communication styles to texts, Instagram photos, snaps, tweets, and Facebook posts, how they think is shaped and bounded by these media. In this sense, how young people grow, the selves they develop, is shaped by a digital environment with its own parameters, pressures, and incentives. Turkle validates the worries of parents contending with these new forces: "If you're spending three, four, and five hours a day in an online game or virtual world (a time commitment that is not unusual), there's got to be someplace you're not. And that someplace you're not is often with your family and friends."[19]

Previous generations have mourned the losses of what is familiar and reassuring as succeeding generations adapt to changed circumstances. Like every other father of boys, I realized this quite personally as I tried to keep up with my sons during video game sessions. Though I was completely hapless, this was not a problem for them—they were happy to crush me. But few activities have been as bewildering and frustrating for me, and I came up with lots of reasons to beg off. My sons turned to their friends for companionship online.

Perhaps the main lesson from research is that children's minds develop in an intimate, highly sensitive dialogue with both their interpersonal and physical environments. From being tools for communication, smartphones become avatars, online profiles become identities, and text messages become the preferred way of having a conversation. Classical developmental theorists regard separation and individuation as necessary steps to maturity. Building on the insights of feminist psychology, theorists have since modified this paradigm, showing that people actually grow in and through relationships rather than separate from them. Today we consider another refinement in our understanding of normal development: how fluidly young minds adapt themselves to the context or medium for their communication with others.

More big changes are afoot, no question. But as with so many other areas of male development, there are many myths, fears, and exaggerations for parents to gain perspective on as they train a vigilant eye on this unfamiliar, digital landscape.

Arousal Addiction

Gaming and social media companies have hit pay dirt. Video games worldwide are projected to hit $130 billion in sales by 2020. The top six social media companies were worth about $600 billion at the end of 2017, with Facebook accounting for two-thirds of the total. Recruiting top neuroscientists, game designers, and specialists in behavioral economics and marketing, these companies are remarkably skillful at tapping into the appetite to overcome negative feelings by earning rewards. Increasingly sophisticated and precise, signals built into these products succeed in reinforcing the behavior of more and more users, to a point that Internet addiction has become a hot topic. Just taking the example of Fortnite Battle Royale, the current action video game craze, "Fortnite incorporates much of what game designers know about how to ensure a captive audience," according to psychologist Lisa Damour.[20]

In the 2013 update of the American Psychiatric Association's *Diagnostic and Statistical Manual of Mental Disorders* (fifth edition, or *DSM-5*), Internet gaming disorder was identified as a condition recommended for further study. A 2017 study surveyed young adults in the United States, the United Kingdom, Canada, and Germany, 86 percent of whom had recently played online games, about this proposed disorder. The study generated the following list of problems attributable to gaming:

- Preoccupation;
- Withdrawal feelings when unable to play;
- Tolerance (compulsion to spend more and more time gaming);
- Difficulties controlling time spent gaming;
- Giving up other activities to play and playing despite problems that arise;
- Becoming deceptive and secretive;
- Relying on gaming to relieve negative moods.[21]

Adam Alter, a professor at New York University and author of the 2017 book *Irresistible: The Rise of Addictive Technology and the Business of Keeping Us Hooked*, tells a story about Facebook that offers a clue to what parents of teenage boys are up against. In 2012, developers at Facebook, then with 200 million users, incorporated the reinforcement schedule found by research psychologists to be most effective at eliciting persistence and engagement. Intermittent reinforcement, it's called. They introduced a "Like" button to their interface. With that simple innovation, Facebook became highly interactive, offering the unpredictable but alluring reward of social approval. The Facebook community tripled over the next three years; by February 2017, it approached 2 billion users.[22]

Helping people regulate their emotions and manage their moods is big business, as many other companies, selling tobacco, or alcohol, or sex, have discovered. Where there is demand, there will be supply. In my lifetime, marijuana has gone from being outlawed and widely suspected of sapping a generation's will to being legitimate for medical and recreational uses. During my stint in an inpatient dual-diagnosis adolescent treatment facility twenty years ago, perhaps as many as half of the admissions at any given time were primarily for alcohol and chronic pot use. Today I can no longer guess which adolescent is likely to be a user; mainstream boys of all kinds get high as routinely as they used to grab a beer.

Still, it is my experience that many boys become dependent on marijuana. I am happy for decriminalization but troubled that another means for intoxication has become so widely available to teenage boys. When I lead the peer counseling program, I talk about alcohol and drug use, trying hard not to preach. Teenage boys have highly developed antennae for adults' moral judgments. Undaunted, each year I try again to deliver the message: intoxication works against emotional self-regulation. By getting drunk or buzzed, boys do not learn anything about the relief that comes from getting hard things off their chests without substances.

That tech companies have found increasingly effective ways to make their products irresistible to young consumers worries me as well. Many families have sought help for sons whose gaming meets the criteria listed in the *DSM-5*. I think of Winston, a quirky high school junior whose mother had all but surrendered to his absorption in the video game world. Clearly gifted, he had built his own computer from components picked up at Radio Shack. What drove him was a desire for a system customized for high-level gaming. His school grades were poor, classes were tedious distractions, and his group of friends shrank as he expanded his involvement in online gaming communities. He spent so many hours playing and became so accomplished that he videotaped his play, posted his best moments on gaming sites, and signed up with the manufacturer of his favorite game to be an arbiter of online etiquette.

Winston fit the profile described by psychologist Brent Conrad, author of *How to Help Children Addicted to Video Games: A Guide for Parents*: male, with declining academic performance, drawn to action and combat games, anxious in high school social contexts, compelled to push his game play to higher and higher levels, spending increasing amounts of time playing at the expense of other activities. But despite the clamor to regard boys like him as addicts—even going so far as South Korea's funding hundreds of treatment centers and employing treatments such as electroshock therapy—there are two disturbing problems with this idea.[23]

The first is that so long as an individual's skills for managing and resolving emotional tensions remain at such novice levels, he will be at risk of becoming dependent on extrinsic strategies—chemicals, activities, experiences—that temporarily change the way he feels. Psychologists Christopher Ferguson of Stetson University and Patrick Markey of Villanova University, coauthors of *Mortal Combat: Why the War on Video Games Is Wrong*, have suggested that "games are not really the root of the problem, but rather something else is."[24]

That something else, in Winston's case, was his relationship with his parents, which had been eroded by his tenacious efforts to push them away and withdraw into digital reality. There are all sorts of reasons why a boy might wish to push his parents away, including a healthy desire to be more autonomous—I see it all the time in families coming for help with their sons. But there is a difference between progressive maturity and reactive rupture. For a boy to establish more independence does not require him to negate or even minimize his dependence on his parents for understanding and support. Disconnections with parents, on the other hand, occur frequently, often in reaction to mothers or fathers who have unwittingly become controlling or suffocating out of anxiety, loneliness, or an earnest determination not to repeat their own childhood abandonment. The only way for a boy to establish himself as a capable and distinct person under such circumstances is to break away.

One fifteen-year-old I saw, Aaron, was still very close to his mother, but he began to worry that his dependence on her made him "soft." It became important to him to establish stronger boundaries and to separate from his mother, needing to see himself differently—at which point, unconscious panic arose that drove his mother to become critical of him. The relationship spiraled into crisis, with Aaron fuming at the way his mother undermined his confidence by always seeing where he came up short and the mother resenting his lack of gratitude for how dedicated she was to him. Compounding the problem was how alone each had become in the absence of being able to talk to each other and to find a common understanding or a way forward.

In the cases of both Winston and Aaron, I could help the parents untangle the relational knots. With coaching and opportunities to work through their codependent feelings—rooted typically in hurtful pasts that produce rigid, unworkable relational patterns—the parents were able to reel their sons back in by simply hanging around, being newly interested, "bribing" them with other activities they still liked, and collaborating with them to set reasonable limits on behaviors such as online gaming. What made their successes possible was recognizing how their own needs operated in the relationship, subtly driving them to cling to their sons or respond to them in ways that undermined the effort to build their sons' competence. Becoming strategic about restoring connection required them to let go of their worries and their longings for the boy they once had in order to embrace the young man who needed their support to become a responsible man.

But untangling parenting knots can be complicated by sensational fears about the neurochemistry of digital addiction. Games and media are truly adept at stimulating the brain's pleasure center. But a release of dopamine, the brain chemical, or neurotransmitter, controlling the brain's reward and motivation centers, is triggered by many pleasures (such as reading a good book or watching an engaging television show) that are rarely viewed as addictive. According to Ferguson and Markey, the dopamine released in response to a video game is equivalent to the effect of eating a slice of pizza. A 2016 study published in the *American Journal of Psychiatry* analyzed the results of four surveys totaling eighteen thousand respondents. According to the authors, less than 1 percent of video game players exhibited symptoms of addiction—far less than gamblers. More importantly, even those who met the criteria did not suffer negative consequences at levels warranting classification as ill. Ferguson and Markey commented about the report: "The biggest difference between addicts and nonaddicts that the study found was that addicts *played more video games.*"[25]

As a caregiver, there is a tendency to react with alarm to teen tech use. As moms and dads cast about for help understanding this new, powerful, and pervasive force in their sons' lives, they are vulnerable to the claims of experts; who are all over the map on this subject. Reporting in the US edition of the *Guardian* in 2017, a writer asked, "Why do so many people—from parents to researchers to ninety-one-year-old actors—believe in the existence of video game addiction and other negative effects of video games when the evidence doesn't support it?"[26] Her report linked claims of addiction to an age-old, anxious desire to dominate and control young people. In the article, Ferguson added, "People that tend to hold the more extreme negative views of video games tend to have more negative views of children and adolescents as well."[27]

Keeping Up with Boys in Cyberspace

When the Pew Research Center first began tracking social media use, it was 2005, and only 7 percent of those older than eighteen visited social networking sites. By 2015, that percentage had increased tenfold. The largest and most rapid increase was with younger people, among whom social media use was "ubiquitous."

Among eighteen-to-twenty-nine-year-olds, 88 percent had Facebook accounts. Mobile use has witnessed even more rapid change: in 2011, 35 percent had a smartphone; in a 2017 report by Pew, that number was 77 percent overall and 92 percent among eighteen-to-twenty-nine-year-olds.[28]

The near-universal presence of digital devices in boys' lives is one startling difference between the present generation and its parents. This difference exaggerates the natural gap in understanding between young people and those trying to stay close to them. Parents already unsettled as boys move beyond their control can make cell phones and video games into proverbial bogeymen, thinking them a cause rather than a symptom. In my experience, it is not clear which comes first: the addiction or the disconnection. Without even knowing it, boys are pulled away from their parents by masculine myths about independence. This situation represents a perfect storm where false stories promoting boys' disconnection from their families merge with marketing messages that lure them to more and more gripping technologies. Games and apps simply represent one more way boys are driven from relationships.

Alongside the rise of digital technologies, there have been dramatic changes in what Michael Kimmel calls "Guyland." While in 1960 almost 70 percent of American young adult males had left home, completed their educations, found a partner, and joined the workforce, today less than a third of men reach these milestones by age thirty. In his research, Kimmel discovered young men who prefer the brotherhood of fellow fraternity members, partiers, and gamers to more serious ambitions or relationships. He concluded, "Ironically, women's newfound freedom invites men to delay adulthood even longer. With no family to support, no responsibilities to anyone other than themselves, and young women who appear to be as sexually active and playful as they could possibly ever fantasize, they're free to postpone adulthood almost indefinitely."[29]

The National Bureau of Economic Research, a nonprofit research organization, recently released a paper attributing a decline
in the number of hours worked by millennial males to video game
play. Researchers found that twenty-one-to-thirty-year-olds put in
203 fewer hours in 2015 than that same age group did in 2000.
Most of this leisure time was spent online—a stark contrast with
their female peers, who are more likely to spend their free time
sleeping and on personal care.[30]

Keeping up with boys who live in cyberspace and use tech tools
practically every moment of their days, adults face challenges that
are both similar to and radically more complicated than those of
previous generations. A look at two aspects of boys' lives influenced
by technology provides a sense of the challenge. According to another 2015 report from the Pew Research Center, of the thirteen-
to-seventeen-year-olds who said they had been in a romantic
relationship, digital media played a central role in how they made
initial connections with a romantic interest. Friending on Facebook,
liking or following someone, and messaging were all ways teens
initiate contact with others. Computer-assisted communication
creates new ways to flirt and to relate. Once they have committed
to a romantic partner, teens find that connectivity brings new relationship expectations: 11 percent expect hourly communication
with their partners; 85 percent, at least once a day. To parents who
came of age prior to this tethered one, relationship expectations
such as these are hard to fathom.[31]

The other aspect is how teenage boys present themselves online.
The need to create a personal profile requires adolescents to commit
to an image that will circulate widely, consequentially, and uncontrollably. Naturally they draw on the norms of their peer group to
fill in the blank page. As they seek to manage how they are perceived, boys tend to draw on masculine conventions in the types of
pictures they post and the language they use to describe who they
are. Boys are likely to put up photos that include alcohol use, sexual

references, and sports. The language they use tends to be more aggressive and tends to portray them as more macho than they actually are. In general, teenage boys are more prone to exaggerations and fabrications in their profiles than girls are.

The parents who know what lies ahead for their sons when they apply to colleges and later to jobs can imagine the reactions of admissions officers and human resources personnel when they come across such unflattering online profiles. A 2013 survey noted that 10 percent of young job applicants were rejected because their social media profiles turned off their prospective employers. The challenge for parents is to explain to their kid the long-term repercussions of a social media image without alienating him by making him think they "don't get it" because they are of another generation. What's more, they have to communicate this perspective without seeming to imply "I know more than you," which will only cause the boy to shield himself from his primary reference point.

In an interview for *PC Magazine* online, psychologist Yalda Uhls of UCLA, who lectures and writes about how to raise responsible digital kids, provided parents with historical context for the digital revolution. She reminded them how mothers and fathers at the end of the eighteenth century were frightened about books, banning and burning them. "It's the same principle. Control and authoritarianism." As an alternative, she recommends "active media mediation," where parents engage with their children to craft a "positive and proactive" approach that balances screen time with other important activities and establishes parameters around basic issues such as sleep, privacy, and appropriate content.[32]

In approaches such as this, the issue of screen time is less important than the relationship. The goal is to establish a collaborative, problem-solving framework that can be drawn upon for even more threatening topics coming down the road, like driving, substance use, and so forth. A win-win orientation in which the parent's legitimate concerns about health and responsibility are balanced with equal recognition of a boy's legitimate concerns about friendships, recreation, and fun strengthens connection.

All moms and dads register the tension between protecting their sons and building their confidence and independent judgment. According to a Pew survey of parents of thirteen-to-seventeen-year-olds, a majority of American parents engage in some form of digital supervision: 61 percent monitor their teens' web activity, and 60 percent monitor their social media profiles; nearly 50 percent check their youngsters' phones and messages. Installing parental controls on computers and phones is somewhat less common, but nearly half of parents require teens to share their passwords. Digital grounding is a common form of discipline, and 55 percent set limits on daily screen time.[33]

Notwithstanding how unfamiliar and threatening it may seem to parents, the digital dimension of boys' lives represents an important opportunity to support their sons as they extend themselves into the wider world. The search for recipes and templates to guide them in handling the intrusion of technology into family life overlooks the reality that it will be the quality of their relationships, not their vigilance, that will make the biggest difference.

For example, should a parent apply search filters and other controls to his or her son's computer and phone? Knowing that every teenage boy comes across pornographic content early in adolescence and that there will be pressures to get too involved in video games, how do parents exercise a steadying influence? One mother I see, whose son has gone too far at times, now monitors his texts and email, has his passwords, and randomly checks his online history. But the goal she has established with him is to ease away from these monitoring practices as he demonstrates better judgment. Rather than a punishment, they came up with this plan after a series of problems when he was younger and more impulsive; the plan was cast as supporting his self-regulation until he could handle things more on his own.

The American Academy of Pediatrics issued new cyber-use guidelines in 2016, shifting from limiting overall screen time to ensuring that children are not alone as they message or watch. "Coview with your children, help children understand what they are seeing, and help them apply what they learn to the world around them." This new ground rule aligns with the recommendation to spend special time with boys: parents and other caregivers must go where the boys are.[34]

But as key architects of their son's boyhood, parents must no more take the cyberworld of media and gaming on its own terms than they should stand aside and let pornography or recreational drugs compromise their son's development. A movement for a "commercial-free childhood" has sprung up in reaction to technology that pulls children away from more spontaneous and open-ended play, relationships, and nature. The mission of the Campaign for a Commercial-Free Childhood, founded in 2000 by Harvard Medical School psychologist Susan Linn, is "to support parents' efforts to raise healthy families by limiting commercial access to children and ending the exploitive practice of child-targeted marketing." The campaign offers a set of resources and promotes Screen-Free Week to coincide with Children's Book Week. To establish a healthy overall balance in families, the CCFC recommends seven tested strategies to reduce children's screen time, including making mealtimes and mornings screen-free zones, encouraging outdoor and imaginative play, and asking adults to model a balanced use of their own devices.[35]

For the times when boys are online, there is an expanding set of digital citizenship guidelines. Appreciating that digital natives are not necessarily fully informed, the Living Online curriculum developed by teacher Reuben Loewy in conjunction with other educators consists of thirty modules covering topics such as the history of the Internet, digital ethics, cyberpsychology, and online relationships.[36] MTV has created its own Digital Rights Project, which reads, "Online and on my cell, I have the right to . . ." followed by a list that includes "Live without pressure or abuse," "Step in and help if I see someone getting harassed," "End unhealthy relationships," and "Disconnect whenever I want." The media company runs an education campaign posing three questions for teens to ask themselves: (1) Why does my bf/gf need to know where I am and what I'm doing every minute of the day? (2) Does sending or receiving a message every five minutes all day and night seem normal? (3) Do the messages I'm receiving sometimes make me feel bad?[37]

For parents wondering whether their son is developing a digital dependency, one interesting approach is offered by physician and writer James Hamblin. He argues against addiction treatment approaches recommending prolonged abstinence, "because I'm not sure they're necessary, or likely to lead to long-term results." Drawing an analogy to a new approach to overeating, intermittent fasting, the approach helps people regulate their digital use by "relearning intentionality." Touting the benefits of a digital fast, Dr. Hamblin writes, "The key to being purposeful about media consumption is breaking the habits that apps and devices are built to create—the mindless checking and scrolling, the Pavlovian response to any ding or buzz or notification."[38]

But if fasting is too radical an approach, Anya Kamenetz, digital education correspondent for National Public Radio, recommends this straightforward guideline: "Enjoy screens; not too much; mostly together."[39]

For parents trying to come up with an appropriate family policy for their son's digital use, these questions might help to guide a self-inventory. The goal is to avoid parents' reactivity, so that their policies are effective.

- If your son has withdrawn from his relationship with you, what is he turning away *from*? In strong relationships there is a magnetic force keeping boys in orbit around their parents despite the pull of the peer group or other attractions. Attached, boys touch down when they need understanding, comfort, support, or help. Has some barrier arisen that has left your son disconnected?

- In particular, as your son shows signs of greater independence, are you having more fights with him? Is your eye drawn to what he is *not* rather than appreciating what he *is*? Has criticalness become an unconscious way of expressing your anxiety about successfully launching your son?

- How are you negotiating fair device use policies with your son? Candid conversations about what is healthy and appropriate, and about how online behavior should reflect his core values, help a boy understand citizenship. If you have not had a *conversation* (instead of a *lecture*), what's stopping you?

- Does your son have the benefit of a digital citizenship program in his school? Can you play a role to ensure that the program is up-to-date and adequate? Does it represent your family values?

- If real concerns arise about overall screen time or content, does your son need stronger scaffolding to adjust to the pressures and temptations of cyberlife? Can you establish a parental control policy with him, setting goals and a timeline for his ultimate independence?

CHAPTER 10

THE TWENTY-FIRST CENTURY— AND BEYOND

At a workshop for parents, I presented our research about boys being relational learners and told participants that very few boys in the study—none, actually—reported a time they had fixed a broken relationship with a coach or teacher. Our conclusion, I explained, was that teachers and coaches must assume that they are the relationship managers. At that point, one father raised his hand, exasperated. "I'm sorry," he complained, "but where is the grit? By coddling boys in the ways your research describes, aren't we making them more passive and dependent?" I shared his concern and added that I also feared that the research might foster more entitlement among boys. I said that I was telling teachers to take two things from our study.

The first is that boys' inability to shoulder any responsibility for their learning relationships is the present baseline, not an ultimate destination. It reflects where things are for boys today. Teachers should not hold their breath waiting for a boy to speak up, come for help, or apologize for some mistake he may have made. When a relationship is strained, it falls to the adult, the professional, to fix the problem—by default.

Secondly, boys' lack of initiative in a difficult relationship represents a logical consequence of how they are socialized. Educators cannot expect a different outcome unless they do something about it. It is not that boys are somehow biologically unable to undertake repair when they feel disconnected from those helping them to learn. But most feel unequipped to do so without creating problems for themselves.

The same socialization that renders many boys relationally hamstrung at school contributes to their educational underperformance overall. The gender achievement gap can be summarized this way: many boys do not buy in. Because learning is a partnership, the active consent of the learner is required. Teachers can cajole, push, and threaten all they like, but ultimately the boy has the power to say, "I won't learn from you." What our research discovered was the power of a mutually respectful relationship to win his agreement to try.

Once we acknowledge that practically every kind of boy can be helped to success by committed teachers whose emotional labor is supported properly, the limiting factor becomes the system—not the boy or even the individual teacher. That many boys do poorly in school actually tells us more about us than about boys. Parents, teachers, coaches, mentors—those in relationships with boys—need to step up *our* game. Only when we operate from correct assumptions about boys—that they are relational learners (and relational beings, in general)—can we expect to get the model for educating them right. What's true in educating boys is true across the board in their care and development.

What's in the way of getting things right? For one, there is the persistence of outdated ideas about boys; ones that never worked very well but had the cover of cultural mythology. For another, there's been a shortage of leadership—professionals and educators who operate from evidence rather than from ideology and pseudoscience—to advocate for a better deal for boys. How we see boys is befogged by myths and misleading ideas.

And how we see them influences how they see their lives and their world. Young men find themselves at a crossroads, when movements for greater equality have rendered inherited expectations obsolete. But boys have trouble reading the handwriting on the wall, partly because they receive mixed messages about the rules of the game. Barbara Risman, a sociologist at the University of Illinois at Chicago, has diagnosed "gender vertigo" as a common condition among millennials and identified four different ways they are responding: as true believers, straddlers, innovators, and rebels. The largest group, the straddlers—"ones that are not so sure of themselves"—reflect the in-between spirit of the times.

True believers, as well as some straddlers, cling to traditional roles while everything beneath them heaves. Their blind reactions are reinforced by thought leaders such as Jordan Peterson, a University of Toronto psychologist, author, and theatrical speaker who promotes the view that "The masculine spirit is under assault" and offers as the solution a return to "eternal values."[1] But when he proposes 12 Rules for Life ("Rule 1: Stand Up Straight, with Your Shoulders Back"), his repackaging of stale masculine tropes won't help younger men find a creative response to the challenges of the school, work, dating, and family environments they actually occupy.[2]

Since 1980, the benefits of a college degree have soared. As manufacturing jobs disappear, a group of economists found, men who are ill-equipped for the knowledge economy become less desirable as partners. Out-of-wedlock births are at an all-time high, just above 40 percent of all births, and there is an overall decline in both marriage and fertility. According to another economist, David Autor of MIT, "You don't want to marry a man who is in all likelihood not economically viable, because it is not a free lunch."[3]

Headline after headline has dispelled any lingering doubt about where slacking off in school, living a frat life of video games and drinking in college, or approaching women with sexual entitlement, lead.

But some young men remain unconvinced. Sociologists Joanna Pepin and David Cotter found that panic about "men's place in society" has motivated many to retreat to "symbolic masculinity." They wrote, "After becoming more egalitarian for almost twenty years, high school seniors' thinking about a husband's authority and divisions of labor at home has since become substantially more traditional."[4] In households where incomes between male and female partners are relatively equal, Fairleigh Dickinson University political scientist Dr. Dan Cassino found, "men may be compensating by stressing the importance of traditional women's roles."[5]

Vulnerable and uncertain, younger males can be misled in even more serious ways. The first time I heard of the incel phenomenon was when a troubled twenty-two-year-old, Elliot Rodger, self-described as a "virgin killer," murdered six people and injured fourteen more in California in 2014. Prior to his rampage, he ranted on YouTube about being sexless and single: "Life is so unfair because girls don't want me."[6] His views became popular among members of an online group for the involuntarily celibate. In April 2018 another young man mowed down random pedestrians while driving a van on a downtown Toronto sidewalk. Alek Minassian also blamed women and feminism, and warned darkly in a Facebook post: "The Incel Rebellion has already begun!"[7]

Where incels profess a right to intimate relations with women, there's a related group advocating just the opposite. The Men Going Their Own Way (MGTOW) movement consists of males choosing to live in the "Manosphere":

Men haven't lost their need to find happiness by providing, protecting, sacrificing, and conquering; we've simply discovered that providing for the modern feminist, working like a dog to protect a family that can be taken away at a moment's notice, or risking our lives to conquer resources for some ungrateful woman who claims she can do it on her own, is an empty way to live.[8]

Despite the flailing response of such men to women's equality, from the front lines of boyhood there's better news. Alongside efforts of some to airbrush and glorify male supremacy, many younger males are reinventing masculinity itself. The UCLA California Health Interview Survey, for example, found in 2015–16 that more than a quarter of California teenagers see themselves as "gender nonconforming," with boys believing they are more feminine and girls more masculine.[9] Writer Sarah Rich, in the *Atlantic*, offered this intriguing interpretation: "There are so few positive variations on what a 'real man' can look like, that when the youngest generations show signs of reshaping masculinity, the only word that exists for them is *nonconforming*. The term highlights that nobody knows what to call these variations on maleness."[10]

However they bend, work around, and reinvent their masculine identities, boys will also draw upon what they find life-giving about being male for their reinventions. Another headline caught my attention not too long ago for how it captured the contrast between men who get stuck in a negative identity and those who assert more positive masculine traits. In late May 2017 a tragedy occurred in Portland, Oregon. A thirty-something man with a long history of struggle—rootlessness, jail time for assorted felonies, a self-described "nihilist" and white supremacist—began making racist remarks to two young women of color, one wearing a hijab, on a local commuter train. Three male passengers stepped forward to assist the women, and the man stabbed them, killing two and wounding the third. One of the men was a career army veteran, recently retired, and a father of four teenage children; another, twenty-three, was a recent college graduate. Conscious as he lay waiting for the ambulance before passing away, the twenty-three-year-old said to a woman helping him, "I want everybody on the train to know I love them."

The third man, a twenty-one-year-old poet, had emergency surgery for a stab wound that barely missed his jugular. As he was released from the hospital, he offered this poem he had composed:

> I am alive.
> I spat in the eye of hate and lived.
> This is what we must do for one another.
> We must live for one another.[11]

On the surface, these three men—a poet, a college graduate, and a career serviceman—were very different from one another, but they drew from the same well for how they thought about being male. Each had taken to heart a commitment to virtues of courage, empathy, and service to others. The man directing racist and xeno-phobic remarks at the women, on the other hand, displayed an extreme version of the entitled, self-centered, and violent male identity encountered particularly among "angry white men" stewing in resentment about being displaced.[12]

These polar extremes represent the range of possibility open to boys and their families in this time of great flux. Confronting so much upheaval and conflicted messaging, it is remarkable not only how many boys stay true to their inner compasses but how few get lost. As he makes his way through boyhood, each youngster will experience some vertigo. What steadies a boy and helps him stay true to himself are the voices he listens to in his heart. Unlike the prophets of doom who point to boyhood's casualties to argue for a return to old traditions, I am impressed by how ready boys are for this new world. Many revel in the uncertainties precisely for their opportunities and love the adventure.

Things can go one way or another. Either boyhood will be reinvented to nurture the qualities boys need to flourish—to attach, to develop their emotional and relational capacities, to engage in learning and living out their values—or it will continue to press boys into identities that succeed less and less well. There is "unconstrained creativity" in how boys can conceive of their lives in the contemporary world, according to Australian sociologist Raewyn Connell.[13]

The Case for a New Boyhood

A couple of years ago, I received an email from a school administrator saying that he had read my latest book and asking me to speak to his faculty before the start of the coming school year. He said he preferred that the talk be "gender neutral." I was surprised that he wanted me to present my research on reaching and teaching boys in a manner that downplayed the impact of masculine stereotypes and myths. Extrapolating from data collected from boys to girls represents a classic social science misstep. Instead, I offered to characterize my research on boys as an example of how gender is unavoidably relevant to the education process.

Cultural backlash against the progress of gender equality has grown, sparking men's own "me too" outcry. When President Barack Obama established the Commission on Women and Girls in 2009, it was followed in 2011 by calls for a White House Commission on Boys to Men. The coalition calling for the commission was led by psychologist Warren Farrell, coauthor of *The Boy Crisis: Why Our Boys Are Struggling and What We Can Do About It*, and a leading proponent of the view that sexism affects males and females equally. As their proposal proclaimed, "Our daughters and sons are in the same boat. Therefore, if just one sex wins, both sexes lose. The more closely our commission investigated, the more concerned we became with the crisis our sons, fathers, and men currently face."[14]

Feminist leaders offer a different perspective. In the fall of 2014 and the spring of 2015, thousands of activists and scholars attended conferences in New Delhi, India, and in New York City on the theme of engaging men and boys in gender equality. In remarks at the outset of the US conference, Phumzile Mlambo-Ngcuka, head of the United Nations Entity for Gender Equality and the Empowerment of Women (UN Women), founded in 2011 to promote gender equality, expand opportunity, and tackle gender discrimination, explained, "What we are about as women leaders is what good men and boys are about."[15] With an equally impressive practicality, longtime feminist activist and writer Gloria Steinem summarized what men stand to gain from gender equality: "I would say that each of us has only one thing to gain from the feminist movement: our whole humanity."[16]

Boys themselves are fervently insisting that parents recognize their true natures, that schools acknowledge their possibilities, and that communities celebrate their diversity. Fortunately, in spite of how the Man Box tends to inhibit change, human instincts cannot be fully suppressed. Human development is a revolutionary force. Even as traditional masculinity holds them back, younger men are adapting creatively to more equal relationships. In the view of sociologist Michael Kimmel, "The data are persuasive that most American men have quietly, and without much ideological fanfare, accommodated themselves to greater gender equality in both their personal and their workplace relationships than any generation before them."[17]

The point, as Mlambo-Ngcuka said, is about "good men and boys." The conversation about what men of virtue look like and what it takes to nurture those qualities is louder and louder. The actions of the men in Portland validate the findings of a large-scale survey of virtues and character strengths conducted by the Positive Psychology Center of the University of Pennsylvania. The center found that males predominated at both the good and the bad extremes of character. Boxed in, many men become discouraged, desperate, and dangerous. Once empathic ties are cut and self-awareness is limited, males are seemingly capable of anything.[18]

But some men, like those who stood up to the man abusing the young women, cling to virtue in spite of their socialization. Their actions offer a powerful affirmation of men's goodness. Heroes help us to see potential. On an everyday basis, what can boys and men be counted on for? Will their goodness be sufficient to trump the desperation fostered by their experiences as boys?

The current version of boyhood leaves too much to chance. Some boys grow one way, others another, depending on accidents of birth and the quality of the resources and relationships available to them. Left unchallenged, the boyhood presently built into schools, sports programs, communities, and families carries a developmental price that is unconscionable. Some boys manage to retain their goodness; some lose their hearts altogether. No family, school, or community should have to guess which boy will be which.

For the sake of individual boys in our lives and to benefit the society overall, those in charge of boyhood must take responsibility for its casualties. Providing only individual solutions is an inefficient—not to mention unjust—solution to a historic social problem.

There is more support today than ever for individual boys to reject or resist the Man Box. But to grow this support into a movement, to the point that the losses and casualties of boyhood are truly aberrant instead of normal, we must be honest about its real costs.

Two types of peculiarly male casualties remind us of the stakes involved for getting boyhood right.

Famished Boys

In workshops for school administrators, I often bring boys into the room by showing interviews I conducted with several boys who participated in our studies and agreed to be videotaped. Brendan, who attended a government-supported school in Toronto, is featured in one. In the first clip, the teenager explains that when he feels a connection with a teacher, when he feels known and respected, he finds it easier to tackle his assignments and to participate in class work. In the absence of a connection, he can present more of a problem. "It may be a flaw in my character," he owns, "but I respond positively when a connection is there, and when it's not, I find myself drifting away a bit." Asked what happens when he "drifts away," Brendan adds, "That might damage our relationship because they might think I'm a kid who doesn't want to be in the class. But I'm an intelligent kid. I like to learn and all. It's just that when a teacher isn't respecting me, it's hard to do the work."

Asked what it looks like when he checks out, Brendan says he tends to "talk more, not really pay attention to what the teacher is saying." If the teacher tries to correct him for his inattention, he "might just shut down, do the assignments, but really just wait until the semester is over." He adds, "If they talked to me, tried to connect with me better, then I think I would be more involved. I would start to better my behavior, if they talked with me in a good, positive way."

What if the teacher reacts more negatively and speaks to him in a less understanding way? "I would shun them a bit, become more resentful, kind of not very responsive to what they were trying to tell me." And might you become disruptive? I ask. "Yes, definitely," he replies without hesitation, telling a story about a French teacher who had sent him from the classroom to the dean's office for misbehavior and "wasn't really trying to connect." When he was allowed to return, their conflict worsened significantly, with Brendan "trying to usurp his authority" in various ways. The class became their battlefield.

As educational philosopher Nel Noddings has asked, don't those who receive care have an ethical responsibility to respond with a measure of respect and consideration to those offering the care? What happens when this responsibility is overlooked?[19] In the video, Brendan comes across as a disheveled but remarkably honest, likeable, and articulate teenage boy. His reactions to the teacher are recognizable to anyone who spends time with boys. Not particularly able to acknowledge his vulnerability in the relationship, he thinks in terms of his rights and the teacher's transgressions. While he is willing to admit to "flaws in my character," he plainly does not feel particularly bad about becoming such a problem for the French teacher. In fact, he seems to take satisfaction in it.

Unfortunately, what is missing in Brendan's understanding of things is a working morality to guide how he behaves when someone lets him down. Without such a compass, he is guided instead by masculine norms that valorize conflicts with teachers and obscure the real relational issue. Brendan sees conflicts with teachers only within the framework of his own disappointments. Being able or willing to consider where the teacher is coming from, reading and responding to the feelings of others, is absent—and yet it is such an important relational skill. Getting stuck in narcissistic patterns is not just a matter of age; the ability to think about what other people feel comes with practice.

Narcissism is generally on the rise among those under thirty, according to psychologists Keith Campbell of the University of Georgia and Jean Twenge of San Diego State. They reviewed more than a hundred studies of college student scores on an inventory of narcissistic traits and found "a massive increase" through 2008. Another group of researchers found a nearly threefold increase in diagnoses of narcissistic personality disorder among twenty-somethings compared with older generations. In yet another metastudy, Emily Grijalva of the University of Buffalo led a team that examined 355 papers for three aspects of narcissism: leadership, grandiosity and exhibitionism, and entitlement. They found that men stood out particularly for entitlement and were more likely to exploit others and to believe they deserve privileges.[20]

Summarizing this finding that males predominate on measures of narcissism, Jeffrey Kluger, author of *The Narcissist Next Door: Understanding the Monster in Your Family, in Your Office, in Your Bed—in Your World*, wrote: "If you're looking for who's preening, strutting, self-absorbed, arrogant, exhibitionistic, conceited, insensitive, and entitled, you'll find more of them in the boys' game than the girls.'"[21]

Positive self-regard is a healthy thing; a necessary foundation for confidence and for building a life. The ancient rabbinic scholar Hillel the Elder queried famously, "If I am not for myself, who will be for me?" Of course, mothers and fathers want their sons to be glad for who they are. So much of parenting, in fact, is aimed at validating a child's belief that he can make something of himself. But positive self-regard, as the mind-set research of Stanford University psychologist Carol Dweck confirms, is not a key to success.[22]

Beginning in the late 1960s, it was believed that a child's self-esteem was related directly to his achievement. Educational practices that undercut self-esteem were discontinued. Coaches started handing out trophies to everyone. Teachers were trained to replace criticism with praise. In 2003 psychologist Roy Baumeister reviewed scientific literature on self-esteem over a thirty-year period and found serious problems with both methods and conclusions. The two hundred studies that met basic research standards actually indicated that high self-esteem was not correlated with grades or career achievement.[23]

Dweck's research indicated that it is the belief in the power of effort that encourages motivation and produces greater achievement. When children defend their innate capabilities and rest on their presumed laurels, they undercut their success. Brendan saw himself as an "an intelligent kid, I like to learn." But his understanding of what happened in his French class—the tragedy of a bright boy whose willingness to learn was lost in a pissing contest with his teacher—was a defensive self-justification. He sacrificed his school goals as he distanced himself from a teacher who did not appreciate him.

Many boys retreat to a myopic narcissism to defend themselves against negative feedback. Crouched in a "not my fault" stance, they are unable to move forward productively, and become more and more defended when this strategy does not lead to improved outcomes.

The clinical term "narcissism" comes from the Greek story of a young man, Narcissus, who becomes frozen in fascination with his own image. Early psychoanalytic thinkers described self-absorption as a stage that lays the foundation for relationships with others. Developmental psychologists realized, however, that some individuals, most often male, do not move into relationships requiring mutuality. These children, in the view of psychoanalyst Heinz Kohut, whose ideas about narcissism and empathy transformed developmental psychology in the nineties, received insufficient "mirroring" and are unsure of themselves and preoccupied by feelings of insecurity. They have an insatiable need for affirmation, shy away from real connections with others, and tend to be rigid and controlling. According to Sigmund Freud, the Austrian founder of psychoanalysis, "Where such men love, they have no desire, and where they desire, they have no love."[24]

Whatever developmental business is left unfinished is made worse by the highly competitive nature of boyhood. Feeling insecure and hungry for validation, many boys are drawn to status and rewards, even though these never really answer their questions about who they are. "If I am only for myself, what am I?" Hillel adds in the next part of his challenge. Boyhood produces casualties of all sorts, but the boy who never takes on enough ballast to venture into the uncertain seas of relationship is a particularly sad one. Some men spend their lives trying to shore up feelings of being empty as a result of having received insufficient confirmation as boys.

Bad Boys

Young men preoccupied with their own unmet needs are often confused with others who act in antisocial ways. Both narcissists and sociopaths are manipulative, even exploitative, and can be unmoved by anything except how to advance their own interests. Both lack interest in others except as a means to their ends. Both can be charming and very convincing, especially when focused fully on an important goal. And both are likely to be male.

Antisocial personality disorder is characterized by a "pervasive disregard for the rights of others." In his book *Bad Boys, Bad Men: Confronting Antisocial Personality Disorder (Sociopathy)*, psychiatrist Donald Black concludes, "The most significant epidemiologic feature of ASP (antisocial personality disorder) is that it is almost exclusively a disorder of men."[25] But an inconsiderate, antisocial attitude is an unsurprising outcome of male conditioning. In the dog-eat-dog grind of boyhood, many boys come to behave in ways that are heedless of others. Marked by a pattern of deceitful, aggressive, impulsive, and reckless behavior that is unchecked by social norms or laws.

Fortunately, misbehaving boys gain self-regulation and empathic restraint as they mature. Most bad behavior among adolescent males is contextual, linked to negative peer influences, and abates with maturity and age. In fact, as many as 60 percent of boys engage in some form of delinquent behavior during adolescence, testimony to the influence of masculine pressures.

I have seen many boys, brought by concerned parents or referred by authorities of one kind or another, who have misbehaved. Derek is a boy who was mandated for counseling by his school after being caught for vandalism. As he and I explored what he had been thinking as he acted so destructively, trying to get a sense of the motivations behind his actions, I could see that he had been carried away by the exciting, antiauthority stirrings of the small group of peers he hung around with. There was nothing—not deeper feelings of anger or distorted thinking—indicating more than a lack of judgment and self-control. Psychologist Terrie Moffitt of the University of Wisconsin estimates that only 5 percent of males warrant the ASP label.[26]

But during my stint in inpatient work, I came across some adolescent males who were unresponsive to the rewards and punishments of our highly structured treatment regimen. The level system governing the unit was based on strictly defined goals and meaningful privileges, intended to foster positive peer pressure and relational influence—and it had little effect with these adolescent males. Whether they ever earned the rewards associated with level 4 (freedom to go outside or to visit the recreation hall, to linger after meals in the dining hall, and so forth) or stayed restricted to the locked unit on level 1 seemed only a matter of inconvenience. They could tolerate negative sanctions. While they sometimes seemed to make real connections, in the end we realized that the connection was purely instrumental—"What can I get from this relationship?"—and that we were being played. What people thought of them only mattered if it helped or got in the way of something they wanted.

The extent of some boys' calculation and manipulation was chilling. In the inpatient adolescent treatment unit, patients came with a wide variety of problems. Some were admitted because they were depressed and suicidal; some because they were out of control at home, school, in the neighborhood—everywhere, in a number of cases. Some were ordered to treatment by the juvenile justice system for offenses such as theft, vandalism, burglary, drug dealing, assault. When I met with a new patient for an intake assessment, my initial impressions provided data about who he was. When my hair stood up as I listened to how detached and coldly calculating a young man had become, it was because I knew nothing was keeping him in line but fear of getting caught. He had no relational anchors grounding him to morality.

One young man, Joe, handsome, with an infectious smile and seeming guilelessness, turned out to be one of the biggest problems I encountered, brazenly thwarting every rule and unfazed by any negative consequence. The usual approaches to influence him went nowhere. At one point, he used a knife stolen from the dining hall to dig a hole through the drywall of his room into the room next door, which happened to be occupied by a female who was hospitalized after years of being sexually abused. Somehow he persuaded her to give him oral sex through the hole in the wall. When confronted by his team about the lack of regard he showed her, he shrugged. He felt nothing.

In the early years of my career, I tried to locate the critical moments of hurt that had led boys like Joe to give up on people. My hope was that I could help them face the crushing disappointments that had turned them away from authentic connection and support them to change self-defeating patterns keeping them from life's real satisfactions. I was optimistic about the power of recovery. Many years later, I am even more impressed by the power of human minds to overcome trauma of all sorts. But I am also sobered by the extent of the damage some boys experience and struck by what is required—courage, deep and patient connection, confidence—to undertake healing.

In a search for answers about how a boy becomes antisocial, researchers have turned to biological studies. But antisocial personality patterns are more likely to come from a variety of causes. Genetics, organic injury, gross childhood abuse and neglect—all contribute to "a condition that sprouts and flourishes in the right mix of circumstances," according to Dr. Black. Yet there is good news about ASP. However a boy's path toward antisocial behavior may be rooted in early deprivations and hurts he has experienced, antisocial patterns can be overcome. "We do know that change is possible," Black writes. "For whatever reasons, some antisocials get better."[27]

This encouraging prognosis is especially important when considering how race and class can combine with masculinity to produce antisocial behavior. To the list of factors driving crime and delinquency, experiences with social oppression must be included. Black males are five times more likely to be jailed than whites; in five states, the racial disparity is more than ten to one. According to a report by the Sentencing Project, a Washington, DC, research center advocating for criminal justice reform, these disparities are attributable to harsh drug sentences, racial bias in judicial attitudes, and systemic disadvantages affecting the families of racial minorities. In other words, young men of color are met with a built-in bias favoring punishment over uplift and rehabilitation.

For these males, prison is but one point in a pipeline that begins in school. What these boys know, consciously and unconsciously, is that racial prejudice will handicap their lives wherever they go. A new study conducted by researchers from Stanford, Harvard, and the US Census Bureau found that among males from the same socioeconomic circumstances, black boys invariably fare worse than whites. In fact, some of the widest black-white disparities show up at upper income levels. As the *New York Times* reported, "The research makes clear that there is something unique about the obstacles black males face."[28]

Smith College professor Ann Arnett Ferguson conducted a three-year study in an urban elementary school and described how a group of young males were identified by school personnel as "bound for jail," internalizing a distorted sense of themselves in the funhouse mirror of a racially biased gaze. University of Pennsylvania psychologist Howard Stevenson speaks of the "hypervulnerability" of boys who, not seen as boys at all but as social threats, exaggerate the stereotypes in stances of defiance and compensation.[29]

The connection between hypermasculinity and hypervulnerability is what has stayed with me about Niles, the boy from my family court days. In our sessions, I saw a young man who was sensitive and artistically inclined. Up against pressures that pushed him to adopt a street persona, he weighed his options. While we waited for his hearing, new charges began coming into court—for drug possession, car theft, burglary—and I realized that the alternative plan I'd worked with him to create was in a race with the more immediate and compelling pressures of life in his family, school, and neighborhood. Under my nose, he was becoming the bad boy everyone expected: standing inside the cell after being subdued, he was so pumped up from fighting and from having to stand up to threat and violence that he was practically unrecognizable.

The Way Ahead with Our Boys

In this in-between, high-stakes time, parents are besieged by conflicting ideas for how to raise their sons. Some voices tout traditional masculine values and approaches, such as Eric Davis and Dana Santorelli, authors of *Raising Men: From Fathers to Sons—Life Lessons from Navy SEAL Training*, who don't think twice about tying boys' hands behind their backs and binding their feet before tossing them into a pool to train them for grit.[30] Voices touting the idea that male biology is primary vie with suggestions to soften boys by treating them as though they are indistinguishable from girls. The conversation about how to raise a son is reminiscent of the one I heard about how to teach a boy at the outset of my career: about hormonally driven differences in energy levels and orientations to school, teachers, and learning. The problem with those ideas was that almost none was grounded in sound research—or worked.

When I organized the On Behalf of Boys project at the school, there were lots of polemics and poetry but little science to offer parents. We scraped together what evidence-based ideas we could to develop a workshop we called Raising Sons 101. It represents an effort to help parents of boys develop a meta-view of the job and to answer some of their urgent questions.

Raising Sons 101

Raising Sons 101 is built around a set of developmental themes and offers information, relevant skills, and lists of dos and don'ts, organized in five lessons.

Lesson I: Advocate for Your Son

Advocating for boys involves, first, understanding the threat posed by the social pressures they face. With a broader understanding of male development, parents are in a better position to take a stand for their sons' well-being. For example, when parents notice boys being forced by peer pressure or other influences to make narrow choices, they can intervene to reinforce his power to travel his own path.

For most boys, these pressures begin practically from the start, when an infant is shushed for crying and told to be a "big boy." Later, if the boy plays with dolls or other toys coded as female, he is likely to be redirected or even shamed. Inviting girls to his parties or having them as friends often elicits the same kind of gender policing. Later still, on sports fields or school playgrounds, pressures mount for boys to conform to stereotyped expectations: to love competition, play through pain, seek dominance, and so forth. On an almost daily basis, through adolescence, parents will find plenty of opportunities to remind their son that he is known and loved for who he is and that he can think for himself about how he wants to express and explore his masculinity.

At such times, there are many ways a parent can help: running interference, normalizing the boy's struggles, making sure their relationship is a haven. For example, when the pressures to conform are overwhelming a boy, the parent can ask if he would like help handling the situation. They can brainstorm ideas for what can be done, partnering with him to think through the situation. As the son grows older, he may feel ashamed for needing help from his parents; at these times, recounting stories from one's own battles with gender norms can ease his feelings of embarrassment and humiliation. Sometimes parents become confused by competing priorities, such as between setting limits and warmly validating their son. I ask them to think first about the overall situation: What kind of pressure is the boy under, and how is it affecting him? Which does he need more: limits and lectures or welcome and respite?

As parents, we must make strategic judgments and keep in mind the larger goal: empowering our sons to stand up to pressures, seeking help whenever their personal resources need a boost. Being a good ally to a boy means welcoming and validating his struggles, no matter what, while also holding high expectations for his ability to figure out his own life.

Too often, parents of boys miss this point. While many take up for their son in one way or another, they often pick the wrong battles. They violate their son's personal boundaries, confusing things they worry about—for example, that he might not be popular—for ones he actually struggles with. Compelled by such worries, they often trample over their son's initiative and inadvertently take over the problem. Instead of feeling supported and more secure, the boy ends up feeling less sure of himself and perhaps even resentful of his parents.

The place to start in becoming an advocate for boys is to develop perspective about boyhood and male stereotyping. It's not possible until the parent recognizes that each and every individual boy is distinct from the stereotypes. To develop their perspective, parents can peruse the field of boyhood studies, reading books that offer real stories of boys' experiences. Penetrating the fog that surrounds boys will help parents keep their sons' humanity in sight.

Throughout their sons' lives, parents will need to remind them how good it is that they are boys. In the current climate, there is understandable ambivalence about how males are viewed; parents are leery of reinforcing attitudes that can lead to trouble. Boys of all ages pick up on this hesitancy. It is very helpful when parents can show how pleased they are with their sons, without qualification. As they stretch themselves to convey their delight, parents may notice their own ambivalence or resentment toward males. Such self-awareness can offer a path to healing and personal growth.

Being an advocate does not mean rushing in to rescue a boy. It is much more powerful to help him notice that he is not alone and to stand with him, ready to provide a shield if he needs it. In this way, we enable our sons' self-confidence.

Lesson 2: Offer Relationship for a Strong Sense of Self

Because the peer pressures of boyhood are so intense, it requires a strong sense of self to steer clear of negative norms. As parents, we need to remember that our connection with our sons is their primary fortification, preventing overcompromise. If they know that they are held in their parents' hearts, boys will hold them in theirs and, with them, their values. Strengthened, they will take on the world with greater independence.

How to cultivate a strong connection with our sons? One way is to learn the very particular skill of mirroring. Parents can practice this with a close partner, arranging to take turns sharing all that they admire and love about their sons. Be as specific as possible and tell stories about actual moments when your son revealed what a special person he is. Not only does such practice time prepare the parent for real-life opportunities with her son, but it also deepens her skill at validation and at offering genuinely positive regard unmitigated by worry or criticism. As a result, patterns of finding fault or getting hijacked by personal upset become more conscious and controllable.

All of the strategies we identified in our research on successful relational strategies for teachers are relevant to parents as well. Finding a common interest or identity, offering help that is carefully fitted to the boy's actual need, being patient and accessible, and so forth—such relational gestures make it more likely that a boy will view the parent as a resource instead of as a judge and jury. Because the cultural script for boys is not to rely on their parents, it is important that parents make themselves available to their sons and maintain keen interest in their lives.

In my office the other day, while meeting with Cyril and his mother, I was reminded of how many boys inadvertently wind up taking care of their parents instead of being the ones who are taken care of. At thirteen, Cyril seemed either absorbed in the video game Fortnite or angry all the time. His mother chalked it up to adolescence. But as I helped them talk to each other about their growing disconnection, what became evident was that Cyril felt protective of his mother and was responding to her sadness over the recent loss of her mother by trying not to burden her with his own stresses and upsets. His mother had no idea that Cyril was trying to take on so much and was cutting himself off for her sake. When she realized that, she insisted that he remain open and talk to her even when she seemed sad and preoccupied. Being close to him, she explained, always made her life better.

Receiving so much feedback that is distorted by the values of competition and popular culture, either a boy finds a true mirror within his family—or he likely goes without. With insufficient mirroring, boys are more vulnerable to the rewards offered by the culture—winning or fitting in with the peer group, for example—and are less likely to think for themselves. Having at least one relationship in which they are truly known and loved makes all the difference.

Lesson 3: Encourage Emotional Expression

Emotional awareness and expressiveness develop in relationship. Boys can be expected to share their feelings only where they are protected from shaming and judgments. When barriers and threats are removed, boys do not hold back: they long to tell their stories. At first, their feelings can be raw and unpleasant, even angry, and may be directed at their parents. Cyril's chronic irritation certainly threw his mother off, until she realized he was simply signaling that he was unable to hold in everything, no matter how hard he tried. But it is in the relationship with an unconditionally loving parent that boys discover how to do the hard work of staying connected even when their feelings want to push everyone away.

The skill of listening to boys' feelings is both straightforward and challenging. Many parents try to listen despite having too much to do, with too little help and little to no attention for themselves, and carrying lots of unfinished business of their own. The stresses they endure can make them inattentive, irritable, and emotionally reactive when their sons behave unreasonably. But when merely reacting to our sons, we lose opportunities to get behind their behavior to the upset that is driving it.

To develop skill at listening, parents first learn to silence our inner monologues and to radiate attention, warmth, and interest. When a parent can muster attention, all that is required is to find the boy and simply direct attention his way—if he is playing a game or watching a show, to sit by him and be interested in what he is doing without altering the flow of the game. During car rides, find a question to ask that expresses a genuine, open curiosity about some part of his life he enjoys: "What song is that you're listening to?" "What happened in that show you watched?" "How did the team you follow do in their last game?" The point is not to require the boy to explain something or even help you to understand; it is for the son to experience his parent's attention as pleasant.

As parents exercise their listening muscles, the quality of their attention will deepen and be less vulnerable to distraction or deflection. And as boys find being listened to a positive experience, they lean in. With this connected state as a baseline, the real payoff comes when the boy seeks a sounding board or comforting ear. Once the trustworthiness and benefit of being listened to are established, boys stay more emotionally open and connected. They are less likely to lose contact with their hearts.

The most common barriers to listening—a tendency to ask questions merely to get more information or to satisfy curiosity and taking their son's feelings personally—require committed practice to avoid. But the rewards for a boy when he can express himself without worrying about how his parent will react are huge. Gaining insight into how feelings influence thinking and behavior is the defining skill in emotional intelligence.

Above all, a parent should never respond to times when the son shares his feelings by giving advice. Being told how to think is a poor substitute for becoming better at thinking for himself, and it often feels disrespectful. Most boys, particularly as they get older, insist on the freedom to make up their own minds and are willing to sacrifice talking altogether to avoid being second-guessed or lectured.

Lesson 4: Exercise Authority

Boys' groups tend to separate themselves from adults, actively test the limits and power of adult rules, exert pressure on their members not to snitch, exclude and mistreat girls, and encourage members to turn to digital devices and substances to deal with suppressed feelings. Parents of boys will need to set limits and guide them away from the values of the peer culture. Unless the parent properly manages the times when the son acts out, he will have a harder time learning to restrain himself.

Three qualities are essential when holding a boy accountable: emotional acceptance, behavioral containment, and prosocial guidance.

Even as they draw a line to check their son's behavior, parents must not react negatively to the emotions that underlie and drive inappropriate behavior. Anger, for example: it is one thing to set a limit on how anger is expressed—it never makes sense to allow destructiveness, threats, or violence, and it is usually a good idea to limit disrespectful language—but it is another to condemn boys for showing anger.

When the feeling is disappointment—"You really let me down"—however tempting it is to explain, defend, or discount the boy's version of events, simply hearing out the feeling is often sufficient to clear things up and has the added benefit of reinforcing emotional release. Offering ourselves as containers for any and all painful feelings is the essential element in the role of parents as counselors. Limit setting is usually followed by an outpouring of hurt feelings and is the real point of the limit: helping a boy free himself from the tension driving his misbehavior.

When parents set a limit, it is a way to communicate that they see their son as a capable and moral person, able to rise above whatever hurts or stresses he feels in order to behave more appropriately. We saw the same phenomenon in our education research, when a boy's misbehavior did not confuse a teacher about who he was; so many boys were turned around when a teacher offered them a fresh slate after they had made a mistake. They realized that the teacher was not confused about what they were capable of and elevated their behavior to the expected level.

Without real conscious awareness, boys expect parents to stand firm against their aggressive or testing behaviors. But they expect their parents to do so in ways that do not compromise or weaken their connection or their sense of being accepted, difficulties and all. To strike the right balance, parents' exercise of authority must be strategic rather than reactive. Limits should always derive from a thoughtful consideration of the situation and willingness to listen to whatever upset may be causing the unreasonable behavior. Reactions that derive from parents' own upset tend to be inconsistent, unsustainable, and may inadvertently reinforce limit testing and forceful resistance.

Lesson 5: Promote Autonomy

The ideal of independence as a Lone Ranger–type isolation continues to be a powerful cultural image. But in healthy development, independence is less the goal than autonomy achieved through initiative, judgment, and confidence. To foster this end, parents must accompany their son through challenges without automatically taking over whenever he falters or makes a mistake. Rather, like a good coach, parents lend confidence and serve as safe receptacles for feelings of frustration or defeat as they arise.

In a counterintuitive way, autonomy actually emerges naturally in relationships rather than from pulling away or withdrawing. How ably parents manage both to stay connected to their sons and to be honest with them about important values and family needs may be the ultimate test of their ability to support their sons' independence. One young man I see has lobbied hard with his parents for permission to smoke weed: "Everybody else does it. You're so naïve and out of touch. There's nothing wrong with it." A recent ploy has been simply to go around them and sneak in hits late at night or down in the family basement.

But to their credit, his parents have not lost their cool. Even while they insist that his getting intoxicated does nothing good for him and reiterate that he cannot continue, they make sure to show that they love and respect him. Discussion has been tense at times, especially when the parents say they will restrict him if they discover he goes against their policy. But the son plainly believes they are thinking about his well-being, even if he does not agree with their stand, and seems willing to give them the benefit of the doubt. In submitting to their judgment, he does not look as though he is surrendering his own.

While compromise and negotiation are always necessary in any relationship, apparent conflicts often evaporate when respect, listening, and the release of tense feelings are encouraged. There's likely always to be a solution in every conflict once painful feelings are cleared away. To strike a healthy balance between maintaining connection and supporting their son's desire to spread his wings, parents usually have to review how their own need for autonomy was handled in their families—and how these experiences bear on their relationship with their son.

Just and Good Men

Critically, in the new, connected economy, boys and young men work alongside other people—all kinds of people—on teams. They live in relationships and households that are more democratic than any generation before and that reflect a deeper commitment to human rights for all. To be effective and productive, boys must embrace these new terms of exchange and the less hierarchical, less entitled positions they offer. Young men must recognize that justice and virtue are necessary for success. Even while the old tune that men are more important than women still plays, to make their way in the new world, millennial and Generation Z males must grasp that unearned privileges of gender, race, class, and so on do not confer just or worthwhile entitlements. How do parents help them get there?

One strategy is to "raise our sons more like our daughters," as

Gloria Steinem has put it, offering them a broader emotional palette. In a recent piece in *Vanity Fair* magazine, pundit Monica Lewinsky wrote about the "new frontiers of male vulnerability," citing Brad Pitt, Prince Harry, and Jay-Z as role models for "something different—something soulful, engaging, vulnerable, and even feminist." When Pitt came under fire from traditionalists who said he should simply "man up" for speaking about recovery from addiction and an appetite for personal reflection and growth, Le winsky defended him by pointing to the "sea change that has occurred over the past generation: to 'man up' and to be a 'real man' among young males now go hand in hand with expressing raw emotion, acknowledging flaws, opening up, facing consequences."[31]

New York Times pundit Claire Cain Miller offered a popular piece titled "How to Raise a Feminist Son." Defining a feminist as someone able to embrace full equality between men and women, she sought the counsel of experts and came up with a set of twelve recommendations that apply "to anyone who wants to raise children who are kind, confident, and free to pursue their dreams."[32]

To begin, she said, boys must be permitted to cry. Channeling all emotion into monochromatic outbursts of anger has far-reaching, negative consequences. Only when hearts and minds work together, when boys can be honest about what hurts, can they truly feel their connection to others. Built through evolution for empathy, when boys' natural expressiveness is disrupted, their virtue is diminished. The fix is simple, with profound consequences.

Other ideas were intended to pierce masculine myths. For example, she recommended providing role models to help boys see through stereotypes to the realities of being male. Another recommendation was to teach boys to take care of their own stuff rather than allowing household responsibilities to fall disproportionately on girls. Relatedly, she recommended that parents teach a boy to take care of others so that he learns as much about caregiving as girls do. She cited research conducted by a Canadian program,

Roots of Empathy, which has spread around the world due to its success preventing bullying and aggression.[33]

Boys should celebrate being boys, according to Cain Miller, who advises parents to "roughhouse, crack jokes, watch sports, climb trees, build campfires." But to combat limiting stereotypes, she recommends that boys also be taught the realities of "No," in order to manage their impulses, tolerate frustrations, and take a stand when others' rights are violated. Boys should be encouraged to read and they must be quickly corrected whenever they use "girl" as an insult. They should be educated about female lives and encouraged to have friendships with girls.

Another writer, Andrew Reiner, took the topic further in an article titled "Talking to Boys the Way We Talk to Girls." He cited a variety of studies of parent-child interactions that show how early and how thoroughly parents pass along traditional stereotypes to boys. In particular, studies of language and interactional styles show they are more vocal and emotionally expressive with daughters. According to Harvard psychologist Susan David, whom he interviewed, parents who want to correct this bias toward their sons can simply "show up for them. Get them talking. Show that you want to hear what they're saying."[34]

For psychologist Christia Spears Brown, there are two general things parents can do to raise sons "beyond pink and blue." Most importantly, they should challenge gender stereotypes: "Even though those stereotypes are hard to fight, I urge you to try to fight them anyway. I think it is a good fight and ultimately worth it. Individuals with both masculine and feminine traits (who are assertive, independent, nurturing, and empathetic) do better the rest of their lives."[35]

Moving to action, parents must make the concrete choice to combat stereotyping. Brown lists her own top action targets: she throws out clothing or toys that are stereotypical and censors entertainment options like TV programs or movies on the same basis;

she keeps close check on her own language, avoiding direct or indirect references to gender such as "pretty girl" or "big boy"; and she kindly but firmly interrupts her children when they use stereotypes.

But the commitment to raise good men must go further than avoiding stereotypes in language, toys, and media, actions that on their own are unlikely to strengthen virtue and permit humanity to flourish. Stanford University philosopher Eamonn Callan, who has studied citizenship, argues that "to be just . . . is necessarily to care about others."[36] The ability to care about others, to be affected by their common humanity, derives from a child's own experiences of care. Absent empathic connections, a child can be myopically obsessed with his own desires and desperately willing to do anything to satisfy them. A boy's experience of parental love lays the foundation for goodness. In the view of another philosopher, John Rawls, parents committed to shaping how a child treats others view "the forming of attachments as final ends."[37] A boy learns that justice is a fundamental right from his own experience in close relationships. Making sure that boys are cared for, that their need for connection is not overshadowed by their performance, is the essential foundation for good men.

As I read story after horrifying story of men so deluded in self-absorption and pumped up by "locker room" talk that they can mistreat their romantic partners—and forgo any chance of a loving connection with them—I am reminded of the critical finding that different kinds of masculine cultures breed varying levels of male sexual aggression. This research reminds us that patterns of male perpetration described in #MeToo stories do not arise spontaneously within boys themselves and are not a necessary ingredient in boyhood. No boy grows twisted and hurtful on his own.

To carry the movement for equality into the trenches, and to ensure that boys can embrace girls and women as partners with open hearts and full respect, parents and others who are in charge of boyhood must make sure that boys themselves are treated as human. We must look carefully to notice where boyhood distorts our sons' human development. Because, from the front lines, we can see that boys are quite ready and eager for the chance to experience the "full development of their capacities"—including love, creativity, and connection.

Campaign for Boys' Lives

When my grandson was born, I was taken off guard by how powerfully he claimed me as his. He gazed at me, sometimes for long moments, and searched my face, looking deeply into my eyes. When I talked to him, telling him how glad I was that he was here, I seemed to be speaking a language he understood, even though he himself did not have words yet. He took me in. A few months more into his life, he began to smile. When he arrived at our home, he heard the sound of my voice, peered intently until he located me, and burst into a radiant smile when our eyes met. A little later still, he would actually squirm with delight, his legs and arms swinging rapidly against his daddy's chest, when he saw me. I appreciated that this is what a child—boy or girl—is: wired to connect at the deepest, most enduring levels.

With the birth of my two sons, I saw that even superhero efforts could not protect them from the culture they swam in. I accepted the offer to become the consulting psychologist at a school for boys partly for their sakes. At least, I thought, they would see me stand on behalf of boys. Once on the job, I discovered great interest in boys' lives both in and outside of the school. I created the program for boys that grew into the Center for the Study of Boys' and Girls' Lives in response to this need. Over the years, we have expanded the work, conducting research and undertaking advocacy in partnership with global organizations such as the International Boys' Schools Coalition, Boy Scouts of America, Boys & Girls Clubs of America, and Promundo, the gender justice organization.

In the course of this work, I have visited schools and communities around the world and heard conversations about boys that are remarkably similar everywhere. Globally, I realize, families, educators, and youth leaders are searching for sounder ideas to guide their care. Despite the culture wars and its backlash, there are cries for clarity and leadership wherever adults work in the trenches with boys—at a nongovernmental organization (NGO) in Nairobi, Kenya; a boys' school in Pietermaritzburg, South Africa; a workshop for Catholic school leaders in Dublin, Ireland; and everywhere I travel in Canada and the United States.

As the world has flattened and become more tightly bound by financial and communication ties, the paradigm for being male has become more homogeneous. Globalization has exported the dominant themes of traditional Western boyhood worldwide. Even as its unworkability becomes more and more apparent and many boys are in revolt, these ideas are stubbornly embedded in family norms and the culture of institutions. It will require concerted effort, a campaign, to uproot them. For my grandson's sake, for a boyhood he can inhabit with an open heart, I write in hopes that parents and others who care will join together in common resistance.

What would a Campaign for Boys' Lives look like? First, it would uphold the fundamental worth and integrity of boys. Bringing together researchers, thought leaders, policy makers, and activists, it would paint a grounded picture of boys' actual experience—distinct from stereotyped and clichéd images—and view their lives through an ethical lens. The campaign would seek not only to interrupt the unconscionable sacrifices imposed upon boys but also to promote sounder, healthier, and ultimately more effective practices in schools, families, and communities. The goal is that boys—boys of all kinds—flourish. A just society cannot permit systematic developmental losses by any group. It is critical that boys—and the men that they become—find our warmest understanding and proudest embrace.

There are inspiring innovations well under way. In Great Britain, the Healthy Minds experiment has been so successful that it has strained resources. Nearly a million people a year have been attracted by the offer of free mental health counseling, and, overall, the number of adults in England who have recently received services has increased from one in four to one in three. The program has gone a long way to erode the stigma of talking about problems in a nation culturally steeped in stoicism. Begun in 2008 from collaboration between a psychologist and an economist, initial funding allowed the program to set up thirty-five clinics across the country. Funding continued to grow to a current budget of $500 million, which will double over the next few years.[38]

In Australia, as in other parts of the world, concern about suicide has become focused on men's difficulties asking for help when they are troubled. Three-quarters of suicides are male, and suicide rates there have reached new highs. A "national suicide emergency" has been declared. In response, a new campaign, Our Toughest Challenge Yet, has been launched by the crisis support organization Lifeline, to promote men's asking for help as an act of courage. For younger men, a Father's Campaign has also been devised by the Headspace project of the National Youth Mental Health Foundation, encouraging fathers not to leave observations they make about their son's mental health unspoken and to intervene if they notice that he has become overwhelmed.[39]

The World Health Organization produced a summary of effective approaches to men and boys. To successfully engage them, programs must "enhance boys' and men's lives." Promundo works from that principle to develop research-based programs, including

Program H for young men aged fifteen to twenty-four. Launched in 2002 and now in twenty-five countries, the curriculum encourages young men to reflect on how rigid norms affect them. Program H, renamed Manhood 2.0 in its US version, has been identified as a best practice in promoting gender equality and preventing gender-based violence by the World Bank and the World Health Organization, and has been cited by UNICEF and the United Nations for its demonstrated effectiveness.[40]

In families, classrooms, on athletic fields, and in communities, those in charge of boyhood have daily opportunities to make a difference for boys. Boys clamor to be themselves and reliably take advantage of every opportunity that is offered. What has slowed the project of human liberation is not some deficiency of male nature, nor is it boys' appetite for privilege at the expense of others. What converts a naturally empathic boy to a hard, emotionally distant, and selfish individual is denying him the connections he needs to stay human and accountable. Holding boys in relationships where they are known and loved is the best way to build good men.

ACKNOWLEDGMENTS

In writing this book, I have tried to channel all of the boys, men, and women who taught me what I know. Many represent themselves in the book itself—their ideas and work, their voices and stories. But beyond this particular book project, there are even more, inspiring and supporting me as I developed the perspective underlying what I have written.

There are the gender, race, human development, and boyhood scholars who welcomed me to their community and offered me their time, fellowship, and challenge. I was first introduced to this community by Michelle Fine and the inimitable Harry Brod, whose passing only clarifies his influence. Michael Kimmel, Niobe Way, Pedro Noguera, Gary Barker, Michael Kaufman, and many more continue to provide me with the warmest of intellectual homes.

The International Coalition of Boys' Schools encouraged my work by offering grants, discerning ears, and open arms. My friend and coauthor, Richard Hawley, of course, but also Brad Adams, Joe Cox, David Armstrong, and many others have been invaluable thought partners. As I have met with teachers at member schools around the world, I have always found keen interest, thoughtful challenge, and open welcome. At the same time, leaders at the Haverford School like Bo Dixon, Joe Healey, Joe Cox, John Nagl, Matt Green, and Janet Heed also encouraged me at every turn, urging me to "take care of our boys." And at my own Center, which grew out of the work at Haverford, my partner, Peter Kuriloff, has dedicated an outsize portion of his brilliant career to our project. Others, including Sharon Ravitch, Brett Stoudt, Joseph Nelson, Charlotte Jacobs, and our wonderful member school Heads have cocreated the Center to help hundreds of boys and girls give voice to the realities of gender socialization.

At an even more basic level, I have been blessed to participate in the community of cocounselors who helped me achieve a robust and reassuring understanding of who I am. Rooted in an abiding faith in human goodness, the collective work of friends like Tim Jackins, Patty Wipfler, Diane Balser, Gwen Brown, Joel Nogic, Joanne Bray, and Lorenzo Garcia has pushed me to recognize how radically things must change for boys and for the world around them. My team at RCCR has held me even as I bluster and thrash.

I must acknowledge the thousands of boys I have spoken with and observed, always forthcoming, whose insights drove my understanding deeper and deeper. I have heard horrifying accounts of male behavior that taught me how off course human development can skew when conditions withhold necessary nurture and incentivize callous excess. I have also heard uplifting stories of goodness, power, warmth, and service that far outweigh these tragic losses.

A wonderful editorial team (mostly parents of boys themselves)— including John Paine, who directed me to Joelle Delbourgo, the epitome of a publishing professional, who in turn led me to Sara Carder and her SWAT team at TarcherPerigee—has guided me through the daunting process of producing this book.

NOTES

༝

CHAPTER 1 | CONFINED BY BOYHOOD

1. Michael Kaufman, "Men, Feminism, and Men's Contradictory Experiences of Power," in *Theorizing Masculinities,* ed. H. Brod and M. Kaufman (Thousand Oaks, CA: Sage, 1994), 142–64.

2. William Pollack, "No Man Is an Island: Toward a New Psychoanalytic Psychology of Men," in *A New Psychology of Men,* ed. R. F. Levant and W. S. Pollack (New York: Basic Books, 1995), 33–67.

3. Christina Hoff Somers, *The War Against Boys: How Misguided Policies Are Harming Our Young Men* (New York, Simon & Schuster, 2015); Peg Tyre, *The Trouble with Boys: A Surprising Report Card on Our Sons, Their Problems at School, and What Parents and Educators Must Do* (New York: Harmony, 2009).

4. Judith Kleinfeld, "Student Performance: Males Versus Females," *Public Interest* 134 (1999): 3–20; Tom Mortenson, "Economic Change Effects on Men and Implications for the Education of Boys," *Education Week*, May 14, 2011, www.edweek.org /media/economicchange-32boys.pdf.

5. Caroline New, "Oppressed and Oppressors? The Systematic Mistreatment of Men," *Sociology* 35, no. 3 (2001): 729–48.

6. Judy Y. Chu, *When Boys Become "Boys": Development, Relationships, and Masculinity* (New York: New York University Press), 202.

7. Niobe Way, *Deep Secrets: Boys' Friendships and the Crisis of Connection* (Boston, MA: Harvard University Press, 2011).

8. David B. Stein, *Unraveling the ADD/ADHD Fiasco: Successful Parenting Without Drugs* (Kansas City, MO: Andrews McMeel, 2003).

9. Mariagiovanna Baccara et al., *"Child-Adoption Matching: Preferences for Gender and Race"* (working paper 16444, National Bureau of Economic Research, Cambridge, MA, 2010), www.nber.org/people/mariagiovanna_baccara.

10. Justin Baldoni, "What My Newborn Son Taught Me About Masculinity," *Huffington Post*, March 1, 2018, www .huffingtonpost.com/entry/opinion-baldoni-masculinity -fatherhood_us_5a944e25e4b02cb368c46d6d.

11. George Orwell, *Shooting an Elephant and Other Essays* (New York: Harcourt, 1984).

12. Brian Heilman, Gary Barker, and Alexander Harrison, *The Man Box: A Study on Being a Young Man in the US, UK, and Mexico* (Washington, DC: Promundo-US, 2017), 60, https:// promundoglobal.org/resources/man-box-study-young-man -us-uk-mexico/?lang=english.

13. Sandra L. Bem, "Gender Schema Theory: A Cognitive Account of Sex Typing Source," *Psychological Review* 88, no. 4 (1981): 354; Olga Silverstein and Beth Rashbaum, *The Courage to Raise Good Men: You Don't Have to Sever the Bond with Your Son to Help Him Become a Man* (New York: Penguin, 1995).

14. Kate Stone Lombardi, *The Mama's Boy Myth* (New York: Penguin, 2012).

15. Heilman, Barker, and Harrison, *The Man Box.*

16. Chu, *When Boys Become "Boys,"* 206–7.

17. Ruth Perou et al., "Mental Health Surveillance Among Children—United States 2005–2011," *Morbidity and Mortality Weekly Report (MMWR)* 62, no. 2 (May 17, 2013): 1–35, www.cdc.gov/mmwr/preview/mmwrhtml/su6202a1.htm; L. Alan Sroufe, "Ritalin Gone Wrong," Opinion, *New York Times* online, January 28, 2012, www.nytimes.com/2012/01/29 /opinion/sunday/childrens-add-drugs-dont-work-long-term.html.

18. David D. Gilmore, *Misogyny, the Male Malady* (Philadelphia: University of Pennsylvania Press, 2001), 203.

19. Martha Nussbaum, *Creating Capabilities: The Human Development Approach* (Cambridge, MA: Belknap Press, 2013).

20. Way, *Deep Secrets*, 77.

21. Amy Banks, *Wired to Connect: The Surprising Link Between Brain Science and Strong, Healthy Relationships* (New York: Tarcher/Penguin, 2015).

22. Donald O. Hebb, *The Organization of Behavior* (New York: Wiley & Sons, 1949); Daniel J. Siegel and Mary Hartzell, *Parenting from the Inside Out: How a Deeper Self-Understanding Can Help You Raise Children Who Thrive* (New York: Tarcher/Penguin, 2003), 34.

23. Daniel J. Siegel. *The Developing Mind: How Relationships and the Brain Interact to Shape Who We Are* (New York: Guilford Press, 1999), xii.

24. Alison Gopnik, *The Gardener and the Carpenter: What the New Science of Child Development Tells Us About the Relationship Between Parents and Children* (New York: Farrar, Straus and Giroux, 2016), 18.

25. Ibid., 9.

26. Ibid., 10.

27. Ibid., 56.

28. William J. Bennett, *The Book of Virtues: A Treasury of Great Moral Stories* (New York: Simon & Schuster, 1993); Josephson Institute, accessed August 25, 2017 at https://charactercounts.org/program-overview/six-pillars.

29. Ibid., 59.

30. Nel Noddings, *Educating Moral People: A Caring Alternative to Character Education* (New York: Teachers College Press, 2002), xiii.

31. Ibid., 15.

32. Ibid., 32.

CHAPTER 2 | FREEING BOYS

1. Chu, *When Boys Become "Boys,"* 21.

2. Ibid., 24.

3. Ibid., 33.

4. Ibid., 205.

5. Miriam Raider-Roth et al., "Resisting Boys, Resisting Teachers,"

in special double issue, *Reproduction, Resistance and Hope: The Promise of Schooling for Boys,* ed. Michael C. Reichert and Joseph D. Nelson of *THYMOS: Journal of Boyhood Studies* 6, no. 1 (Spring 2012): 34–54.

6. Ibid.

7. Ibid.

8. Diana Divecha, "What Is Secure Attachment? And Why Doesn't 'Attachment Parenting' Get You There?," *Developmental Science* (blog), April 3, 2017, www.developmentalscience.com.

9. Allan Schore, "Modern Attachment Theory," in *Handbook of Trauma Psychology,* ed. Steven N. Gold (Washington, DC: American Psychological Association, 2017), 6.

10. Michael P. Nichols, *The Lost Art of Listening: How Learning to Listen Can Improve Relationships* (New York: Guilford Press, 2009), 15.

11. Ibid., 26.

12. Siegel and Hartzell, *Parenting from the Inside Out,* 34.

13. Nichols, *Lost Art of Listening,* 139.

14. Siegel and Hartzell, *Parenting from the Inside Out,* 154–83.

15. Ibid., 23.

16. Ibid., 193.

17. Patty Wipfler and Tosha Schore, *Listen: Five Simple Tools to Meet Your Everyday Parenting Challenges* (Palo Alto, CA: Hand in Hand Parenting, 2016), 326.

18. Ibid., 50.

CHAPTER 3 | BOYS AND THEIR HEARTS

1. Heilman, Barker, and Harrison, *The Man Box*, 36.

2. Kevin Love, "Everyone Is Going Through Something," *Players' Tribune,* last modified March 6, 2018, www.theplayerstribune.com /en-us/articles/kevin-love-everyone-is-going-through-something.

3. Jean M. Twenge, *iGen: Why Today's Super-Connected Kids Are Growing Up Less Rebellious, More Tolerant, Less Happy—and Completely Unprepared for Adulthood* (New York: Atria Books, 2017), 93.

4. Ibid., 103–4.

5. "5 Minute Guide to Men's Mental Health," Mental Health America online, accessed April 10, 2018, www.mentalhealthamerica.net /issues/infographic-mens-mental-health-5-minute-guide.

6. Ronald F. Levant and Wizdom A. Powell, "The Gender Role Strain Paradigm," in *The Psychology of Men and Masculinities,* ed. Ronald F. Levant and Y. Joel Wong (Washington, DC: American Psychological Association, 2017), 15–44.

7. James M. O'Neil, *Men's Gender Role Conflict: Psychological Costs, Consequences, and an Agenda for Change* (Washington, DC: American Psychological Association, 2015), 24.

8. Stephanie A. Shields, *Speaking from the Heart: Gender and the Social Meaning of Emotion* (Cambridge: Cambridge University Press, 2002), 93.

9. Arlie R. Hochschild, *The Managed Heart* (Berkeley: University of California Press, 1983).

10. Thomas Newkirk, "Misreading Masculinity: Speculations on the Great Gender Gap in Writing," *Language Arts* 77, no. 4 (March 2000): 294–300, www.csun.edu/~bashforth/305_PDF

/305_ME2/305_Language&Gender/MisredaingMasculinity
_GenderGapInWriting_LA2000.pdf.

11. Pollack, "No Man Is an Island," 195.

12. O'Neil, *Men's Gender Role Conflict*, 10.

13. Maurice J. Elias et al., *Promoting Social and Emotional Learning: Guidelines for Educators* (Alexandria, VA: Association for Supervision and Curriculum Development, 1997), 2.

14. Joseph A. Durlak et al., "The Impact of Enhancing Students' Social and Emotional Learning: A Meta-analysis of School-based Universal Interventions, *Child Development* 82, no. 1 (January/February 2011): 405–32, https://doi: 10.1111/j.1467-8624.2010.01564.x.

15. *2015 CASEL Guide: Effective Social and Emotional Learning Programs* (Chicago: Collaborative for Academic, Social, and Emotional Learning [CASEL], June 2015), https: //secondaryguide.casel.org/casel-secondary-guide.pdf.

16. Marc A. Brackett and Susan E. Rivers, "Transforming Students' Lives with Social and Emotional Learning," in *International Handbook of Emotions in Education,* ed. Reinhard Pekrun and Lisa Linnenbrink-Garcia (New York: Routledge, 2014); Rafael Heller, "On the Science and Teaching of Emotional Intelligence: An Interview with Marc Brackett," *Phi De Ha Kappan* 98, no. 6 (March 2017): 22.

17. Richard D. Lane and Branka Zei Pollermann, "Complexity of Emotional Representations," in *The Wisdom of Feelings,* ed. Lisa Feldman Barrett and Peter Salovey (New York: Guilford Press, 2002), 271–293.

18. Steven Krugman, "Male Development and the Transformation of Shame," in *A New Psychology of Men*, Ronald F. Levant and William S. Pollack (New York: Basic Books, 1995), 93.

19. Ibid., 93.

20. Ibid., 103.

21. William Pollack, *Real Boys: Rescuing Our Sons from the Myths of Boyhood* (New York: Random House, 1998), 27.

22. Shields, *Speaking from the Heart*, 140.

23. Ibid., 141.

24. Megan Boler, *Feeling Power: Emotions and Education* (New York: Routledge, 1999), 192.

25. Michael Kimmel, *Angry White Men: American Masculinity at the End of an Era* (New York: Nation Books, 2017).

26. Dan Kindlon and Michael Thompson, *Raising Cain: Protecting the Emotional Life of Boys* (New York: Ballantine Books, 2000).

CHAPTER 4 | BOYS' LEARNING AND SCHOOLING

1. Michele Cohen, "'A Habit of Healthy Idleness': Boys' Underachievement in Historical Perspective," in *Failing Boys? Issues in Gender and Achievement*, ed. D. Epstein et al. (Philadelphia: Open University Press, 1998), 20.

2. "The Weaker Sex: Boys Are Being Outclassed by Girls at Both School and University," *Economist* online, March 7, 2015, www.economist.com/news/international/21645759-boys-are -being-outclassed-girls-both-school-and-university-and-gap.

3. *The ABC of Gender Equality in Education: Aptitude, Behaviour, Confidence* (Paris: Organization for Economic Co-operation and

Development [OECD], 2015, https://docs.google.com
/viewer?url=http%3A%2F%2Fwww.oecd.org%2Fpisa
%2Fkeyfindings%2Fpisa-2012-results-gender-eng.pdf.

4.   Thomas A. DiPrete and Claudia Buchmann, *The Rise of Women: The Growing Gender Gap in Education and What It Means for American Schools* (New York: Russell Sage Foundation, 2013).

5.   David Autor et al., *"Family Disadvantage and the Gender Gap in Behavioral and Educational Outcomes"* (working paper 22267, National Bureau of Economic Research, Cambridge, MA, last modified 2017), http://www.nber.org/papers/w22267.

6.   Hua-Yu Sebastian Cherng, "The Ties That Bind: Teacher Relationships, Academic Expectations, and Racial/Ethnic and Generational Inequality," *American Journal of Education* 124, no. 1 (2017): 67–100.

7.   *ABC of Gender Equality in Education*, 53.

8.   Ibid.

9.   Thomas Mortenson, "Economic Change Effects on Men and Implications for the Education of Boys," p. 1, https://www
.edweek.org/media/economicchange-32boys.pdf.

10.   Debbie Epstein et al., eds., *Failing Boys? Issues in Gender and Achievement* (Philadelphia: Open University Press, 1998).

11.   Newkirk, "Misreading Masculinity," 294–300.

12.   Becky Francis and Christine Skelton, *Reassessing Gender and Achievement: Questioning Contemporary Key Debates* (Abington, UK: Routledge, 2005), 9.

13.   Charles Bingham and Alexander M. Sidorkin, *No Education Without Relation* (New York: Peter Lang, 2004), 4.

14. *PISA 2009 Results: What Makes a School Successful? Resources, Policies and Practices,* vol. 4 (Paris: OECD, 2010), https://dx.doi .org/10.1787/9789264091559-en; Debora L. Roorda et al., "The Influence of Affective Teacher-Student Relationships on Students' School Engagement and Achievement," *Review of Educational Research* 81, no. 4 (2011): 493–529.

15. Sara Rimm-Kaufman and Lia Sandilos, "Improving Students' Relationships with Teachers to Provide Essential Supports for Learning," American Psychological Association online, accessed January 15, 2018, www.apa.org/education/k12/relationships.aspx.

16. Sally Weale, "Teachers Must Ditch 'Neuromyth' of Learning Styles, Say Scientists," *Guardian* (US edition) online, last modified March 12, 2017, www.theguardian.com /education/2017/mar/13/teachers-neuromyth-learning-styles -scientists-neuroscience-education.

17. Michael C. Reichert and Richard Hawley, *Reaching Boys, Teaching Boys* (San Francisco: Jossey-Bass/Wiley, 2010); Reichert and Hawley, *I Can Learn From You: Boys as Relational Learners* (Cambridge, MA: Harvard Educational Press, 2014).

18. Ibid., 191.

19. David Hawkins, "I, Thou, and It," in *The Informed Vision: Essays on Learning and Human Nature* (New York, NY: Agathon Press, 1974), 56.

20. Daniel Rogers, "The Working Alliance in Teaching and Learning: Theoretical Clarity and Research Implications," *International Journal for the Scholarship of Teaching and Learning* 3, no. 2 (2009), https://doi.org/10.20429/ijsotl.2009.030228.

21. Tamara Bibby, *Education: An "Impossible" Profession? Psychoanalytic Explorations of Learning and Classrooms* (London: Routledge, 2011), 37.

22. Andy Hargreaves, "The Emotional Practice of Teaching," *Teaching and Teacher Education* 14, no. 8, (1998): 835–54.

23. Miriam Raider-Roth, *Trusting What You Know: The High Stakes of Classroom Relationships* (San Francisco: Jossey-Bass, 2005), 157.

CHAPTER 5 | BROTHERHOOD AND BOYS' CLUBS

1. Lisa Selin Davis, "My Daughter Is Not Transgender. She's a Tomboy," *New York Times* online, April 18, 2017, www.nytimes.com/2017/04/18/opinion/my-daughter-is-not-transgender-shes-a-tomboy.html?_r=0.

2. Harry Stack Sullivan, *The Interpersonal Theory of Psychiatry* (New York: Norton, 1953).

3. Jane E. Brody, "The Surprising Effects of Loneliness on Health," *New York Times* online, December 11, 2017, www.nytimes.com/2017/12/11/well/mind/how-loneliness-affects-our-health.html.

4. Hara Estroff Marano, "The Dangers of Loneliness," *Psychology Today* online, last modified June 9, 2016, www.psychologytoday.com/us/articles/200307/the-dangers-loneliness.

5. Way, *Deep Secrets*, 2.

6. Brett McKay and Kate McKay, "The History and Nature of Male Friendships," The Art of Manliness (blog), August 24, 2008, www.artofmanliness.com/2008/08/24/the-history-and-nature-of-man-friendships.

7. Judy Y. Chu, "A Relational Perspective on Adolescent Boys' Identity Development," in *Adolescent Boys: Exploring Diverse*

Cultures of Boyhood, ed. Niobe Way and Judy Y. Chu (New York: New York University Press, 2004), 85.

8. Ibid., 95.

9. Way, *Deep Secrets,* 171.

10. Ibid., 1.

11. Gregory Lehne, "Homophobia Among Men: Supporting and Defining the Male Role," in *Men's Lives,* eds. Michael Kimmel and Michael Messner (New York: Macmillan, 1989), 422.

12. Eric Anderson, *Inclusive Masculinity: The Changing Nature of Masculinities* (New York: Routledge, 2009), 7.

13. Ibid., 7.

14. Way, *Deep Secrets,* 222.

15. Ibid., 20.

16. Ibid., 263.

17. Barrie Thorne, *Gender Play: Girls and Boys in School* (New Brunswick, NJ: Rutgers University Press, 1994), 47.

18. Ehrmann, *InSideOut Coaching,* 141.

19. Ibid., 246.

20. Lionel Howard, "Performing Masculinity: Adolescent African American Boys' Response to Gender Scripting," *THYMOS: Journal of Boyhood Studies* 6, no. 1 (Spring 2012) (eds. Reichert and Nelson): 97–115.

21. Joseph Derrick Nelson, "Transformative Brotherhood: Black Boys' Identity in a Single-Sex School for Boys of Color" (unpublished dissertation, City University of New York, 2013).

22. Peggy Reeves Sanday, "Rape-Prone versus Rape-Free Campus Cultures," *Violence Against Women* 2, no. 2 (June 1996): 191–208.

23. Neil M. Malamuth, "Rape Proclivity Among Males," *Journal of Social Issues* 37, no. 4 (1981): 139–57.

24. John Hechinger, "Get the Keg out of the Frat House," *New York Times* online, September 26, 2017, www.nytimes.com /2017/09/26/opinion/frats-college-partying-pledging.html.

25. Jessica Bennett, "The Problem with Fraternities Isn't Just Rape: It's Power," *Time* online, last modified December 3, 2014, http:// time.com/3616158/fraternity-rape-uva-rolling-stone-sexual -assault.

26. Way, *Deep Secrets*, 122.

27. Siegel, *Developing Mind*, 77–83.

28. William Bukowski, Andrew F. Newcomb, and Willard W. Hartrup, "Friendship and Its Significance in Childhood and Adolescence: Introduction and Comment" in *The Company They Keep: Friendships in Childhood and Adolescence* (Cambridge, UK: Cambridge University Press, 1998), 1–18.

CHAPTER 6 | LOVE, SEX, AND AFFECTION

1. Levant and Powell, "Gender Role Strain Paradigm," 15–44.

2. Amy Schalet, "Why Boys Need to Have Conversations About Emotional Intimacy in Classrooms," The Conversation, last modified June 12, 2017, http://theconversation.com/why-boys -need-to-have-conversations-about-emotional-intimacy-in -classrooms-54693.

3. Ibid., 1.

4. "A Young Man's Guide to Masturbation: Questions and Answers About the Most Common and Least Talked-about Sexual Practices," HealthyStrokes.com, accessed September 1, 2017, www.healthystrokes.com/YMG.pdf.

5. Philip Zimbardo and Nikita Coulombe, *Man Interrupted: Why Young Men Are Struggling and What We Can Do About It* (Newburyport, MA: Conari Press, 2016), xviii.

6. Michael Sadowski, "From Adolescent Boys to Queer Young Men: Support for and Silencing of Queer Voice in Schools, Families, and Communities," *THYMOS: Journal of Boyhood Studies* 6, no. 1 (Spring 2012) (eds. Reichert and Nelson): 76–96.

7. 9. Ritch C. Savin-Williams, "Why 'Mostly Straight' Men Are a Distinct Sexual Identity," *Time* online, last modified November 20, 2017, http://time.com/5026092/mostly-straight-sexual-identity-bisexual-gay.

8. Ross Douthat, "Let's Ban Porn," *New York Times* online, February 10, 2018, www.nytimes.com/2018/02/10/opinion/Sunday/lets-ban-porn.html.

9. Sam Louie, "Involuntary Celibacy: The Sexual Frustrations of 'Incels,'" *Minority Report* (blog), *Psychology Today* online, last modified June 21, 2017, www.psychologytoday.com/us/blog/minority-report/201706/involuntary-celibacy accessed on April 26, 2018, at http://www.samlouiemft.com/2017/06/4225/.

10. Leanna Allen Boufford, "Exploring the Utility of Entitlement in Understanding Sexual Aggression," *Journal of Criminal Justice* 38, no. 5 (September/October 2010): 870–79, https://doi.org/10.1016/j.jcrimjus.2010.06.002.

11. Brian Heilman, Gary Barker, and Alexander Harrison, *The Man Box: A Study on Being a Young Man in the US, UK, and Mexico* (2017).

12. Kathleen A. Bogle, *Hooking Up: Sex, Dating and Relationships on Campus* (New York: New York University Press, 2008).

13. Justin R. Garcia et al., "Sexual Hookup Culture: A Review," *Review of General Psychology* 16, no. 2 (2012): 161.

14. Ibid., 163–64.

15. Ibid., 167.

16. Ibid., 168.

17. Ibid., 170.

18. Jennifer Shukusky and T. Joel Wade, "Sex Differences in Hookup Behavior: A Replication and Examination of Parent-Child Relationship Quality," *Journal of Social, Evolutionary and Cultural Psychology* 6, no. 4 (2012): 502.

19. Garcia et al., "Sexual Hookup Culture," 167.

20. Jean M. Twenge, Ryne A. Sherman, and Brooke E. Wells, "Declines in Sexual Frequency Among American Adults, 1989–2014," *Archives of Sexual Behavior* 46, no. 8 (November 2017): 2389–2401.

21. Kaitlin Lounsbury, Kimberly J. Mitchell, and David Finkelhor, *The True Prevalence of Sexting* (Durham, NH: Crimes Against Children Research Center, 2011), 1.

22. *Sex and Tech: Results From a Survey of Teens and Young Adults* (Washington, DC: National Campaign to Prevent Teen and Unplanned Pregnancy and CosmoGirl.com, 2008), www.drvc.org/pdf/protecting_children/sextech_summary.pdf.

23. Amanda Lenhart, "Teens and Sexting", Pew Research Center online (December 15, 2009), www.pewinternet.org/files/old -media/Files/Reports/2009/PIP_Teens_and_Sexting.pdf.

24. Sheri Madigan and Jeff Temple, "1 in 7 Teens Are Sexting, New Research Finds," *CBS News* online, last modified February 26, 2018, www.cbsnews.com/news/one-in-seven-teens-are-sexting -new-research-finds.

25. Lounsbury, Mitchell, and Finkelhor, *True Prevalence of Sexting*, 4.

26. David Cantor et al., *Report on the AAU Campus Climate Survey on Sexual Assault and Sexual Misconduct* (Rockville, MD: Westat and the University of Pennsylvania, September 21, 2015), www.upenn.edu/ir/surveys/AAU/Report%20and%20Tables%20 on%20AAU%20Campus%20Climate%20Survey.pdf.

27. Peggy Orenstein, "How to be a Man in the Age of Trump," *New York Times* online, October 15, 2016, www.nytimes.com /2016/10/16/opinion/sunday/how-to-be-a-man-in-the-age -of-trump.html?_r=0.

28. Sarah K. Murnen, Carrie Wright, and Gretchen Kaluzny, "If 'Boys Will Be Boys,' Then Girls Will Be Victims? A Meta-analytic Review of the Research That Relates Masculine Ideology to Sexual Aggression," *Sex Roles: A Journal of Research* 46, nos. 11/12 (June 2002): 359–72.

29. Michael Kimmel, "A Recipe for Sexual Assault," *Atlantic* online, August 24, 2015, www.theatlantic.com/education /archive/2015/08/what-makes-a-campus-rape-prone/402065.

30. Peggy C. Giordano, Wendy D. Manning, and Monica A. Longmore, "Affairs of the Heart: Qualities of Adolescent Romantic Relationships and Sexual Behavior," *Journal of Research on Adolescence* 20, no. 4 (December 2010): 983–1013.

31.   Peter Glick and Susan T. Fiske, "Hostile and Benevolent Sexism: Measuring Ambivalent Sexist Attitudes Towards Women," *Psychology of Women Quarterly* 21, no. 1 (March 1, 1997): 119–35.

CHAPTER 7 | BOYS AND THEIR BODIES— SPORTS AND HEALTH

1.   Raewyn Connell, *Gender in World Perspective* (Cambridge, UK: Polity, 2009), 60.

2.   Janet S. Hyde, "The Gender Similarities Hypothesis," *American Psychologist* 60, no. 6 (September 2005): 581–92.

3.   Raewyn Connell, *Gender and Power: Society, the Person and Sexual Politics* (Cambridge, UK: Polity, 1987), 170.

4.   Connell, *Gender in World Perspective*, 56–57.

5.   Will Courtenay, "Theorizing Masculinity and Men's Health," in *Men's Health: Body, Identity, and Social Context,* ed. Alex Broom and Philip Tovey (Chichester, UK: Wiley-Blackwell, 2009), 15.

6.   *EHS Today* staff, "NHTSA Targets Young Males in Seat Belt Safety Campaign," *EHS Today,* May 21, 2018, www.ehstoday .com/safety/nhtsa-targets-young-males-seat-belt-safety-campaign.

7.   Laura J. Viens et al., "Human Papillomavirus-Associated Cancers—United States, 2008–2012," *Morbidity and Mortality Weekly Report (MMWR)* 65, no. 26 (July 8, 2016): 661–66.

8.   Jacinta Bowler, "The HPV Vaccine Has Cut Infections By up to 90% in the Past 10 Years," Science Alert, last modified August 29, 2016, www.sciencealert.com/the-hpv-vaccine-has-halved -cervical-cancer-rates-in-the-past-10-years.

9. Lilly Berkley, "Young Guys May Think Preventing HPV Is 'Women's Work,'" *Futurity,* last modified December 2, 2016, www.futurity.org/hpv-vaccine-men-1308052-2.

10. E. U. Patel et al., "Increases in Human Papillomavirus Vaccination Among Adolescent and Young Adult Males in the United States, 2011–2016," *Journal of Infectious Diseases* 218, no. 1 (June 5, 2018): 109–13.

11. David L. Bell, David J. Breeland, and Mary A. Ott, "Adolescent and Young Male Health: A Review," *Pediatrics* 132, no. 3 (September 2013): 537.

12. Sabrina Tavernise, "Young Adolescents as Likely to Die from Suicide as from Traffic Accidents," *New York Times* online, November 3, 2016, www.nytimes.com/2016/11/04/health /suicide-adolescents-traffic-deaths.html?_r=0.

13. Pam Harrison, "Pediatric ADHD Accounts for 6 Million Physician Visits Annually," *Medscape,* last modified March 28, 2017, www .medscape.com/viewarticle/877849; Sroufe, "Ritalin Gone Wrong."

14. Gary Barker, *What About Boys? A Literature Review on the Health and Development of Adolescent Boys* (Geneva, Switzerland: World Health Organization, 2000).

15. Michael Kimmel, *Manhood in America* (New York: Free Press, 1996), 120.

16. David Whitson, "Sport in the Social Construction of Masculinity," in *Sport, Men and the Gender Order,* eds. Michael A. Messner and Donald F. Sabo (Champaign, IL: Human Kinetics Books, 1990), 23.

17. Don Sabo, "Sports Injury, the Pain Principle, and the Promise of Reform," *Journal of Intercollegiate Sport* 2, no. 1 (June 2009): 145–52.

18. Maya Dusenbery and Jaeah Lee, "Charts: The State of Women's Athletics, 40 Years After Title IX," *Mother Jones* online, last modified June 22, 2012, www.motherjones.com /politics/2012/06/charts-womens-athletics-title-nine-ncaa.

19. Joanna L. Grossman and Deborah L. Brake, "The Big 4-0: Title IX Puts a Fourth Decade Under Its Belt," *Verdict* (blog), Justia, June 26, 2012, https://verdict.justia.com/2012/06/26/the-big-4–0.

20. Whitson, "Sport in the Social Construction," 26.

21. Eric Anderson, "Orthodox and Inclusive Masculinity: Competing Masculinities Among Heterosexual Men in a Feminized Terrain," *Sociological Perspectives* 48, no. 3 (2005): 337–55.

22. Paul Langhorst, "Youth Sports Participation Statistics and Trends," *Engage Sports Blog,* March 8, 2016, www.engagesports.com/blog /post/1488/youth-sports-participation-statistics-and-trends.

23. Jonathan Drennan, "Rugby's Decline Continuing Apace in an Apathetic Australia," *Irish Times* online, last modified December 8, 2016, www.irishtimes.com/sport/rugby/international/rugby -s-decline-continuing-apace-in-an-apathetic-australia-1.2898261.

24. Michael Atkinson and Michael Kehler, "Boys, Bullying, and Biopedagogies in Physical Education," in *THYMOS: Journal of Boyhood Studies* 6, no. 1 (Spring 2012) (ed. Reichert and Nelson): 181.

25. US Centers for Disease Control and Prevention online, "A Fact Sheet for Youth Sports Parents: Heads Up Concussion," last modified December 2015, https://docs.google.com /viewer?url=https%3A%2F%2Fwww.cdc.gov%2Fheadsup %2Fpdfs%2Fyouthsports%2Fparents_eng.pdf.

26. Alan L. Zhang et al., "The Rise of Concussions in the Adolescent Population," *Orthopaedic Journal of Sports*

Medicine 4, no. 8 (August 1, 2016): http://journals.sagepub.com /doi/10.1177/2325967116662458.

27. Ben Rains, "Study Shows Concussions up 500% in Youth Sports," *Sports Illustrated* online, last modified July 13, 2016, www.si.com /tech-media/2016/07/13/concussions-youth-sports-rising-nfl.

28. John W. Powell, "Cerebral Concussion: Causes, Effects, and Risks in Sports," *Journal of Athletic Training* 36, no. 3 (July– September 2001): 307–311.

29. Ray W. Daniel, Steven Rowson, and Stefan M. Duma, "Head Impact Exposure in Youth Football," *Annals of Biomedical Engineering* 40, no. 4 *(*April 2012): 976–81.

30. Linda Flanagan, "How Students' Brains Are in Danger on the Field," *Atlantic* online, last modified August 14, 2017, www .theatlantic.com/education/archive2017/08/how-students-brains -are-in-danger-on-the-field/536604.

31. Tim Froh, "'It's Un-American': Will the Government and CTE Fears Kill US Youth Football?," *Guardian* (US edition) online, last modified March 6, 2018, www.theguardian.com /sport/2018/mar/06/tackle-football-children-health-concerns.

32. David Xavier Chu, "Repetitive Head Injury Syndrome," *Medscape,* last modified February 8, 2017, http://emedicine .medscape.cm/article/92189-overview.

33. Rebecca Adams, "It's Not Just Girls: Boys Struggle with Body Image, Too," *Huffington Post*, December 29, 2014, www.huffing tonpost.com/2014/09/17/body-image-boys_n_5637975.html.

34. Jamie Santa Cruz, "Body-Image Pressure Increasingly Affects Boys," *Atlantic* online, last modified March 10, 2014, www .theatlantic.com/health/archive/2014/03/body-image-pressure -increasingly-affects-boys/283897.

35. Jesse A. Steinfelt et al., "Drive for Muscularity and Conformity to Masculine Norms Among College Football Players," *Psychology of Men and Masculinity* 12, no. 4 (2011): 324–38.

36. Harrison G. Pope, Katherine A. Phillips, and Roberto Olivardia, *The Adonis Complex: How to Identify, Treat and Prevent Body Obsession in Men and Boys* (New York: Free Press, 2002).

37. Stephanie Pappas, "Size Doesn't Matter: 'Penis Shame' Is All in Guys' Heads," *Live Science,* last modified October 4, 2013, www.livescience.com/40192-penis-shame-guys-heads.html.

38. *Health Provider Toolkit for Adolescent and Young Adult Males* (Washington, DC: Partnership for Male Youth, 2014), www.ayamalehealth.org/#sthash.o8CsgfcT.dpbs.

39. Jerry L. Grenard, Clyde W. Dent, and Alan W. Stacy, "Exposure to Alcohol Advertisements and Teenage Alcohol-Related Problems," *Pediatrics* 131, no. 2 (February 2013): 369–79.

40. Lesley A. Smith and David R. Foxcroft, "The Effect of Alcohol Advertising, Marketing, and Portrayal on Drinking Behaviour in Young People: Systematic Review of Prospective Cohort Studies," *BMC Public Health* 9, no. 1 (February 2009): https://doi.org/10.1186/1471-2458-9-51; David Jernigan et al., "Alcohol Marketing and Youth Alcohol Consumption: A Systematic Review of Longitudinal Studies Published Since 2008," *Addiction* 112 (January 2017): 18.

41. Richard J. Bonnie and Mary Ellen O'Connell, eds., Committee on Developing a Strategy to Reduce and Prevent Underage Drinking, Board on Children, Youth and Families, National Research Council, *Reducing Underage Drinking: A Collective Responsibility* (Washington, DC: National Academies Press, 2004), 2.

42. Magdalena Cerda, Melanie Wall, and Tianshu Feng, "Association of State Recreational Marijuana Laws with Adolescent Marijuana Use," *JAMA Pediatrics* 171, no. 2 (2017): 142–49; Steve Gorman and Diane Craft, eds., "Colorado's Teen Marijuana Usage Dips After Legalization," *Scientific American* online. accessed September 2, 2017, www.scientificamerican.com /article/colorado-s-teen-marijuana-usage-dips-after-legalization.

43. Patricia A. Adler and Peter Adler, *The Tender Cut: Inside the Hidden World of Self-Injury* (New York: New York University Press, 2012).

44. Theo Merz, "Why Are More Boys Than Ever Self-Harming?" *Telegraph* (UK) online, last modified August 21, 2014, www .telegraph.co.uk/men/thinking-man/11046798/Why-are-more -boys-than-ever-self-harming.html.

45. Ibid., 2.

46. "Teen Suicide Statistics," Statistic Brain Research Institute, accessed September 2, 2017, www.statisticbrain.com/teen -suicide-statistics; Tara Haelle, "Fewer Teens Die by Suicide When Same-Sex Marriage Is Legal," *Forbes* online, last modified February 20, 2017, www.forbes.com/sites /tarahaelle/2017/02/20/fewer-teens-die-by-suicide-when-same -sex-marriage-is-legal/#1ef1f6783b75.

47. Michael A. Messner and Donald F. Sabo, *Sex, Violence and Power in Sports* (Freedom, CA: Crossing Press, 1994), 214.

CHAPTER 8 | VIOLENCE, BULLYING, AND VULNERABILITY

1. David Finkelhor et al., "Violence, Crime and Abuse Exposure in

a National Sample of Children and Youth: An Update," *JAMA Pediatrics* 167, no. 7 (July 2013): 614–21.

2. "Physical Fighting by Youth: Indicators of Child and Youth Well-being" (Bethesda, MD: ChildTrends Databank online, April 2017), www.childtrends.org/indicators/physical-fighting-by-youth.

3. Gary Barker, "Violence Does Not Come Naturally to Men and Boys," *Telegraph (UK)* online, last modified June 5, 2005, www .telegraph.co.uk/men/thinking-man/11652352/Violence-does -not-come-naturally-to-men-and-boys.html.

4. Michael Kaufman, "The Construction of Masculinity and the Triad of Men's Violence," in *Beyond Patriarchy: Essays by Men on Pleasure, Power and Change,* ed. Michael Kaufman (Toronto: Oxford University Press, 1987).

5. Brian Heilman with Gary Barker, *Masculine Norms and Violence: Making the Connections* (Washington, DC: Promundo-US, 2018), 6, https://promundoglobal.org/2018 /05/04/report-links-harmful-masculine-norms-violence.

6. Myriam Miedzian, *Boys Will Be Boys: Breaking the Link Between Masculinity and Violence* (New York: Anchor Books, 1991), xxiii.

7. Leonard D. Eron, Jacquelyn H. Gentry, and Peggy Schlegel, eds., *Reason to Hope: A Psychosocial Perspective on Violence and Youth* (Washington, DC: American Psychological Association, 1994), 9.

8. Wynne Perry, "Battling the Boys: Educators Grapple with Violent Play," *Live Science,* last modified August 29, 2010, www.livescience.com/8514-battling-boys-educators-grapple -violent-play.html.

9. Eron, Gentry, and Schlegel, *Reason to Hope*, 30.

10. Ibid., 35–36.

11. "Children's Exposure to Violence: Indicators of Child and Youth Well-being" (Bethesda, MD: ChildTrends Databank online, May 2016), www.childtrends.org/indicators/childrens-exposure -to-violence.

12. Gavin Aronson, Mark Follman, and Deanna Pan, "A Guide to Mass Shootings in America," *Mother Jones* online, last modified June 5, 2017, www.motherjones.com/politics/2012/07/mass -shootings-map; James Garbarino, *Lost Boys: Why Our Sons Turn Violent and How We Can Save Them* (New York: Free Press, 1999), ix.

13. James Gilligan, "Shame, Guilt, and Violence," *Social Research* 70, no. 4 (Winter 2003): 1154.

14. Elijah Anderson, *Code of the Street: Decency, Violence and the Moral Life of the Inner City* (New York: W. W. Norton, 2000), 75.

15. Kindlon and Thompson, *Raising Cain*.

16. Gilligan, "Shame, Guilt, and Violence," 1163.

17. Anderson, *Code of the Street*, 32.

18. Ann Arnett Ferguson, *Bad Boys: Public School in the Making of Black Masculinity* (Ann Arbor: University of Michigan Press, 2001), 193.

19. Michael Cunningham and L. K. Meunier, "The Influence of Peer Experiences on Bravado Attitudes Among African American Males," in *Adolescent Boys*, eds. Way and Chu (New York: New York University Press, 2004), 221.

20. Howard C. Stevenson, "Boys in Men's Clothing," in *Adolescent*

Boys, eds. Way and Chu (New York: New York University Press, 2004), 60.

21. "Bullying," ChildTrends Databank online, May 2016, www. childtrends.org/indicators/bullying.

22. "Unsafe at School," ChildTrends Databank online, December 2015, www.childtrends.org/indicators/unsafe-at -school.

23. US Centers for Disease Control and Prevention online, "Understanding School Violence: Fact Sheet 2016," accessed September 2, 2017, www.cdc.gov/violenceprevention/pdf /school_violence_fact_sheet-a.pdf.

24. Jonathan Salisbury and David Jackson, *Challenging Macho Values: Practical Ways of Working with Adolescent Boys* (London: Falmer Press, 1996), 104, 129.

25. Brett G. Stoudt, "'You're Either In or You're Out': School Violence, Peer Discipline, and the (Re)Production of Hegemonic Masculinity," *Men and Masculinities* 8, no. 3 (January 1, 2006): 274.

26. Heilman with Barker, *Masculine Norms and Violence*.

27. ChildTrends Databank online, "Physical Fighting by Youth."

28. Connie David-Ferdon et al., *A Comprehensive Technical Package for the Prevention of Youth Violence and Associated Risk Behaviors* (Atlanta: National Center for Injury Prevention and Control, CDC, 2016), 25.

29. Ibid., 23.

30. Bob Ditter, "Bullying Behavior in Boys . . . and What to Do About It," American Camp Association online, accessed

September 3, 2017, www.acacamps.org/resource-library
/camping-magazine/bullying-behavior-boys-what-do-about-it.

31. David-Ferdon et al., *Comprehensive Technical Package*, 15.

32. Eron, Gentry, and Schlegel, *Reason to Hope*, 11.

33. Garbarino, *Lost Boys*, 150.

CHAPTER 9 | BOYS' TOYS IN A DIGITAL AGE

1. "Parenting in America: Outlook, Worries, Aspirations Are
   Strongly Linked to Financial Situation" Pew Research Center,
   December 17, 2015, http://assets.pewresearch.org/wp-content
   /uploads/sites/3/2015/12/2015–12–17_parenting-in-america
   _FINAL.pdf.

2. Kristen Lucas and John L. Sherry, "Sex Differences in Video
   Game Play: A Communication-Based Explanation,"
   Communication Research 31, no. 5 (October 2004): 517.

3. Bruce D. Homer et al., "Gender and Player Characteristics in
   Video Game Play of Preadolescents," *Computers in Human
   Behavior* 28, no. 5, (2012): 1782–89.

4. Benjamin Paassen, Thekla Morgenroth, and Michelle
   Stratemeyer, "What Is a True Gamer? The Male Gamer
   Stereotype and the Marginalization of Women in Video Game
   Culture," *Sex Roles* 76, no. 7–8, (2017): 421–35.

5. Ibid.

6. Maeve Duggan, "Gaming and Gamers," Pew Research Center,
   December 15, 2015, www.pewinternet.org/2015/12/15/gaming
   -and-gamers.

7. Rosalind Wiseman, "Everything You Know About Boys and Video Games Is Wrong," *Time* online, last modified July 8, 2015, http://time.com/3948744/video-games-kate-upton-game-of-war-comic-con.

8. Christia Spears Brown, *Parenting Beyond Pink and Blue: How to Raise Your Kids Free of Gender Stereotypes* (New York: Ten Speed Press, 2014).

9. Elizabeth Sweet, "Toys Are More Divided by Gender Now Than They Were 50 Years Ago," *Atlantic* online, last modified December 9, 2014, www.theatlantic.com/business/archive/2014/12/toys-are-more-divided-by-gender-now-than-they-were-50-years-ago/383556.

10. Brown, *Parenting Beyond Pink and Blue*, 5.

11. Marshall McLuhan and Quentin Fiore, *The Medium Is the Massage: An Inventory of Effects* (Berkeley, CA: Gingko Press, 2001).

12. Gabriel A. Barkho, "What Exactly Makes Someone a 'Digital Native'? A Comprehensive Guide," *Mashable*, last modified June 20, 2016, http://mashable.com/2016/06/20/what-is-a-digital-native/#dWYGIV12kmqq.

13. Ibid., 4.

14. Steven Johnson, *Everything Bad Is Good for You* (New York: Riverhead Books, 2005).

15. Zimbardo and Coulombe, *Man Interrupted*.

16. Howard Gardner and Katie Davis, *The App Generation: How Today's Youth Imagine Identity, Intimacy, and Imagination in a Digital World* (New Haven, CT: Yale University Press, 2013).

17. Ibid., 160.

18. Sherry Turkle, *Alone Together: Why We Expect More from Technology and Less from Each Other* (New York: Basic Books, 2011).

19. Ibid., 12.

20. Lisa Damour, "Parenting the Fortnite Addict," *New York Times* online, April 30, 2018, www.nytimes.com/2018/04/30 /well/family/parenting-the-fortnite-addict.html.

21. Andrew K. Przybylski, Netta Weinstein, and Kou Murayama, "Internet Gaming Disorder: Investigating the Clinical Relevance of a New Phenomenon," *American Journal of Psychiatry* 174, no. 3 (November 2016): 230–36, http://ajp.psychiatryonline .org/doi/abs/10.1176/appi.ajp.2016.16020224.

22. Adam Alter, *Irresistible: The Rise of Addictive Technology and the Business of Keeping Us Hooked* (New York: Penguin Press, 2017).

23. Brent Conrad, *How to Help Children Addicted to Video Games* (Halifax, Nova Scotia: TechAddiction, 2012).

24. Christopher J. Ferguson and Patrick Markey, "Video Games Aren't Addictive," *New York Times* online, April 1, 2017, www.nytimes.com/2017/04/01/opinion/sunday/video-games -arent-addictive.html?_r=0.

25. Ibid., 2.

26. Jordan Erica Webber, "'As Addictive as Gardening': How Dangerous Is Video Gaming?," *Guardian* (US edition) online, last modified April 25, 2017, www.theguardian.com/technology/2017 /apr/25/video-game-addiction-compulsive-dangerous.

27. Ferguson and Markey, "Video Games Aren't Addictive," 3.

28. Andrew Perrin, "Social Media Usage: 2005–2015" (Washington, DC: Pew Research Center online, October 8, 2015), www .pewinternet.org/2015/10/08/social-networking-usage-2005–2015.

29. Michael Kimmel, *Guyland: The Perilous World Where Boys Become Men* (New York: Harper Perennial, 2009), 31.

30. Alexia Fernandez Campbell, "The Unexpected Economic Consequences of Video Games," *Vox,* last modified July 7, 2017, www.vox.com/policy-and-politics/2017/7/7/15933674/video -games-job-supply.

31. Amanda Lenhart, "Teens, Technology and Romantic Relationships" Pew Research Center online, October 1, 2015, www.pewinternet.org/2015/10/01/teens-technology-and -romantic-relationships.

32. Sophia Stuart, "How to Raise Responsible Digital Kids," *PC Magazine* online, last modified February 13, 2017, www.pcmag .com/news/351706/how-to-raise-responsible-digital-kids.

33. Monica Anderson, "Parents, Teens and Digital Monitoring" *Pew Research Center,* January 7, 2016, www.pewinternet .org/2016/01/07/parents-teens-and-digital-monitoring.

34. American Academy of Pediatrics, "Policy Statement: Media Use in School-Age Children and Adolescents," *Pediatrics* 138, no. 5 (November 2016), https://docs.google.com/viewer?url=http% 3A%2F%2Fpediatrics.aappublications.org%2Fcontent%2 Fearly%2F2016%2F10%2F19%2Fpeds.2016–2592.full-text .pdf.

35. Campaign for a Commercial-Free Childhood (CCFC) online, "7 Parent-Tested Tips to Unplug and Play," accessed September 3, 2017, www.commercialfreechildhood.org/resource/real-life -strategies-reducing-children%E2%80%99s-screen-time.

36. Alia Wong, "Digital Natives, Yet Strangers to the Web," *Atlantic* online, last modified April 21, 2015), www.theatlantic.com /education/archive/2015/04/digital-natives-yet-strangers-to -the-web/390990.

37. MTV Digital Rights Project, *A Thin Line,* accessed September 3, 2017, www.athinline.org/digital-rights-project.

38. James Hamblin, "Quit Social Media Every Other Day," *Atlantic* online, last modified June 15, 2017, www.theatlantic.com/health /archive/2017/06/intermittent-social-media-fasting/529752.

39. Anya Kamenetz, *The Art of Screen Time: How Your Family Can Balance Digital Media and Real Life* (New York: Public Affairs, 2018), 221.

CHAPTER 10 | THE TWENTY-FIRST CENTURY— AND BEYOND

1. Nellie Bowles, "Jordan Peterson: Custodian of Patriarchy," *New York Times* online, May 18, 2018, www.nytimes.com/2018/05 /18/style/jordan-peterson-12-rules-for-life.html.

2. Jordan B. Peterson, *12 Rules for Life: An Antidote for Chaos* (Toronto: Random House Canada, 2018).

3. Alana Semuels, "When Factory Jobs Vanish, Men Become Less Desirable Partners," *Atlantic* online, last modified March 3, 2017, www.theatlantic.com/business/archive/2017/03/ manufacturing-marriage-family/518280.

4. Joanna Pepin and David Cotter, "Trending Towards Traditionalism? Changes in Youths' Gender Ideology," Council on Contemporary Families online, last modified March 31, 2017, https://contemporaryfamilies.org/2-pepin-cotter-traditionalism.

5. Stephanie Coontz, "Do Millennial Men Want Stay-at-Home Wives?," *New York Times* online, March 31, 2017, www .nytimes.com/2017/03/31/opinion/sunday/do-millennial-men -want-stay-at-home-wives.html?_r=0; Dan Cassino, "Some Men Feel the Need to Compensate for Relative Loss of Income to Women: How They Do So Varies," Council on Contemporary Families online, last modified March 31, 2017, https: //contemporaryfamilies.org/3-cassino-men-compensate-for -income-to-women.

6. Beyond the Veil, *Elliot Rodger's Retribution Video*, online video clip (6:55), YouTube, uploaded May 24, 2014, accessed June 17, 2018, www.youtube.com/watch?v=G-gQ3aAdhIo.

7. Alexandra Ma, "The Toronto Van Attack Suspect Warned of an 'Incel Rebellion' on Facebook Hours Before the Attack—Here's What That Means," *Business Insider,* last modified April 24, 2018, www.businessinsider.com/incel-alex-minassian-toronto -van-attack-facebook-post-2018–4?IR=T.

8. *The Manosphere*, MGTOW (Men Going Their Own Way) online, accessed June 17, 2018, www.mgtow.com/manosphere.

9. Bianca D. M. Wilson et al., "Characteristics and Mental Health of Gender Nonconforming Adolescents in California: Findings from the 2015–2016 California Health Interview Survey," Williams Institute and UCLA Center for Health Policy Research, December 2017, http://healthpolicy.ucla.edu/publications /search/pages/detail.aspx?PubID=1706.

10. Sarah Rich, "Today's Masculinity Is Stifling," *Atlantic* online, last modified June 11, 2018, www.theatlantic.com/family /archive/2018/06/imagining-a-better-boyhood/562232.

11. Nicholas Kristof, "On a Portland Train, the Battlefield of American Values," *New York Times* online, May 30, 2017,

www.nytimes.com/2017/05/30/opinion/portland-train-attack
-muslim.html.

12. Michael Kimmel, *Angry White Men* (New York: Nation Books, 2013).

13. R. W. Connell, *The Men and the Boys* (Cambridge, UK: Polity, 2000).

14. *The Proposal* (Coalition to Create a White House Council on Boys to Men), accessed June 20, 2018, http: //whitehouseboysmen.org/the-proposal/introduction.

15. Stony Brook University, "The International Conference on Masculinities Explores Gender Activism and Gender Justice," news release, March 4, 2015, http://sb.cc.stonybrook.edu/news /general/2015_04_03_masculinities_conf.php.

16. Alanna Vagianos, "Gloria Steinem on What Men Have to Gain from Feminism," *Huffington Post,* last modified December 6, 2017, www.huffingtonpost.com/2015/03/06/gloria-steinem -men-feminism_n_6813522.html?ncid=fcbklnku shpmg00000046.

17. Michael Kimmel, 2013: xiv. SAA, p. 280.

18. Values in Action Institute on Character online, "Character Strengths Research: Breaking New Ground," accessed September 4, 2017, www.viacharacter.org/www/Research.

19. Nel Noddings, *Caring: A Feminine Approach to Ethics and Moral Education* (Berkeley, University of California Press, 1984), p. 69.

20. Jean M. Twenge and W. Keith Campbell, *The Narcissism Epidemic: Living in the Age of Entitlement* (New York: Atria Books, 2010); Emily Grijalva et al., "Gender Differences in

Narcissism: A Meta-analytic Review," *Psychological Bulletin* 141, no. 2 (March 2015): 261–310.

21. Jeffrey Kluger, "Why Men Are More Narcissistic Than Women," *Time* online, last modified March 5, 2015, http://time .com/3734329/narcissism-men-women.

22. Carol Dweck, *Mindset: The New Psychology of Success* (New York: Ballantine, 2007).

23. Roy Baumeister, "Rethinking Self-Esteem: Why Nonprofits Should Stop Pushing Self-Esteem and Start Endorsing Self-Control," *Stanford Social Innovation Review* (Winter 2005): 34–41.

24. "The Key to Understanding Bad Boys: They're Narcissists," EMandLO.com (blog), July 29, 2015, www.emandlo.com /the-key-to-understanding-bad-boys-theyre-narcissists.

25. Donald W. Black, *Bad Boys, Bad Men* (New York: Oxford University Press, 1999), 28.

26. Ibid., 83.

27. Ibid., 202.

28. Emily Badger et al. "Extensive Data Shows Punishing Reach of Racism for Black Boys," *New York Times* online, March 19, 2018, www.nytimes.com/interactive/2018/03/19/upshot/race -class-white-and-black-men.html.

29. Caroline Simon, "There Is a Stunning Gap Between the Number of White and Black Inmates in America's Prisons," *Business Insider* last modified June 16, 2016, www.businessinsider.com /study-finds-huge-racial-disparity-in-americas-prisons-2016–6; Ferguson, *Bad Boys* 230; Howard Stevenson, "Boys in Men's Clothing," 59.

30. Eric Davis and Dana Santorelli, *Raising Men: Lessons Navy SEALs Learned from Their Training and Taught to Their Sons* (New York: St. Martin's Press, 2016).

31. Monica Lewinsky, "Jay-Z, Prince Harry, Brad Pitt, and the New Frontiers of Male Vulnerability," *Vanity Fair* online, last modified July 19, 2017, www.vanityfair.com/style/2017/07 /jay-z-prince-harry-brad-pitt-male-vulnerability.

32. Claire Cain Miller, "How to Raise a Feminist Son," *New York Times* online, June 1, 2017, www.nytimes.com/2017/06/02 /upshot/how-to-raise-a-feminist-son.html.

33. Roots of Empathy, "About Us," www.rootsofempathy.org.

34. Andrew Reiner, "Talking to Boys the Way We Talk to Girls," *New York Times* online, June 15, 2017, www.nytimes .com/2017/06/15/well/family/talking-to-boys-the-way-we-talk -to-girls.html.

35. Brown, *Parenting Beyond Pink and Blue*, 206.

36. Eamonn Callan, *Creating Citizens: Political Education and Liberal Democracy* (Oxford, UK: Oxford University Press, 2004).

37. John Rawls, *A Theory of Justice* (Cambridge, MA: Belknap Press, 1999).

38. Benedict Carey, "England's Mental Health Experiment: No-Cost Talk Therapy," *New York Times* online, July 24, 2017, www.nytimes.com/2017/07/24/health/england-mental-health -treatment-therapy.html.

39. Lifeline, "Our Toughest Challenge Yet," accessed on September 4, 2017, www.lifeline.org.au/www.lifeline.org.au /paul.

40. "Manhood 2.0: Breaking Up with Stereotypes and Encouraging Relationships Based on Consent, Respect, and Equality in the United States," *Promundo* online, last modified August 23, 2016, http://promundoglobal.org/2016/08/23/manhood-2–0 -breaking-stereotypes-encouraging-relationships-based-consent -respect-equality-united-states.

INDEX

❧